Focus on French as a Foreign Language

SECOND LANGUAGE ACQUISITION
Series Editor: Professor David Singleton, *Trinity College, Dublin, Ireland*

This new series will bring together titles dealing with a variety of aspects of language acquisition and processing in situations where a language or languages other than the native language is involved. Second language will thus be interpreted in its broadest possible sense. The volumes included in the series will all in their different ways offer, on the one hand, exposition and discussion of empirical findings and, on the other, some degree of theoretical reflection. In this latter connection, no particular theoretical stance will be privileged in the series; nor will any relevant perspective – sociolinguistic, psycholinguistic, neurolinguistic, etc. – be deemed out of place. The intended readership of the series will be final-year undergraduates working on second language acquisition projects, postgraduate students involved in second language acquisition research, and researchers and teachers in general whose interests include a second language acquisition component.

For more details of these or any other of our publications, please contact:
Multilingual Matters, Frankfurt Lodge, Clevedon Hall,
Victoria Road, Clevedon, BS21 7HH, England
http://www.multilingual-matters.com

SECOND LANGUAGE ACQUISITION 10
Series Editor: David Singleton, *Trinity College, Dublin, Ireland*

Focus on French as a Foreign Language
Multidisciplinary Approaches

Edited by
Jean-Marc Dewaele

MULTILINGUAL MATTERS LTD
Clevedon • Buffalo • Toronto

For Katja and Livia

Library of Congress Cataloging in Publication Data
Focus on French as a Foreign Language: Multidisciplinary Approaches/Edited by
Jean-Marc Dewaele.
Second Language Acquisition: 10
Includes bibliographical references and index.
1. French language–Acquisition. 2. Interlanguage (Language learning)
I. Dewaele, Jean-Marc. II. Second Language Acquisition (Buffalo, NY): 10.
PC2074.85.F63 2004
440'.71–dc22   2004002825

British Library Cataloguing in Publication Data
A catalogue entry for this book is available from the British Library.

ISBN 1-85359-767-8 (hbk)
ISBN 1-85359-766-X (pbk)

Multilingual Matters Ltd
UK: Frankfurt Lodge, Clevedon Hall, Victoria Road, Clevedon BS21 7HH.
USA: UTP, 2250 Military Road, Tonawanda, NY 14150, USA.
Canada: UTP, 5201 Dufferin Street, North York, Ontario M3H 5T8, Canada.

Typeset by Archetype-IT Ltd (http://www.archetype-it.com).
Printed and bound in Great Britain by the Cromwell Press Ltd.

Contents

Preface

French is still the most widely studied foreign language in the UK and in many other countries around the globe. For those learners whose motivation is not purely instrumental, French is valued for its history, refinement, and civilisation. Kinginger (2004), in her study of the autobiographical novels of Nancy Huston, an American who emigrated to Paris in the 1960s, observes that, for Huston, 'the French language, learned in adulthood, is valued for the quality of the alternative frame it provided, one that is associated with adult affect, self-control, and subtle artistry' (p. 173). Similarly, Pavlenko notes that for Natasha Lvovich, a Russian Jewish woman who had studied French in Moscow in the 1970s, French provided an alternative frame. Travel restrictions made it impossible for her to travel to France:

> Instead, associating French with intellectualism, sophistication, and nobility, she created an imaginary French identity for herself, learning to speak with a Parisian accent, memorizing popular French songs, reading French classics and detective stories in argot, mastering numerous written genres, cooking French food (from locally available ingredients), and even dipping 'the imagined croissant into coffee' (Lvovich, 1997: 2). For her, this was the only possible escape from the political reality' (Pavlenko, 2003: 326).

In her study on metaphors of language learning, Kramsch was struck by a student's metaphor that 'learning French is like eating regurgitated pâte', which is related to the commonly shared belief in the refinement of French cuisine as well as to an equally shared belief in the drudgery of learning French grammar, or as another student put it: 'learning French is like having phlegm stuck in the back of my throat' (Kramsch, to appear). French is often perceived by learners to be a difficult language to acquire because of the complexity of the grammar.

It is true that French poses some interesting challenges to foreign learners: the gender system is notoriously difficult to master; tense, aspect and verb morphology are complex; the acquisition of adverbs is an arduous task; learners at all levels have to overcome syntactic obstacles: beginning learners struggle with word-order and the use of the two bound morphemes *ne* and *pas* for negation and more advanced learners still struggle with the omission of the *ne* in certain registers. At some point the learners are expected to dislodge 'the phlegm stuck in the back of their throat' and become fluent speakers of French.

All these struggles are particularly interesting for researchers in French as a foreign language, and they are the focus of the studies in the present book. This is the first volume in English, to my knowledge, which is solely devoted to the acquisition and the production of French interlanguage. The contributors to this book are of French, British, Swedish, Irish, Polish and Belgian origin and all have crossed linguistic, cultural and theoretical boundaries. Clive Perdue and Daniel Véronique crossed a channel and an ocean to reach France, where their academic careers flourished. They brought a breath of fresh air to second language research in France. They also remained in permanent contact with researchers outside France and participated in the first big pan-European linguistic project funded by the European Science Foundation (Perdue, 1984), which looked at the acquisition of various target languages by immigrants from European and non-European countries. This research provided the research community with the first complete descriptions of the 'Basic Variety' (the original studies on French were recently re-edited in Giacomi, Stoffel and Véronique, 2000).

Mireille Prodeau and Marzena Watorek did their doctoral research under the supervision of Daniel Véronique and Clive Perdue, and adopted their supervisors functionalist and interactionist perspectives. They brought their own multilingual, multidisciplinary and multicultural experiences: Mireille Prodeau was a teacher of mathematics and worked in the United Kingdom, in the United States and in Germany before settling down in Paris and converting to Second Language Acquisition (SLA). Marzena Watorek obtained her first degrees in French philology at the University of Kraków, Poland, before crossing the Iron Curtain and finding a new home in Paris.

The Swedish researchers represent different generations in the rich tradition of Scandinavian philologists and Francophiles with a strong knowledge of the latest developments in the Anglo-Saxon SLA world. Victorine Hancock and Nathalie Kirchmeyer obtained their PhDs recently at the University of Stockholm, where they worked on the Interfra project under the supervision of Inge Bartning. Victorine Hancock spent a year of research in Paris; Nathalie Kirchmeyer is of French nationality and moved to Stockholm some years ago. Jonas Granfeldt obtained his PhD at the University of Lund in 2003 under the supervision of Suzanne Schlyter.

The two Irish contributors share the same theoretical perspective, i.e. variational sociolinguistics, which is not surprising given the fact that

Martin Howard obtained his PhD under the supervision of Vera Regan at University College, Dublin. Both are Irish-born and also very cosmopolitan. Vera Regan obtained her PhD in France and spent prolonged study periods in the United States; Martin Howard studied and worked in France, Germany and the Netherlands.

Richard Towell is an ardent francophile who spent most of his academic life in Salford (UK). He obtained his PhD there and became professor in French Applied Linguistics. I crossed the Channel from the continent to London after obtaining my PhD at the Free University of Brussels under the supervision of Hugo Baetens Beardsmore.

The book comprises 10 original chapters that cover the full range of learners and users, from beginners to advanced learners (cf. Bartning, 1997), from different linguistic backgrounds. It will be of interest not only to researchers, students and teachers working in FSL (French as a Second Language) but also to those who work in the field of second or foreign language acquisition and production in general.

The volume starts with a chapter by Marzena Watorek and Clive Perdue entitled 'Psycholinguistic Studies on the Acquisition of French as a Second Language: The 'Learner Variety' Approach'. The authors adopt a functionalist approach to consider idiosyncratic productions in the speech of beginners up to highly advanced users, focusing on spatio-temporal reference and aspect.

Chapter 2, by Victorine Hancock and Nathalie Kirchmeyer, 'Discourse Structuring in Advanced L2 French: The Relative Clause', deals with the development of complexity and the structuring of discourse in the French interlanguage of Swedish learners.

Chapter 3, by Suzanne Schlyter, 'Adverbs and Functional Categories in L1 and L2 Acquisition of French', looks at how adverbs and functional categories develop in L1 and L2 acquisition of French by Swedish learners.

Chapter 4, by Martin Howard, 'The Emergence and Use of the Plus-Que-Parfait in Advanced French Interlanguage', considers the development of the use of tense in advanced French interlanguages from Irish learners using a variationist perspective.

Chapter 5, by Florence Myles, 'The Emergence of Morpho-syntactic Structure in French L2', analyses the emergence of the verb-phrase among young English learners of French within a Universal Grammar perspective.

Chapter 6, by Daniel Véronique, 'Syntactic and Semantic Issues in the Acquisition of Negation in French', focuses on the development of negation in the basic variety of naturalistic learners with Arabic as an L1.

The two following chapters look at the phenomenon of agreement and gender assignment in different populations using contrasting approaches. Mireille Prodeau, in Chapter 7, 'Gender and Number in French L2: Can we find out more about the Constraints on Production in L2?' considers the productions of two groups of adult learners of French from a traditional psycholinguistic perspective. Jonas Granfeldt, in chapter 8, The Development of Gender Attribution and Gender Agreement in French: A Comparison of Bilingual First- and Second-Language Learners', compares adult second language learners with young bilingual first language users of French using a Universal Grammar framework.

Chapter 9, by Vera Regan, 'From Speech Community back to Classroom: What Variation Analysis can tell us about the Role of Context in the Acquisition of French as a Foreign Language', reports on the long-term effects of a stay in the native speech community on the acquisition of sociolinguistic competence by Irish learners of French.

Chapter 10, by Richard Towell and Jean-Marc Dewaele, 'The Role of Psycholinguistic Factors in the Development of Fluency amongst Advanced Learners of French', considers the development of fluency among 12 adult British learners of French.

A word of thanks finally to the many friends and colleagues who acted as reviewers for the contributions in the present volume: Inge Bartning, Susan Carroll, Gessica De Angelis, Jonas Granfeldt, Anna Herwig, Alex Housen, Roger Hawkins, Scott Jarvis, Raymond Mougeon, Colette Noyau, Aneta Pavlenko, Clive Perdue, Katie Rehner, Suzanne Schlyter, Liz Temple, Daniel Véronique, and Martha Young-Scholten. Thanks also to Moira Courtman, my loyal proof-reader.

References

Bartning, I. (1997) L'apprenant dit avancé et son acquisition d'une langue étrangère. Tour d'horizon et esquisse d'une caractérisation de la variété avancée. _AILE Acquisition et Interaction en Langue Etrangère_ 9, 9–50.

Giacomi, A., Stoffel, H. and Véronique, D. (eds) (2000) _Appropriation du français par des Marocains arabophones à Marseille_. Aix en Provence: Publications de l'Université de Provence.

Kinginger, C. (2004) Bilingualism and emotion in the autobiographical works of Nancy Huston. In A. Pavlenko and J.-M. Dewaele (eds) _Languages and Emotions: A Crosslinguistic Perspective_. Special issue of the _Journal of Multilingual and Multicultural Development_ 25 (2 &3), 159–78.

Kramsch, C. (to appear) Metaphor and the subjective construction of belief. In P. Kalaja, P. and A-M. Barcelos (eds) _New Approaches to Research on Beliefs about SLA_. Dordrecht: Kluwer.

Lvovich, N. (1997) _The Multilingual Self: An Inquiry into Language Learning_. Mahwah, NJ: Lawrence Erlbaum.

Pavlenko, A. (2003) 'Language of the enemy': Foreign language education and national identity. _The International Journal of Bilingual Education and Bilingualism_ 6 (5), 313–31.

Perdue, C. (ed.) (1984) _Second Language Acquisition by Adult Immigrants. A Field Manual_. Rowley: Newbury House.

Chapter 1

Psycholinguistic Studies on the Acquisition of French as a Second Language: The 'Learner Variety' Approach

MARZENA WATOREK AND CLIVE PERDUE

Introduction

In this chapter we propose to discuss some studies on adult language acquisition undertaken within the *learner variety approach*, concentrating on French as a target language (TL). The studies range from an analysis of the initial stages of acquisition (Benazzo, 2000; Starren, 2001), around the so-called 'basic variety' (Klein & Perdue, 1997), right up to the advanced, quasi-bilingual stage (cf. Carroll & von Stutterheim, 1993, 1997; Lambert, 1997; Watorek & Perdue, 1999).

We are interested in the recurrent phenomena attested in these studies, namely the 'idiosyncratic' productions (cf. Corder, 1967, 1971) that characterise early stages on the way to the TL, and the 'grammatical' but nonetheless inappropriate (or 'unfluent') productions characterising the very advanced stages (cf. Bartning, 1997). We start by outlining the particularities of the 'learner variety' approach, before summarising some results from the studies cited above.

The 'Learner Variety' Approach

We draw on some results from a large body of empirical work undertaken from a functional, longitudinal and cross-linguistic perspective, which takes into account both communicative factors 'pushing' acquisition and structural factors 'shaping' it, in an attempt to explain the process of acquisition. In general terms, the cognitive and linguistic predisposition of the learner interacts with the formal characteristics of the L2 input in

1

shaping the acquisition process, but a further set of factors – communicative factors – intervenes in pushing the learner to acquire the L2.

Two recurrent phenomena will be of interest in the following section: the type of utterance the learner constructs in order to convey her/his meaning, and the orders of acquisition reported. First, we have a fresh look at an old acquisitional chestnut, 'aspect before tense', and then at learners' utterance patterns and use of anaphoric devices in the construction of descriptive discourse.

Communicative factors

The type of communicative factors of interest here are those intervening in the learner/user's need to express recurrent relational meanings between items of vocabulary that languages grammaticalise to a greater or lesser extent – for brevity we will call these '(grammatical) functions' – relations such as assertion, temporal reference and determination. Such functions are numerous (but not unlimited), and the ones mentioned involve the interaction of sentence grammar, discourse grammar and context-relating rules. There is little reason to assume that they are all equally important for the learner when communicating. The relative communicative importance of expressing such functions is thus held to be a determining factor for acquisition.[1] Another communicative factor of relevance to the examples below is Levelt's (1981) 'linearisation problem', that of arranging the information for production in temporal order, between utterances and within each utterance. Some of the principles underlying the speaker's linearisation of information will be discussed in more detail in the section below.

Formal factors

Languages develop devices to express grammatical functions to different degrees of specification – one speaks for example of 'aspect-prominent languages' as opposed to 'tense-prominent languages'. Different languages therefore give different formal priorities to functions which are nevertheless shared (temporal reference is accomplished in aspect-prominent languages, and vice versa). The learner who by virtue of her SL competence understands how to apply these functions, has to find some means of expressing them in the TL.[2] It is therefore necessary to understand which are the linguistic means used at first, and how the means used for expressing a particular function change – and possibly grow more complex – over time. Note that the grammatical organisation of the SL, or characteristics of the TL input, individually or in tandem, may make certain aspects of the input highly salient, and others less so.

The very mention of 'communicative factors' reveals that we are interested in the learners' real-time communicative activity (restricted to language production in this chapter). The analyst attempts to retrace over time how the learner succeeds, or does not succeed, in the communicative task s / he is engaged in, and this reconstruction allows one to identify what the learning problem was at any given time during the acquisition process. The acquisitionist therefore looks first at the way the learner's linguistic repertoire is organised at a given moment, how this repertoire is put to use in particular communicative tasks, and how the repertoire changes over time in respect to the same tasks. Acquisition and use – or rather, use and acquisition – are therefore not dissociated. The object of investigation is the L2 learner / user. We further assume, for argument's sake, that real-time communicative activity forms part of the goals of any L2 learner, be s / he an adult economic immigrant (2.1), or a university student of a foreign language (2.2).[3]

'Idiosyncratic' Utterances

We look in this section at an old debate in acquisitional studies: whether temporal or aspectual distinctions are acquired first – but with the difference (from some published studies) that the expressive means analysed (the 'alternatives of expression') are not limited to verbal morphology. By 'aspect' we mean grammatical aspect, which we define following Klein's (1994) model.

Klein defines tense and aspect by appealing to a semantic function of finiteness. Finiteness is traditionally associated with the morphosyntactic categories of person and tense. However, Klein distinguishes between the *concept* of finiteness and the way languages *mark* it. The European languages typically mark finiteness by verb morphology – one speaks of finite versus non-finite verb forms – but such is not the case for a language like Chinese, for example (see Klein, Li & Hendriks, 2000), nor – and this is of immediate concern – for early learner varieties.

The semantic function of finiteness involves the speaker's claim about a time span. Klein (1998: 227) illustrates this with the following example:

(1) The book WAS on the table.

In this example, WAS is marked by contrastive stress, and the contrast can involve either the time-span ('the book WAS on the table, but isn't any longer'), or the claim ('you said it wasn't, but in fact the book WAS on the table'). Klein (1994) calls the time span for which the speaker makes a claim the 'topic time' (TT), in contrast to the time of situation (TSit), i.e. the interval occupied on the time axis by the situation talked about. The notional category of *tense* then expresses the relation of TT to the deictically given time of utterance (TU), and the notional category of grammatical *aspect* expresses the relation between TT and TSit. Starren (2001) uses the metaphor of the video camera to explain TT – it is the time the camera is 'shooting'. Imagine you are a witness in court, and the judge asks you, 'What did you see when you entered the room?' The crucial time span corresponds to your entering the room, and just this time span is filmed by the camera. You answer, 'A man was trying to open the safe. He looked Japanese.' The time span occupied by 'man trying to open safe', and indeed the time span occupied by 'man looked Japanese' – the 'situation times'- are considerably longer than it took you to enter the room. It would indeed be surprising if the man did not still look Japanese as you speak. But this was not what you were asked. The TT is your entering the room, and your, and the judge's, use of past tense puts this TT (but *not* necessarily the TSit) before the time of utterance. The time of the action of trying to open the safe, TSit, encompasses the TT. This aspectual relation is imperfective, and explains the use of the past progressive aspect in your answer.

Imperfective aspect contrasts with perfective aspect, where TSit is within, or coincides with, TT; this coincidence of TT and TSit is found in subdistinctions of perfectivity such as habituality or continuity. Two further grammatical aspectual distinctions may be drawn: prospective, where the topic time is in the 'pre-state' of the situation time (TT < TSit), or perfect, where topic time is in the 'post-state' of an event (TT > TSit).[4] The crucial distinction between perfective aspect, on the one hand, and the others is that perfective aspect shows no dissociation between TT and TSit, whereas the others do.

Right from the beginning of the acquisition process, it is necessary for an adult to express temporal relations. These relations can be inferred from discourse organisation principles, or simply left implicit, in which case the relation is by default contemporaneous with the moment of speech. Very early learner varieties ('basic varieties') have as a defining characteristic that they completely lack the usual grammatical means[5] to express tense and aspect, as they are devoid of morphological marking. (Adult) learners nevertheless manage to produce sophisticated temporal structures in their discourse with the means available, which allow the specification of some time span and certain relations between time spans. What elementary learners do at the beginning of their discourse is establish an initial TT, either: implicitly, by taking over the time proposed by the interlocutor or using the time of utterance (TU) as a default case; or: explicitly, by means of an utterance-initial adverb, as in (2a). This initial TT serves as a point of departure, and is maintained or shifted, depending on the type of discourse. If it is shifted (as in a narrative, for example), then this shifted time may be marked by an initial anaphoric adverb, as in (2b), or follows on from discourse-organisational principles such as the principle of natural order (PNO, Clark, 1971), whereby events are recounted in the order in which they occur.

(2) (a) SF: Gloria   **aujourd'hui** ici + quatre familles
                         'today, there are four families here'
     (b) MF: Abdel   **après** + avec la police
                         'afterwards, the police arrived'

As we see, the utterance-initial adverb, in bold type in the examples, specifies the TT of the (rather minimally expressed) state of affairs of the utterance. Starren (2001) analyses the many early productions of Moroccan learners of L2 French from the ESF corpus (Perdue, 1984), and finds a regular use of a *second* adverb of time (underlined in the examples),[6] specifying the time span filled by the state of affairs, i.e. TSit:

(3) (a) MF: Zahra   **toujours** moi [fe] la cuisine <u>ce soir</u>
                        'always me make the cooking this (= in the) evening'
     (b) MF: Zahra   **toujours** il [fe] la crise <u>chaque jour</u>
                        'always he has his crisis every day'
     (c) MF: Abdel   **hier** le capitaine bateau <u>toujours</u> [regarde]
                        'yesterday the captain the ship always look'
     (d) MF: Zahra   **quand [lepeti]** <u>toujours</u> malade
                        'when (he was) little (he was) always ill'

Starren's analysis of many such early utterances allows a distinction to be drawn between the aspectual values of habituality and continuity, by the interplay of adverbs denoting TT and TSit. For habituality, as in (3)a, b: for all the subintervals of *toujours*, I cook in the evening (3a), or he has his crisis each day (36); (3c), which contains an activity verb, expresses continuity (the time span *yesterday* is filled by the activity of supervising); and (3d), which expresses a state, also expresses continuity (the time span *when little* was filled by his being ill). Thus even at this basic level, it is possible to make some aspectual distinctions, by means of an adverb distribution which owes nothing to the specifics of either SL or TL organisation. The utterances of (3) are truly idiosyncratic in the sense that the adverb distribution of *toujours* cannot be unequivocally traced either to SL or to the TL.

It is worth devoting a paragraph to the word 'unequivocally' of the previous sentence. As a reviewer rightly pointed out, the language pairing of (3) is Moroccan Arabic-French; in this language pairing it would be possible to appeal to certain distributional facts of Moroccan to explain the functioning of *toujours* in these examples. However, this is less possible for Turkish, the other L1 studied by Starren:[7] learners of Dutch with Moroccan and Turkish as a L1 show the same use of these adverbials. Moreover, the same distribution can be found in the production of Spanish-speaking learners of French, with other temporal adverbs.[8] The following is an extract from a conversation between Bernarda and a native speaker (NS), whose theme is when Bernarda works in a canteen:

(4)   NS: ça c'était à midi
            'that was midday'
      BE: **à midi** non + **à midi** [nepa] moi la cuisine (. . .) **à midi** [se] un
            garçon la cuisine
            'midday no midday isanot me the kitchen(. . .) midday isa a
            man the kitchen
      NS: et en septembre?
            'and in September?'
      BE: **en septembre** [se] moi <u>à midi</u> [asoesoir]
            'in September isa me midday (and) evening'
      NS: et en octobre?
            'and in October?'
      BE: seulement [<u>asoesoir</u>]
            'only evening'

The general regularity is therefore the following: an adverb denoting TT in utterance-initial position has scope over the adverb denoting TSit, which is placed close to the expression denoting the situation. What we have is a more or less direct reflection of the way information structure is reflected by linguistic structure – the source language pulling more or less in the same direction – and the hypothesis is that the more direct this reflection is, the more 'language-neutral' (Kellerman, 1987) the structure is (implicitly) judged to be by learners, and the more they will have recourse to it. We have, perhaps, a syntactic reflection of Kellerman's 'psychotypology', which he himself fleshed out for idioms and lexical items.

Starren (2001) goes further: she also shows that the major communicative limitation of the above interplay of adverbs is that it does not alone suffice to dissociate TT and TSit. Learners thus cannot focus on the pre-state of an event (prospective: TT < TSit) or the post-state of an event (perfect: TT > TSit). In order to be able to do this, learners must go beyond the basic variety and develop a verbal morphology which allows for the independent specification of TT.

The overall picture that emerges from Starren's study is of a developing system which first allows temporal relations to be marked by discourse means and simple adverbs, through a stage where finer temporal distinctions can be expressed through the interplay of adverbs marking both TT and TSit, in conjunction with the internal temporal characteristics of the event denoted in the utterance, to the development of verbal morphology which alone allows TT and TSit to become dissociated, and grammatical aspect expressed. Temporal reference is achieved before the first aspectual distinctions within perfectivity, and for aspect to become fully productive, some verbal morphology must be acquired. But 'tense before aspect' is a spin-off from the main question Starren is asking, which is: 'What temporal functions can be expressed by the learner's repertoire at a given time?'

This study may be compared to that of Benazzo (2000), who examined the use of additive and restrictive scope particles in English, French and German L2 in longitudinal data from the ESF corpus. She also looked closely at temporal adverbs expressing iteration and at temporal adverbs of contrast, and found that adverbs marking the iteration of an event (*encore [une fois]*, and translation equivalents in the other languages) are used before temporal adverbs of contrast ('TACs': *déjà, encore*[9]). TACs only appear at relatively advanced stages, when verbal morphology has been acquired.

Benazzo found that learners of the same L2 use the same particles in the same way at each stage examined, and that at a given stage of utterance organisation, learners of all L2s studied show similar behaviour. This is a remarkable correspondence, and it has to do with the nature of the constituents that at each stage of development are in the 'scope' of the particle. Iterative particles characteristically express the repetition of an event, which happens again, at a later time interval. They quantify over events, referred to by V and its complements. To be repeated, an event has to be bounded (perfectively presented), and the expressive means for temporality of the basic varieties allow this: TT and TSit coincide. This is why they appear at basic variety level, but not before. The central forms are *encore (une fois), noch(mal), nog*, but other more idiosyncratic forms are also used, as **otra* fois* in the following example:

(5)   SF: Alberto   (charlot) [ale] à la prison *otra* fois
                        'Chaplin go to the prison another time'

These adverbs indicate that the event denoted by the utterance containing them is of the same type as that of a previously mentioned utterance; they quantify over that event and occur adjacent to the expression denoting it. In other words, their distribution is identical to that of the temporal adverbs modifying TSit, which we have already seen in Starren's study.

But temporal adverbs of contrast relate <u>two</u> different time intervals (phases) of the same event. These time intervals have to be signalled, and for this it is necessary to master the relevant verbal morphology. In the following example of Alfonso, a Spanish-speaking learner of French who developed a fully functional verb morphology:

(6)   SF: Alberto   tous les gens que j'ai déjà dits
                          'all the people that I have already mentioned'

TT = TU > TSit, the use of *déjà* associates with the TSit, and the finite *ai* ('have') is necessary to specify the TT. In other words, a pre-requisite for the productive use of this adverb of contrast, which functions to dissociate TT from TSit, is that independent means are available for fixing the TT. It is therefore only used productively when a functional verbal morphology is in place.

This last example shows that 'communicative need' is but one side of the coin; for the efficient expression of this communicative need, there are structural prerequisites: a functional verbal morphology must be available. This example contrasts with the conclusions of Schlyter (this volume), and we return to it in the discussion below.

Inappropriate Productions

At the other end of the acquisitional scale we find a phenomenon which Lambert (e.g. 1997), and Carroll & von Stutterheim (e.g. 1997) have been investigating in detail: learners' utterances are grammatical, but the result is not right. Carroll and von Stutterheim (1997: 84) find that 'les écarts entre natifs et apprenants sont peu visibles lorsqu'on envisage de manière isolée les connaissances lexicales, la syntaxe, la morphologie, etc., car peu d'aspects de la performance divergent notoirement de la norme'.[10] What does emerge from close examination of advanced learners' productions are differences with respect to natives in the way they organise information across utterances in building up a coherent text – in the way the different levels of knowledge interact.

We will discuss this phenomenon with examples from TL French, and from two studies on advanced Italian learners (Watorek & Perdue, 1999) and Polish learners (Watorek, 2003). Both these studies are concerned with the analysis of spatial descriptions; both groups of learners, and a group of French native speakers, were asked to describe a poster on which figured a town square. The main structure utterances in this type of task are required (spatially) to relate a figure to a ground (Talmy, 1983), so that the interlocutor can understand what is where.

(7)   KAT (native francophone)
(a)   alors *par rapport au bâtiment jaune toblerone en allant vers la droite* il y a une espèce de petit square avec 5 arbres.

'so in relation to the yellow toblerone building and going towards the right there is a sort of little square with five trees'

(b) *au milieu un kiosque où* il y a marqué tabac.
'in the middle a kiosk where it's written 'tobacco''

(c) avec une vieille dame qui tricote.
'with an old lady who is knitting'

(d) *à gauche du kiosque* trois enfants s'amusent sur les échasses.
'to the left of the kiosk three children are having fun on stilts'

(e) et *devant* il y a un monsieur qui donne à manger aux pigeons.
'and in front (of it) there is a man who is feeding the pigeons'

(8) VIC (Italian L1)
(a) après il y a une place.
'then there is a square'

(b) *où* il y a beaucoup de gens.
'where there are many people'

(c) il y a des voitures.
'there are cars'

(d) il y a **aussi** des arbres.
'there are also trees'

(e) il y a un tabac.
'there is a tobacco kiosk'

(f) il y a **aussi** un homme qui lit le journal.
'there is also a man who is reading the paper'

(9) ANG (Polish L1)
(a) une place
'a square'

(b) il y a des gens qui qui se promènent.
'there are people who are walking'

(c) il y a une femme *au tabac* qui vend des journaux.
'there is a woman in the tobacco kiosk who is selling newspapers'

(d) il y a des gens des enfants qui jouent qui s'amusent.
'there are people children who are playing who are having fun'

(e) il y a **aussi** des des gens qui font du vélo.
'there are also some some people who are cycling'

The learners' L1s are typologically different, yet their L2 production, which consists of grammatical utterances, shows striking similarities to each other's rather than to that of the French native speaker. The learners' texts consist of grammatical utterances, but are 'unfluent'. The native speaker uses a rich repertoire of spatial expressions (italicised in the examples: *au milieu, à gauche, devant, en allant vers la droite*), whereas the learners limit themselves to one each, italicised in (8b) and (9c). On the other hand, the learners use *aussi* (8d, f), (9e), an anaphoric additive particle, whereas the native speaker does not. The typical utterance pattern for this type of text: PrepP + V_{exist} + NP (where the existential verb in French is typically *il y a*), is used systematically by the learners with the PrepP 'understood' – left implicit – and recoverable from (8b) and (9a). Absence of PrepP and use of *aussi* go hand in hand, as *aussi* functions to create an anaphoric link between its utterance and a previous utterance (Watorek & Perdue, 1999). Finally, the native speaker once uses (7d) a simple utterance pattern, which includes not only the spatial relation between figure and ground, but also the activities of the figure. Elsewhere in the texts, this figure's activity is separated off in a relative clause (7c, e), (8f), (9b–e).

These differences betray not so much a difference of repertoire (learners 'have' a wider range of spatial prepositions than these texts evidence, the native speaker 'has' *aussi*) as a difference in the way the information to be conveyed is organised for expression.[11] The native speaker introduces the global space to be described – the square – and then subdivides it in order to locate the entities it contains: the middle (7d), the left-hand space in relation to the kiosk (7c), and the sub-space in front of the kiosk (7e). This division into subspaces leads the speaker to encode different typ7s of (topological and projective) spatial relations. The learners, on the other hand, give a list of entities within the global space, with no subdivisions. The space provided by the square affords a salient (topological) ground within which a series of figures are included, the ground being maintained from utterance to utterance.

We see, then, a close interrelation between the organisation and linearisation of the information to be expressed, and the linguistic means accessed to do so. The 'prototypical' treatment of the spatial task (Watorek, 1996) adopted by the learners – a list of figures included in one relatum by repetition of the same spatial relation made explicit by *aussi* – is directly reflected in the linguistic means used:

LINGUISTIC MEANS USED	>	SELECTION AND LINEARISATION OF INFORMATION
(PrepP) Vexist + NP *aussi*	>	choose a salient ground, figure-ground relation of inclusion

We now see why the learners' productions are relatively poor in spatial expressions: the prototypical way they go about solving the task, using a basic utterance pattern and implicit reference maintenance, does not require them. We see that choice on one level of the production process has ramifications for other levels.

Discussion

Even as briefly described as they have been, the studies just mentioned show how formal and communicative factors mentioned in the introduction intervene together in the acquisition process. These studies come down on the side of 'tense before aspect', but from the functional viewpoint of the difference between temporal reference and aspectualisation. Deictic and anaphoric temporal reference is more urgent than aspectual distinctions; temporal adverbs are sufficient to specify temporal reference, are indeed much more precise than morphology for marking temporal reference, and so are acquired first. But – the other way round – temporal adverbs are central to the means for expressing temporality (all languages have them, whereas not all language have verbal morphology); they are full lexical items, are easier to perceive and take in than morphology, and so are acquired first, which is why temporal reference is acquired first. The aspectual distinctions are decisive in this respect. There exist aspectual adverbs (TACs), and they are not acquired first. Temporal adverbs work if the event or state they specify is perfectively presented. If, however, a learner expresses aspectual distinctions (TT–TSit dissociations in Klein's terminology), then s/he needs verb morphology. Verbal morphology is more efficient for aspect. As temporal adverbs of contrast associate with and reinforce aspectual distinctions, their use becomes productive only when verb morphology is in place. There are structural constraints on the order of acquisition of different semantic sub-classes of temporal adverbs. This sequence is not reserved for learners who acquire French outside the classroom; it is clearly reflected in the results of Brum de Paula's (1998) study on the learning of French as a foreign language in Brazil.

We came back to this example because it allows us to contrast the learner variety approach with a more strictly formal approach, as exemplified in Schlyter's contribution to this volume. She uses Cinque's (1999) syntactic hierarchy of functional categories expressing tense, aspect and modality in order to contrast child and adult acquisition processes, and points out that the hierarchy allows very precise hypotheses to be formulated with respect to acquisition orders: the child builds up the hierarchy *ab initio*, whereas the adult, who masters the underlying concepts in the L1, does not follow the hierarchy. The perspective is by definition target-orientated, as Cinque is interested in what is grammaticalised in the (adult) languages of the world. Thus the approach does not take into account the communicative potential of a learner's linguistic repertoire at a given time, which imposes learner-specific constraints on the acquisition process. This is why we spelled out the 'communicative factors' and the 'formal factors' in the introduction to this chapter, since important and interrelated questions for the learner variety approach are: (a) how do communicative limitations[12] incite the learner to go beyond the linguistic repertoire she has?; (b) and what are the structural prerequisites for acquiring the linguistic means?

To recap: firstly, the organisation of the learner's current repertoire excluded the productive use of temporal adverbs of contrast.[13] Secondly, the use of an utterance pattern with reference to the ground conveyed implicitly or, indirectly, by *aussi* largely obviated the use of explicit spatial expressions in the learner's utterances. These types of constraints on learners' production have been characterised by Carroll & von Stutterheim (1993, 1997) in terms of grammatical choice. Not only in terms of processing (see Pienemann, 1998; Towell, 2002), but in terms of grammatical choice – their idea is also more constraining than 'thinking for speaking' (Slobin, 1991). We give one of their examples, again from spatial descriptions, to emphasise this point. German has a grammaticalised paradigm of expressions for maintaining reference to spaces built around *da* ('there'), for example: *davor* ('there in front'), *dahinter* ('there behind'), *daneben* ('there next to'), *darüber* ('there above'), *darunter* ('there beneath'). As the glosses indicate, this paradigm is much less productive in English, and less central to the grammar of reference maintenance. German native speakers thus tend to conceptualise spatial descriptions around spaces. This is 'thinking for speaking', in Slobin's sense, but the story does not end here. German speakers consequently systematically place expressions referring to the ground in utterance-initial position, followed by the expression referring to the figure. Reference is then maintained, adverbially, to the ground:

(10) (a)   vor dem Café ist ein Brunnen
      (b)   **daneben** ist ein Zeitungskiosk

The English reference maintenance system in such texts is based on entities – *it* rather than *there*. (*There* is part of the existential expression, see below.) Reference maintenance to the ground is therefore achieved by a full PrepP, with the existential and the NP referring to the figure in different possible positions, as this translation of (10) illustrates:

(11) (a)   in front of the café is a fountain.
      (b)   **beside the fountain** there is a newspaper stand.
      (b') there is a newspaper stand **next to it.**

Use of the spatial anaphor *there* in these contexts is 'unfluent':

(b″) ?beside there there is a newspaper stand.

These authors propose a "conceptual transfer'during the conceptuali-sation phase (Levelt, 1989) to explain why even very advanced English learners of German produce spatial descriptions where the referential domain of entities is used for reference maintenance, this choice having grammatical ramifications throughout the utterance:

(12) (a)   es gibt einen brunnen **vor dem Café**
       (b)   und **neben ihm** gibt es einen Zeitungskiosk

(12) is a grammatical sequence in German, but is 'unfluent' to a native for a double reason: the existential *es gibt* (which is largely absent from native productions), which either relegates the ground expression to the end of the utterance (12a), or which has to invert (12b) to keep the finite verb in second position given the use of the utterance-initial PrepP containing the anaphoric pronoun *ihm*. Notice also that (12a) illustrates a linguistic structure that goes against the informational organisation of the main structure of this text-type, where ground-expression normally precedes figure-expression.

The examples discussed here have sufficed, we hope, to suggest that at the early and also the very advanced stages of L2 acquisition, the learner's variety has its own systematicity, manifested by an 'idiosyncratic' interaction of organisational constraints. Hence, use of one form inevitably has ramifications for what can combine with it in the utterance.

Conclusion: The Significance of Learners' Errors

If we return to the 'basic stages' of acquisition, where temporal specifica-tion is carried only by adverbs and discourse organisation principles, we encounter highly recurrent structures with sub-classes of temporal adverbs in utterance-initial position, specifying TT, which are learner-specific. Corder (1971) would have said 'idiosyncratic'.[14] All learners show this structure, which seems communicatively necessary, early on in the acquisition process. The examples from the advanced stages underline the multi-level interaction of constraints: conceptual choices at utterance level have ramifications for the construction of discourse. As Bardovi-Harlig and Hartford (1995: 125) put it, the learner has to master both 'grammatical features that contribute to the structure of the text and, conversely (. . .) contextual features that determine the use of grammatical features'; and for the analyst, this interaction may not 'be accessible through the analysis of sentence-level production'. We hope the examples discussed in this chapter have suggested that learner-specific organising principles, and their specific interaction, may constrain the path 'towards' the TL. In a way, we have fleshed out Corder's (1981) insight that the learner has her/his own, grammatically-based, 'internal syllabus'.

Notes
1. This problem was called 'ranking of functions' in Perdue (1984).
2. This problem was called 'alternatives of expression' in Perdue (1984).
3. See Towell (2002) for a recent study of the narrative production in L2 French by English undergraduates.
4. If TT is contemporaneous with the time of utterance, then this configuration gives the well-known English present perfect.
5. For our purposes, 'usual' applies to target language French.
6. Transcription conventions are as follows: [ ] enclose broad phonetic transcription, (...) represents an irrelevant, omitted passage, + represents a silent pause. M = Moroccan, S = Spanish, F = French before the informant's name indicates his/her Source and Target languages. The English glosses should not be interpreted as a grammatical analysis.
7. Starren cites the study of Erguvanli (1984), who gives the standard word order of Turkish as S (Adv) O (Adv) V. The TT adverb is in second position when the subject is overt, but as the subject can often be left implicit, the adverb can appear initially. This account seems to exclude the order Adv S O V, attested in the L2 production of Turkish learners.
8. The same reviewer points out that the Spanish-speaking learners have a different (and idiosyncratic) lexical solution for expressing habituality.
9. Note that French *encore* is highly multifunctional. Compare: *je voudrais encore une bière* (additive – 'I would like another beer '); *il m'a encore insulté* (iterative – 'he has insulted me again'); *à dix heures il dormait encore* (contrastive – 'at ten o'clock he was still sleeping').
10. 'the deviations between natives and learners are scarcely noticeable if one takes separately each level of knowledge: lexis, syntax, morphology, etc., because few aspects of [learners'] performance clearly diverge from the norm.'
11. A reviewer pointed out that this remark would be 'even more convincing' if a richer repertoire of spatial expressions were found for the same learners in other tasks. We agree, and point to the fact that the learners of French in the ESF project (see for example Perdue & Schenning, 1996) show a richer repertoire of spatial expressions in contexts of movement than in contexts of static location.
12. Limitations that can be defined rather precisely in terms of 'competition' between different organising principles (see, for example, Perdue, 1995).
13. We assume that an adult learner has no more difficulties in understanding *déjà* and contrastive *encore* than she has with *hier* or iterative *encore*.
14. As regards utterance-initial frequency or duration adverbs think, for TL French, of the wealth of published grammatical interpretations of the remarkable (idiosyncratic) first sentence of Proust's *A la recherche du temps perdu*.

References
Bardovi-Harlig, K. and Hartford, B. (eds) (1995) The construction of discourse by non-native speakers. [Special issue]. *Studies in Second Language Acquisition* 17(2).
Bartning, I. (1997) L'apprenant dit avancé et son acquisition d'une langue étrangère. *AILE, Acquisition et Interaction en Langue Etrangère* 9, 9–50.
Benazzo, S. (2000) L'acquisition de particules de portée en français, anglais et

allemand L2: études longitudinales. Unpublished PhD thesis, University Paris VIII.

Brum de Paula, M. (1998) L'appropriation de la temporalité morphologique en langue étrangère. Unpublished PhD thesis, University Paris X.

Carroll, M. and von Stutterheim, C. (1993) The representation of spatial configurations in English and German and the grammatical structure of locative and anaphoric expressions. *Linguistics* 31, 1011–1041.

Carroll, M. and von Stutterheim, C. (1997) Relations entre grammaticalisation et conceptualisation et implications pour l'acquisition d'une langue étrangère. *AILE, Acquisition et Interaction en Langue Etrangère* 9, 83–116.

Cinque, G. (1999) *Adverbs and Functional Heads: A Cross-linguistic Perspective.* New York and Oxford: Oxford University Press.

Clark, E. (1971) On the acquisition of the meaning of 'before' and 'after'. *Journal of Verbal Learning and Verbal Behaviour* 10, 266–275.

Corder, S. P. (1967) The significance of learners' errors. *International Review of Applied Linguistics* 5, 161–170.

Corder, S. P. (1971) Idiosyncratic dialects and error analysis. *International Review of Applied Linguistics* 9, 147–160.

Corder, S. P. (1981) Post Scriptum. *Langages* 57, 39–41.

Erguvanli, E. (1984) The function of word order in Turkish grammar. Unpublished PhD thesis, University of California at Berkeley.

Kellerman, E. (1987) Aspects of transferability in second language acquisition. Unpublished PhD thesis, KU Nijmegen.

Klein, W. (1994) *Time in Language.* London: Routledge and Kegan.

Klein, W. (1998) Assertion and finiteness. In N. Dittmar and Z. Penner (eds) *Issues in the Theory of Language Acquisition* (pp. 225–245). Bern: Lang.

Klein, W. and Perdue, C. (1997) The basic variety (or: Couldn't natural languages be much simpler?) *Second Language Research* 13 (4), 301–47.

Klein, W., Li, P. and Hendriks, H. (2000) Aspect and assertion in Mandarin Chinese. *Natural Language and Linguistic Theory* 18, 723–770.

Lambert, M. (1997) En route vers le bilinguisme. *AILE, Acquisition et Interaction en Langue Etrangère* 9, 147–72.

Levelt, W. (1981) The speaker's linearisation problem. *Philological Transactions of the Royal Society of London. Series B* 295, 305–315.

Levelt, W. (1989) *Speaking. From Intention to Articulation.* Cambridge, MA and London: MIT Press.

Perdue, C. (ed) (1984) *Second Language Acquisition by Adult Immigrants. A Field Manual.* Rowley: Newbury House.

Perdue, C. (1995) *L'acquisition du français et de l'anglais par des adultes: former des énoncés.* Paris: CNRS Editions.

Perdue, C. and Schenning, S. (1996) The expression of spatial relations in a second language: two longitudinal studies. *Zeitschrift für Literaturwissenschaft und Linguistik* 104, 6–34.

Pienemann, M. (1998) *Language Processing and Second Language Development Processability Theory.* Amsterdam / Philadelphia: Benjamins.

Schlyter, S. (This volume) Adverbs and functional categories in L1 and L2 acquisition of French.

Slobin, D. (1991) Learning to think for speaking. Native language, cognition and rhetorical style. *Pragmatics* 1, 7–25.

Starren, M. (2001) The second time. Unpublished PhD, Katholieke Universiteit Brabant.

Talmy, L. (1983) How language structures space. In H. Pick and L. Alcrelodo (eds) *Spatial Orientations: Theory, Research and Application* (pp. 225–282). New York: Plenum Press.

Towell, R. (2002) Relative degrees of fluency: A comparative case study of advanced learners of French. *International Review of Applied Linguistics in Language Teaching* 40 (2), 117–50.

Watorek, M. (1996) Le traitement prototypique. *Toegepaste Taalwetenschap in Artikelen* 55 (2), 187–200.

Watorek, M. and Perdue, C. (1999) Additive particles and focus: observations from learner and native speaker production. *Linguistics* 37, 297–323.

Watorek, M. (2003) The development of anaphoric means to refer to space and entities in the acquisition of French by Polish learners. In Ch. Dimroth and M. Starren (eds) *Information Structure and the Dynamic of Language Acquisition* (pp. 329–355). Amsterdam: Benjamins.

Chapter 2

Discourse Structuring in Advanced L2 French: The Relative Clause

VICTORINE HANCOCK AND NATHALIE KIRCHMEYER

Introduction

In this chapter we will take relative clauses to illustrate clause combining in French interlanguage. We argue that the use of subordinators as a measure of syntactic complexity should be evaluated at two levels, a micro-syntactic level and a discourse (or macro-syntactic) level. We describe some relative structures that we claim are characteristic of the discourse structuring of the advanced learner, and which could thus contribute towards identifying advanced stages of acquisition.

A number of studies have investigated the domain of clause combining within the framework of SLA. This area of language learning is interesting as it reflects learners' competence to package utterances into more complex entities in order to hierarchise information and to build a more coherent text. The functional and typological approaches proposed by Givón (1990) and Lehmann (1988) constitute the basis of a number of studies in SLA (Chini, 1998; Ferraris, 2001; Giacalone Ramat, 1992, 1999, 2000; Sato, 1990). In these studies, language acquisition is described as a development from a paratactic mode (i.e. strongly context-dependent) to a syntactic mode (i.e. characterised by more integrated structures). The acquisition process is compared to the diachronic grammaticalisation process and would thus be a continuum that stretches from minimal to maximal integration, i.e. from juxtaposition via coordination and subordination to nominalisation.

However, an increasing number of studies in the field of spoken French have proposed a re-evaluation of the notion of subordination (Andersen, 1997; Blanche-Benveniste, 1990, 1997; Debaisieux, 1994; Deulofeu, 1995). These studies point out that a macro-syntactic approach is more fruitful as it better describes dependencies between elements beyond the sentence boundaries. The studies also question the sentence as a relevant unit for the

17

description of spoken language in general and take into account the information structure (Morel & Danon-Boileau, 1998).

In advanced stages of L2 acquisition – our subject matter here – it seems that clause combining does not constitute a major difficulty in language production, considering the high frequency and variation of subordinate clauses produced by learners: adverbial (temporal, causal, . . .), complement and relative clauses (Bartning, 1990, 1997; Chini, 1998; Kirchmeyer, 2000; Kirsch & Dittmar, 2001). The aim of the present study is thus to show some characteristic features of the syntactic complexity and discourse structuring at acquisition stages beyond *the Basic Variety* (as described by Klein & Perdue, 1992, 1997).

In analysing relative clauses, we will try to answer the following questions: How do we characterise syntactic complexity at advanced stages? How can we adapt a formal description of clause combining (i.e. coordination versus subordination) to a more functional approach to discourse competence in SLA? We will use examples of relative clauses to show that *integration* and *packaging* are relevant parameters to evaluate syntactic complexity as they reflect some essential properties of advanced learners' discourse. We define the degree of integration as reflecting the learner's capacity to organise information in a hierarchised way (*hierarchisation*). Subordinate, infinitive and participial structures are examples of integrated structures. The degree of packaging reflects the capacity of planning sequences of speech. The production of multipropositional utterances is an example of packaging.

Corpus and Method

The study draws on the *InterFra* corpus from Stockholm University. For a detailed description of the corpus, see Bartning (1997). The corpus contains both video retellings (see Appendix) and interviews from non-native speakers (NNS) and native speakers (NS) aged 20–25.[1] The NNS are semi-formal learners, since they have studied French at university level and have stayed in a French-speaking country for at least one month. For the quantitative analysis of this particular study (see Table 2.1), relative structures in the retellings of 12 NNS in French were analysed and compared with retellings from 12 NS. Relatives were also analysed from the interviews of eight NNS as well as eight NS. The eight NNS contributed two interviews each. Six of the NNS and eight of the NS were the same in the retellings and in the interviews.

In order to detect a possible influence from the mother tongue, Swedish, retellings in Swedish L1 were also analysed. By comparing interviews and narrative data, we can identify general patterns in discourse structuring.

Table 2.1 Extract of corpus used in the present study

Retellings	language recorded	number of words	Interviews	language recorded	number of words
12 NNS	French L2 Swedish L1	5855	8 NNS	French L2	23488
12 NS	French L1	5092	8 NS	French L1	21526

Analysis of the Structure of Relative Clauses

In this section, we will analyse a particular subordinate type, the relative clause (or rather a group of related types of clause), in order to illustrate some features of the advanced learner's discourse organisation. The relative clauses in the retellings and interviews were, to begin with, analysed with regard to their structure (Tables 2.2a and b).

Table 2.2a Distribution of different types of relatives. Retellings

L2 = FR	cl*	qui	que	où	ce Q	le Q	Σ	L1 = FR	cl*	qui	que	où	ce Q	le Q	Σ
Christina	3	–	–	–	–	–	3	Anne	1	4	–	1	–	–	6
Eva	1	–	–	2	–	–	3	Bernard	2	3	1	–	–	–	6
Lena	4	7	1	5	1	–	18	Eric	1	7	–	2	1	1	12
Marie	4	6	–	–	–	–	10	Henri	3	8	–	4	–	–	15
Pernilla	–	1	–	–	–	–	1	Jérôme	3	6	2	–	1	–	12
Yvonne	4	2	–	2	1	–	9	Laurent	1	6	1	–	2	–	10
Anders	5	1	–	–	–	–	6	Mélanie	4	5	2	–	1	–	12
Anita	1	3	–	–	–	–	4	Olivier	–	2	1	2	–	–	5
Ida	7	2	–	–	1	–	10	P-N	2	2	–	1	1	–	6
Kerstin	6	2	–	–	1	1	10	Rachelle	3	5	–	1	–	–	9
Malena	5	1	–	–	–	–	6	Thérèse	4	1	–	2	–	–	7
Mona	3	–	–	–	–	–	3	Véron	1	1	–	–	–	–	2
Σ	43	25	1	9	4	1	83	Σ	25	50	7	13	6	1	102
%	52	30	1	11	5	1	100	%	25	49	7	13	6	1	100

If we consider the distribution of the different structures of relative clauses found in the corpus (Tables 2.2a and b), the following features can be observed. First, the overall distribution of relative structures is quite similar for NNS and NS: almost all structures used by the NS are also used by the NNS, in both retellings and interviews, such as *cleft* constructions like *il y a* /*c'est . . . qui/que*, relatives introduced by *qui*, *que*, *où*, *ce qui/que* and

Table 2.2b Distribution of different types of relatives. Interviews

L2 = FR	cl*	qui	que	où	ce Q	le Q**	Σ	L1 = FR	cl*	qui	que	où	ce Q	le Q**	Σ
Christina	4	6	–	1	1	–	12	Anne	16	15	1	6	6	2	46
Eva	3	1	4	–	–	–	8	Bernard	4	6	1	1	2	–	14
Jessica	2	1	2	1	1	–	7	Eric	4	4	6	2	2	1	19
Lena	15	16	4	3	1	1	40	Henri	12	5	5	2	4	1	29
Marie	8	12	2	2	1	–	25	Laurent	4	13	3	3	3	–	26
Nathalie	1	11	–	1	2	–	15	Mélanie	5	7	4	5	4	–	25
Pernilla	2	4	–	2	1	–	9	Olivier	2	21	2	4	3	–	32
Yvonne	17	9	4	2	1	–	33	P-N	8	15	4	2	4	–	33
Σ	52	60	16	12	8	1	149	Σ	55	86	26	25	28	4	224
%	34	36	11	8	6	1	100	%	25	38	12	11	12	2	100

*il y a x qui/que/où, j'ai/on a x qui, on voit/entend x qui, c'est x qui/que.
** le Q + prép Q: lequel, avec qui, dont

lequel (*avec qui*, two tokens, and *dont*, one token in NS, are not found in NNS).

Second, two differences between the NS and NNS are worth noticing: clefts constitute only 25% of the NS production in both retellings and interviews, but as much as half of the NNS relatives in the retellings. The other difference observed in the interviews, but not in the retellings, was that the use of *ce qui/que* constructions was twice as frequent in French L1 speech (12 versus 6%). Despite these two differences, there is a similarity in the distribution of relative structures between the two groups of interlocutors, and the two most frequent structures, clefts and *qui* clauses, constitute about 80% of the relatives in the retellings and 60–70% in the interviews in both groups of interlocutors.

Tables 2.2a and 2.2b thus show similarities in the distribution and the frequency of relative structures between learners and native speakers. We then wanted to find out if there would in fact be different functions at a discourse level in spite of the apparent resemblance.

Syntactic Dependency of Relative Clauses

As mentioned in the introduction, the notion of subordination and the degree of dependency of subordinate clauses is a matter of discussion. In spoken language in particular, the dichotomy of subordination versus coordination deserves reanalysis. As a consequence, the contribution of subordinate clauses to integrated constructions in learner speech could be debated.

Morel and Danon-Boileau (1998) and Morel and Rialland (1993) have focused on the syntactic and intonational independency of certain relative clauses in spoken (standard) French. According to Creissels (1995: 324), only a certain number of relatives in French can be considered as subordinated:

(1)   (a)   je ne connais pas la personne qui vient de me saluer
            'I don't know the person who just said hello to me'
(1)   (b)   j'ai rencontré Michel, qui ne m'a même pas salué
            'I met Michel, who didn't even say hello to me'

Whereas in Example 1a the relative constitutes a structure integrated into the matrix clause, the relative clause in Example 1b is not influenced by transformations (negation/question) of the main clause. Thus the two relatives clearly have different relations with regard to dependency of their main clauses (Creissels, 1995: 315).

As Berrendonner (1990) points out, *appositive* relative clauses, in opposition to determinative clauses, are to some extent independent from their principal clause. Appositive clauses are often placed, in spontaneous talk, at the final end of an utterance, like an afterthought (Berrendonner, 1990: 33):

(2)   IBM Suisse a pris l'affaire très au sérieux, qui a prévenu par lettre tous ses clients. (Press, Fribourg)
      'IBM Switzerland has taken the question very seriously, and has informed all its clients.'

While the relationship between the relative clause and its main clause in e.g. the *determinative* case is of a micro-syntactic nature, the relationship in Example 2 is characterised by the author as non-rectional or macro-syntactic, i.e. the relative is less integrated than the determinative relative. Accordingly, these types of relative have a tendency to function as a *période binaire* or an autonomous pair of *thème-rhème*, where the relative pronoun is the *thème*. Blanche-Benveniste (1997: 121) considers the appositive relative as a separate element added to the nucleus:

(3)   je suis obligée d'acheter beaucoup de médicaments – qui ne sont pas remboursés
      'I have to buy a lot of medicine – for which there is no reimbursement'

The relative pronoun in example (3) introduces an additional *rhème*.

According to Morel and Danon-Boileau (1998), there is an increasing usage in spontaneous French talk of so-called autonomous relatives. Our hypothesis is that these relatives play a role in the hierarchisation at a macro-syntactic level, a phenomenon we will come back to and develop below. If we suppose that the production of autonomous relatives has an impact at the macro-syntactic level, these relatives would be significant for the characterisation of the advanced learners' discourse organisation.

In the following section we will analyse the relative clauses with respect to the information structure. Our starting points were the intonational studies made by Morel and Rialland (1993), and Morel and Danon-Boileau (1998), and the study on macro-syntax by Berrendonner (1990).

Analysis of the Information Structure of Relatives

We distinguish three different types of relative clause based on their position in the information structure of the utterances. The number of intonational features taken into account are limited, compared with the studies of Morel and Rialland (1993) and Morel and Danon-Boileau (1998). Our classification is based on the transcription, but also on attentive listening. The transcription gives information about pauses, hesitation phenomena and lengthened syllables (see Appendix for transcription conventions). The first group includes relatives associated with a presentative *cleft construction* like *il y a, j'ai, on a, c'est x qui/que* and (including perception verbs) *on voit, on entend*. In this group, the relative functions as a *rhème*.

Retellings:

(4)   (NNS: Kerstin) et puis <u>il y a</u> un monsieur <u>qui: qui arrive</u>
      'and then there is a man who who arrives'

(5)   (NNS: Yvonne) eu:h / <u>c'est</u>+ une mère <u>qui garde l'enfant</u> dans une parc
      'there is a mother who looks after the child in a park'

(6)   (NNS: Anders) <u>on entend</u> / les spectateurs <u>qui: qui fait / des applauds qui applaudissent</u>
      'you hear the audience who who makes applause who applauds'

Interviews:

(7)   (NNS: Chr2)   mais là <u>il y a</u> des gens <u>qui habitent dans dans les chambres de bonnes</u>/(I:mm) partout / dans toute Paris.
      'but there there are people who live in in the servants' bedrooms everywhere all over Paris'

(8)   (NNS: Len2)   e:h à *Nya-Zealand il y avait ce ce:/ce truc de gr euh Greenpeace./on a: # on on croit que <u>c'est</u> c'était vrai vé- (I:mm) SIM véritablement le le gouvernement <u>qui a</u>/(I:mm) SIM ou: la police euh

secrète ou quelque chose.
'in New Zealand there was this this this Greenpeace business. they
have they they think it is was true rea- really the the government who
has or the secret service or something.'
(9)   (NNS: Mar1) on a vu <u>on a vu</u> eh toutes les maisons à Londres/<u>qui</u>
      <u>étaient</u> (I:mhm) <u>bombardées</u>/(I:mhm)
      'you could see all the houses in London that had been bombed'
(10) (NNS: Per2) <u>c'est</u> l'attitude des parents <u>qui/euh décide beaucoup/</u>
      euh/l'avenir de leurs enfants
      'it is the attitude of the parents that is decisive for the future of their
      children'

The second type contains relatives that are integrated in a *thème* or a
rhème (followed by [TH] or [RH] in the examples below). As these relatives
are internal to an information constituent, they have a micro-syntactic
(rectional) relation to their main clause.

Retellings:

(11) (NNS: Lena) e:t les les hommes <u>qui: qui: qui: travaillent</u> ils ils viennent
      tout de suite [TH]
      'and the men who who who work [= the paramedics] they they come
      immediately'
(12) (NNS: Marie) mais le petit fils n'aime pas l- ce monsieur <u>qui est venu</u>
      [RH]
      'but the little boy doesn't like this man who has arrived'

Interviews:

(13) (NNS: Nat2) dans la famille <u>où j'étais</u> ils ne voyaient/mm très
      souvent ses enfants [TH]
      'in the family where I was they didn't see very often their children'
(14) (NNS: Jes2) tout/tout <u>ce qu'ils mangent</u> / c'est toujours des choses
      qu'on aime [TH]
      'all all that they eat it's always things one likes'
(15) (NNS: Chr2) si elle peut rester à la maison avec les enfants c'est très
      bien./mais elle peut pas dire qu'elle a:/tant tant choses à faire si elle a
      une fille au pair <u>qui f / qui fait tout.</u> [RH]
      'if she can stay at home with the children it's very good. but she can't
      say she has so so many things to do if she has an au pair girl who who
      does everything.'

The third and last type is made up of the so-called autonomous relatives,
in which the relative form in itself a *thème-rhème* unity. According to

Berrendonner (1990), these relatives have a non-rectional or macro-syntactic relation to their main clause.
Retellings:

(16) (NNS: Anita) et et soudain un un homme vient avec <u>qui ont / qui a des ballons</u>
      'and and suddenly a a man appears with who have who has balloons'

(17) (NNS: Kerstin2) et puis il donne un coup de pied au monsieur / / <u>qui essaie de lui offrir des bonbons</u>. / / mais ça marche pas du tout parce que le garçon il mord / / .
      'and then he gives a kick to the man who tries to offer him candies. but it doesn't work at all because the boy he bites.'

(18) (NS: Anne) il en achète un gros paquet les offre au petit garçon <u>qui dès lors s'envole</u>
      'he buys a big bag of them offers them to the little boy who then flies away'

Interviews:

(19) (NNS: Chr2) j'aime pas les femmes qui ont des filles au pair et *qui ne font rien*
      'I don't like women who have an au pair girl and who are idle'

(20) (NNS: Eva1) j'a beaucoup des ami:s qui habitent à: aux Etats-Unis / (I:mhm) <u>que j'ai rencontrés/eh/en France</u>
      'I have a lot of friends who live in the United States who I have met in France'

(21) (NS: Lau) Caen il reste encore une pe- une moyenne ville je dirais en France <u>où: euh/où les choses se passent encore relativement bien</u> / par rapport aux grosses villes <u>où:/où là c'est vrai qu'il y a beaucoup de problèmes</u>
      'Caen is still a sma- a medium-sized town I would say in France where where things still go rather well compared to big cities where there certainly are lots of problems'

(22) (NS: Pie) ben j'ai déjà: j'ai déjà fait ce choix. enfin j'ai déjà eu/ce problème avec euh//e:h une ex-petite amie danoise/(I:mm/mm mm) <u>qui doit rester au Danemark euh/pou:r/pour ses études</u>
      'well I have already I have already made this decision. I mean I have already had this problem with a Danish ex-girlfriend who has to stay in Denmark for for her studies'

(23) (NS: Mel) // *ben je sais p-* // # j'ai rencontré beaucoup de Suédois qui en fait sont très très tournés vers l'étranger. / / (I:mm) <u>qui eu:h / / qui en plus ont beaucoup de mal à parler de leur pays.</u>

'well I don't kn- I have met lots of Swedes who are actually extremely open to foreign countries. who who also find it difficult to talk about their country'.

The autonomous relative clauses have been identified on the basis of the following criteria, which are informational, semantic, intonational and syntactic:

It constitutes in itself a *thème-rhème* pair (*période binaire*), where the relative pronoun is the *thème*.

The relative clause could be paraphrased by juxtaposition. Often an *et* ('and') could be added before the relative pronoun (Examples 17, 18, 19). Semantically, it constitutes a new 'idea' or aspect (*rhème*) of the noun. It is often separated from its main clause by several words (Examples 16, 20, 21).

The autonomy of the relative clause could be reinforced by intonation: it is often preceded by pauses and the relative pronoun is lengthened and/or repeated. It could also be preceded by a closing intonation (Examples 17, 20, 21, 23).

In NS production the relative pronoun could be followed by an adverb or a modifier, like *dès lors, en plus, c'est vrai que* (= *then, also, certainly*) (Examples 18, 21, 23). The tense of the relative clause could be another than that of the main clause (Example 22).

The relative could have the role of a 'comment' or 'afterthought' on the preceding clause. It is often possible, in order to make the content explicit, to supply the relative clause with an adverb like *ensuite* (= *then*) in retellings and *d'ailleurs* (= *by the way*) in interviews (Examples 17, 20, 22, 23).

Quantitative Study of the Information Structure of Relatives

Tables 2.3a and b display the quantitative analysis of the three categories presented in the previous section. A comparison between learners' and NS' production of relative clauses showed that autonomous relatives are less frequent in learner speech. In the retellings (Table 2.3a) only 5% of the relatives produced by NNS were autonomous compared to 18 % of the NS. In the interviews (Table 2.3b), the learners produced 13% of autonomous relatives and the NS 20%.

Also, Tables 2.3a and b show that learners have no difficulty producing integrated relative clauses. In both retellings and interviews, the NNS and the NS produce equal frequencies of relatives integrated into an informational constituent.[2] In contrast, it seems that autonomous relative structures are more difficult to produce for the learner. The quantitative difference between the NNS and the NS in producing autonomous relatives was significant in retellings (NNS: 5%; NS: 18%),[3] but not in interviews (NNS: 13%; NS: 20%).

Table 2.3a Information structure of relatives. Retellings

	L2 = FR		L1 = FR	
	Σ	%	Σ	%
presentative	51	61	45	44
integrated	28	34	39	38
autonomous	4	5	18	18
Σ	83	100	102	100

Table 2.3b Information structure of relatives. Interviews

	L2 = FR		L1 = FR	
	Σ	%	Σ	%
presentative	51	34	61	27
integrated	79	53	119	53
autonomous	19	13	44	20
Σ	149	100	224	100

Thus, it seems that the use of autonomous relatives could be a property of the advanced learner. If this is the case, one would expect the frequency of such relatives to increase with the development of the interlanguage. This is what Kirchmeyer found (see Kirchmeyer, 2002) when she compared retellings at three different stages of acquisition, in a cross-sectional and in a longitudinal study. Although relatives were used at the first stage (students at an elementary stage, but not beginners), autonomous relatives were used with a native-like frequency only at the third level, i.e. after at least one year of university study of French.

To sum up, the learners in our corpus seem to be restricting the production of relatives within the *thème-rhème* pair to a higher degree than NS, i.e. either to presentatives or to relatives integrated in a constituent, which reflects an organisation of the information structure at a local level. The autonomous relative, on the other hand, reflects an organisation at a textual or global level.

Relatives: Local and Global Organization

As we suggested in the introduction, *integration* and *packaging* (reflecting hierarchisation and planning) would be relevant to characterising the advanced learner. In this section, we will consider these two notions at two different organisational levels. From our results, we have concluded in the previous section that NNS tend to stick at a *local* organisational level (micro-level) more than NS, who have a capacity to organise their speech adequately also at a *global* level (macro-level). If we consider the degree of integration in relation to the two levels, local and global, it could be represented in the following way (Table 2.4):

Table 2.4 Degree of integration in the information structure

Information structure/organisation level	*Degree of integration*
micro-level: LOCAL	in a constituent:[TH] or [RH]
	in a *thème-rhème* pair:[TH-RH]
macro-level: GLOBAL	in an utterance;the autonomous relative:[TH-RH]–[TH-RH] . . .

The degree of integration is highest when the relative clause is inserted in an information constituent and it is lowest with respect to the autonomous relative. Considering that learners in our corpus master production of highly integrated local structures, but differ from NS with regard to their use of global structures, it would be relevant to focus on the latter to discuss hierarchisation and planning.

Hierarchisation and Planning at a Global Level

Learner utterances in the retellings and interviews typically contain one single autonomous relative per utterance, in contrast with NS, who often produce several per utterance (Examples 17 and 21). Nevertheless, both groups of speaker produce multipropositional utterances with relatives of one type of discourse function per utterance, as in Examples 24 and 25, where the autonomous clauses (underlined) are descriptive. The degree of hierarchisation is limited:

(24) (Nat2: NNS, interview; subject: the prototypical Frenchman) (RIRE) / eh / il est assez petit / (RIRE) aux cheveux bruns . il eh / / qui suit eh / / les / les discussions dans les journaux / / et les événements sociales et politiques. eh / qui s'intéresse à la vie intellectuelle . + et . . .
      '(LAUGHTER) he is quite small (LAUGHTER) with brown hair he who follows the debates in the newspapers and the social and political events and who who is interested in intellectual activities'
(25) (Lau: NS, interview) c'est un Sri-lankais qui est venu depuis trois (I:mm) SIM ans

e:t qui étudie ici (I:mm mm mm) SIM
e:t qui est / #
qui habite eu:h dans la cité universitaire
'it's a Sri Lankan who came three years ago and who studies here and
who is who stays at the campus'

The NS, however, produce complex multipropositional utterances with
autonomous relatives, where the hierarchisation is highly developed:

(26) (Eric: NS, retelling) arrive un monsieur
      qui veut compter fleurette à la dame
      ce qui déplaît fort au garçon
      qui joue dans le / dans le # à faire des pâtés de sable
      qui lance sa truelle
      'appears a man who wants to flirt with the lady which the boy
      strongly dislikes who plays in the in the, baking sand cakes who
      throws his spade'
(27) (Ann: NS, interview) avec les deux Français
      avec qui je suis
      on a rencontré aussi des des Suédois dans le dans le corridor dans l'un
      des corridors
      où on habite/
      qui so:nt qui sont sympas
      et avec qui (I:mm) ça / ça se passe assez bien quoi.
      'with the two Frenchmen I am with, we have also met Swedes in the in
      the corridor in one of the corridors where we live who are who are
      friendly and with whom things go quite well'

The multipropositional utterances of the NS in Examples 26 and 27
display a variety of functions at the semantic, narrative and informational levels. In the examples there are descriptive, continuative,
restrictive and autonomous relatives within one utterance. In the interviews of a few of the learners, there are 'outlines' of complex multipropositional utterances with relatives, as in Example 28, where the
learner is talking about France:

(28) (Len2: NNS, interview) à:/à u- une côté je vois un pays euh trè:s/
      culturel
      et qui a des/eu:h hm #/
      un pays
      où où je vois des des choses
      que que/eh que j'admire beaucoup
      'On one hand I see a country very cultural and which has # a country
      where where I see things that that that I admire very much'

The following extract from a retelling of the same learner was recorded 10 months after the interview in Example 28. To Lena, the use of autonomous relatives seems to support the sequential linking of events in her discourse production:

(29) (Lena2: NNS, retelling) et il commence à parler /
ce que n'aime pas l'enfant
qui eh qu se met à à / euh regarder le monsieur très fâchement /.
'and he starts to talk which the child doesn't like who start to look at the man very angrily'

The degree of packaging in the Examples 24–27 could be described along a scale (Table 2.5), where the lowest degree corresponds to utterances with one autonomous relative clause:

Table 2.5 Degree of packaging

Packaging of autonomous relatives (global level)
1. production of utterances with one autonomous relative clause, >
2. production of utterances with bi- or multipropositional autonomous relatives (with one function), >
3. production of complex multipropositional utterances with a variety of relatives showing multiple discourse functions

In our corpus most of the advanced learners seem to have reached the first degree in Table 2.5 and a few have reached the second degree. None of the advanced learners in the corpus produced fully developed complex utterances with relatives in the first or second recording (Example 29 from Lena was recorded later).

We could summarise our use of the notions of integration and packaging as follows (see Table 2.6). Both NS and NNS are able to hierarchise at a local information level (constituent level, *thème-rhème* pair). The NNS reach the same degree of integration as the NS at this level of linguistic development. However, the NS can plan larger discourse entities, resulting in the production of complex utterances with autonomous relatives and a variety of discourse functions at different discourse levels. This planning capacity thus entails a hierarchisation capacity at a global level, which we call synthesisation (Table 2.6). The learner's smaller capacity to plan larger speech units does not allow him to produce complex utterances containing multiple discourse functions, and both the degree of packaging and the synthesisation are lower. Thus, the advanced learner's capacity to hierarchise should be evaluated at a global level. At this level the analysis of learners' speech could reveal characteristic structural and functional features.

Table 2.6 Integration and packaging

	hierarchisation capacity		*planning capacity*
	integration	synthesisation	packaging
	local level	*global level*	*global level*
NS	+	+	+
NNS	+	–	–

Influence from L1 on Relative Clause Production

The lower production of autonomous relatives by the learners, compared with NS, is possibly due to the influence of L1 Swedish, at least to some extent. Evidence from the corpus shows that the French NS, who for example relate a sequence of events or enumerate the properties of a person prefer a succession of autonomous relatives as in Example 30 and as already shown before, while a recurrent structure of the NNS in French L2 is coordination with the conjunction *et* (= *and*), in both retellings (Example 31) and interviews.

(30) (Henri: NS, retelling) euh de suite après arrivent les secours / et euh / les secours ambulance j'entends euh
et **qui** prennent sur la civière la voiture
et **qui** qui prennent soin de de l'arbre / là où il a été abîmé en fait
et **qui** laissent euh l'homme étendu sur la route
'immediately afterwards assistance arrives and the paramedics I hear and who put the car on the stretcher and who take care of the tree where it was damaged in fact and who leave the man lying on the road'

(31) (Chr: NNS, retelling) oui / là il y avait un bonhomme dans une voiture.
et il a eu un acci accident de voiture / .
e:t / l'ambulance est arrivée .
e:t / ils ont pris la la voiture au lieu de l'homme . ils l'ont laissé / par terre .
e:t ils sont partis avec la voiture .
et avant de partir eh eh ils ont mis des pansement sur l'arbre du tronc oui / . c'est tout.
'yes there there was a little man in a car. and he had a car accident. and the ambulance came . and they took the the car instead of the man.

they left him on the ground. and they went away with the car. and before leaving they put a bandage on the tree of the trunk yes. that's all.'

The equivalent structure used in Swedish L1 would be coordination of the events, in retellings often with omission of the subject, as in Example 32:

(32) (Yvo: NNS, retelling) så kommer en ambulans förbi
      och stannar där framför
      och eh lyfter upp då bilen på en bår
      men lämnar honom
      'then passes an ambulance and stops there in front and then lifts the car on to a stretcher but leaves him'

An interesting example is 33, where the learner switches from a 'French' structuring manner (cf. Examples 25 and 30) to a 'Swedish' pattern (cf. Examples 31and 32) within an utterance. The learner starts her description of the prototypical Swede with autonomous relatives and accomplishes it by coordination with *et* (= *and*).

(33) (Per2: NNS, interview) c'est+ un homme ou une femme (RIRE)/
      e:t/**qui**/qui travaille/et euh qui a cinq semaines de vacances
      e:t **qui**/euh vont/souvent/euh/à l'étranger en/charter/cha/
      charter/*resa (RIRE) oui et/oui
      qui #/peut-être il a: a/euh un une petite maison/à la campagne ./
      et/il aime euh/euh faire du ski ./
      et il: cherche / euh il cherche le soleil pend pendant ses vacances .
      'it's a man or a woman (LAUGH) and who who works and has five weeks' holiday and who often goes abroad on a charter cha charter trip (LAUGH) yes and yes who # maybe he has a little cottage in the country and he likes skiing and he looks for the sun during his holidays.'

Conclusion

In this chapter we have suggested that the advanced learner's syntactic complexity should be evaluated at two separate levels of language, a micro- and a macro-level, defined by different levels of the information structure. Swedish L1 structuring could have an influence on French discourse production, which could partly explain why learners' production of autonomous relatives is less frequent compared with that of French NS. It is possible that the presence of autonomous relative clauses is a feature of an advanced acquisition stage. In previous studies (Hancock, 1997, 2000), we have argued that advanced learners typically introduce clauses with an autonomous *parce que*. This *parce que* is very frequent in native spoken French (Blanche-Benveniste, 1995: 26; Debaisieux, 1994). The function of this type of *parce que* (Examples 34 and 35) is a hierarchising one on a macro-level:

(34) (Pie: NS; subject: being a foreigner in Sweden) et puis euh et puis aussi ce qui était drôle c'est euh / c'est lorsque j'ai: j'ai parlé de ça à ma mère / (I:mhm) parce que ma mère est un petit ah elle est un p un petit (HESITATION) peu raciste quoi un petit peu (I:mm mm) SIM un peu comme tous les Français enfin bon (I:mhm) SIM. / alors quand je lui dis que moi je me retrouvais dans cette situation (I:mm) SIM ça ça l'a fait réfléchir un petit peu. / (I:mm mm) alors ça c'est bien en fait. (RIRE)
'and then and then what was fun it's it's when I I talked about that with my mother because my mother is a little she is a little (HESITATE) racist I mean a li- a little bit like like any French well. so when I told her I found myself in that situation that that made her think a little. so that's good in fact. (LAUGH)'

(35) (Mar: NNS) I: mm / et qu'est-ce que tu penses faire après les soixante points donc tu m'as dit travailler?
E: oui: eu:h / m je ne sais pas. j'ai parlé avec *** *** [= professeur] l'autre jour. / (I: mm) parce qu'on / on était euh # le cours / qu'on a eu avec elle (I:m) on était invité chez elle (I:m m) SIM l'autre jour. / et on a parlé de / de prendre un cours à *KV (I: mm) moi et: quelques autres X. / s'il y avait a:ssez d'étu:diants et elle pouvait / nous donner des cours .
'I: so what do you intend to do after sixty points [= three semesters of French studies] then you said you would work?'
'E: yes I don't know. I talked to *** *** [= teacher] the other day. because we we were # the course we had with her we were invited to her place the other day. and we talked about taking a course at KV me and some others X if there were enough students and she could give us courses .'

This type of autonomous *parce que*, which introduces background information, was found in the recordings of only some learners who seem to be advanced also with respect to other morpho-syntactic and lexical criteria[4] (see also Kihlstedt, 1998). Both the autonomous relatives and the type of *parce que* mentioned entail hierarchising at a macro-level, a feature of an advanced discourse organisation.

Notes
1. 38 non-native and 20 native speakers were recorded under similar conditions and by the same native French interviewer. Recently, interviews and retellings at elementary stages of acquisition have been added to the corpus.

2. There was no statistically significant difference according to an χ^2 test.
3. $\chi^2 = 7.0$, $p < 0.01$.
4. Preliminary results show that two of the learners (Marie and Lena) use both autonomous *parce que* and relatives in interviews.

References

Andersen, H. L. (1997) Propositions parenthétiques et subordination en français parlé. PhD thesis, University of Copenhagen.

Bartning, I. (1990) L'acquisition du français par des apprenants universitaires suédois – quelques aspects. *Revue Romane* 25, 165–180.

Bartning, I. (1997) L'apprenant dit avancé et son acquisition d'une langue étrangère – tour d'horizon et esquisse de la variété avancée. *AILE (Acquisition et Interaction en Langue Étrangère)* 9, 9–50.

Berrendonner, A. (1990) Pour une macro-syntaxe. *Travaux de linguistique* 21, 25–31.

Blanche-Benveniste, C. (1990) *Le français parlé: études grammaticales*. Paris: Editions du CNRS.

Blanche-Benveniste, C. (1997) *Approches de la langue parlée en français*. Paris: Ophrys.

Chini, M. (1998) La subordinazione in testi narrativi di apprendenti tedescofoni: forma e funzione. *Linguistica e filologia* 7, 121–159.

Creissels, D. (1995) *Éléments de syntaxe générale*. Paris: Presses Universitaires de France.

Debaisieux, J.-M. (1994) Le fonctionnement de parce que en français parlé contemporain: description linguistique et implications didactiques. PhD thesis, University of Nancy.

Deulofeu, J. (1995) Le dilemme de la 'modernisation des terminologies' en linguistique. *Travaux de Linguistique* 31, 25–45.

Ferraris, S. (2001) Text organisation in Italian learner varieties. In S. Foster-Cohen and A. Nizegorodcew (eds) *Eurosla Yearbook 1* (pp. 225–37). Amsterdam: Benjamins.

Giacalone Ramat, A. (1992) Grammaticalization processes in the area of temporal and modal relations. *Studies in Second Language Acquisition* 14, 297–322.

Giacalone Ramat, A. (1999) Grammaticalization of modality in language acquisition. *Studies in Language* 23(2), 387–417.

Giacalone Ramat, A. (2000) Typological considerations on second language acquisition. *Studia Linguistica* 54 (2), 123–135.

Givón, T. (1990) *Syntax. A Functional Typological Introduction*. Amsterdam: Benjamins.

Hancock, V. (1997) 'Parce que': un connecteur macro-syntaxique. L'emploi de 'parce que' chez des apprenants de français langue étrangère et des locuteurs natifs. *AILE (Acquisition et Interaction en Langue Étrangère)* 9, 117–145.

Hancock, V. (2000) Quelques connecteurs et modalisateurs dans le français parlé d'apprenants avancés. Étude comparative entre suédophones et locuteurs natifs. PhD thesis, Stockholm University.

Kihlstedt, M. (1998) La référence au passé dans le dialogue. Étude de l'acquisition de la temporalité chez des apprenants dits avancés de français. PhD thesis, Stockholm University.

Kirchmeyer, N. (2000) Étude de la compétence textuelle des lectes d'apprenants avancés. Aspects syntaxiques, sémantiques et discursifs. MA thesis. Stockholm University.

Kirchmeyer, N. (2002) Étude de la compétence textuelle des lectes d'apprenants avancés. Aspects structurels, fonctionnels et informationnels. PhD thesis, Stockholm University.

Kirsch, K. and Dittmar, N. (2001) Subordination in the RUSIL Corpus: The acquisition of German by Russian Jewish immigrants in Berlin. Paper presented at the 11th Annual Eurosla Conference, Paderborn 26–29 September 2001.

Klein, W. and Perdue, C. (1992) *Utterance Structure. Developing Grammars Again.* Amsterdam: Benjamins.

Klein, W. and Perdue, C. (1997) The basic variety. *Second Language Research* 13, 301–347.

Lehmann, C. (1988) Toward a typology of clause linkage. In J. Haiman and S.A. Thompson (eds.) *Clause Combining in Grammar and Discourse* (pp. 181–225). Amsterdam: Benjamins.

Morel, M.-A. and Danon-Boileau, L. (1998) *Grammaire de l'intonation. L'exemple du français.* Bibliothèque de Faits de Langues. Paris: Ophrys.

Morel, M.-A. and Rialland, A. (1993) L'énoncé oral complexe. Les relatives en qui. *Travaux Linguistiques du CERLICO* 6. Rennes: Presses universitaires de Rennes, 145–168.

Sato, C. (1990) *The Syntax of Conversation in Interlanguage Development.* Tübingen: Gunter Narr.

Appendix

Three video films

The knife-thrower

A circus performer throws knives around his female assistant, who stands against a wall. You can hear the audience applauding. The performer puts on a blindfold and starts his number again with the assistant against the wall. You can hear the footsteps of the assistant and suppose that she is leaving her position. In fact, she has taken cover behind the wall. When the knife-thrower has finished throwing, the assistant takes up her position against the wall again and the thrower takes off his blindfold while you can hear the audience whistling and applauding.

The accident

A man driving his car seems to have some technical problems and he ends up bumping into a tree. An ambulance arrives and the paramedics approach with a stretcher. They put the car on the stretcher and a bandage on the tree. The ambulance leaves and the man is left beside the road, astonished.

The sandbox

A woman is sitting on a bench in the park while she watches her child, who is playing in a sandpit. A man comes up, says hello to the woman, and sits down beside her. The child doesn't like the man approaching his mother, and gives him a kick on the leg. The man tries to make friends with the child and gives him a sweet. The child then bites his finger and throws sand in his eyes, and then a balloon-seller passes by. The man has an idea and buys a bunch of balloons, which he gives to the child. The child then disappears into the air with the balloons. The man, pleased that the child is gone, gives the woman a kiss on the cheek.

TRANSCRIPTION CONVENTIONS

I: Interviewer; E: student

/ // ///	short, medium and long pause
+ SIM	beginning and end of simultaneous talk
SIM	follows simultaneous talk of the interviewer
(RIRE)	non-verbal sound
eh euh	hesitation
X	incomprehensible syllable
:	lengthened syllable
NON	accentuated syllable
(I:mm)	feedback
*	precedes code-switch or non-existent word
st	click of the tongue
#	interruption / restructuration

Chapter 3

Adverbs and Functional Categories in L1 and L2 Acquisition of French

SUZANNE SCHLYTER

Introduction

In generative approaches to language acquisition, different models are proposed to account for the development of Functional Categories (henceforth FCs). Functional Categories are those categories that host functions such as tense, aspect, agreement, etc., having been developed out of a simple AUX or INFL node. At the beginning of the 1990s, it was claimed for L1 as well as for L2 acquisition that learners start out with the VP without AUX, INFL or other FCs, which are developed later during the acquisition process. Thus, according to this line of reasoning, syntactic structure is built from the bottom up. Such a position was defended by, e.g., Radford (1990) for L1 acquisition and similarly by, e.g., Vainikka and Young-Scholten (1996) for L2. In recent years, however, an increasing number of scholars have argued for the 'Strong Continuity Hypothesis', according to which children's grammar is not essentially different from the adult's grammar and there is no break in the development but instead continuity (Poeppel & Wexler, 1993). In this model, the child has access to all the FCs from the outset, but does not necessarily project them all, due to her reduced lexicon or short memory span, etc.

Similarly, it has often been argued in recent years that adult L2 learners have access to all FCs, and that their problems consist in transfer from their source language (Schwartz & Sprouse, 1996), in difficulties with bound inflection (the Missing Inflection Hypothesis, cf. Lardière, 1998; Prevost & White, 2000), or in the inability to find the correct values for the FCs rather than lack of access to them. There are also many intermediate positions, which allow some sort of structure building, while still claiming that, in principle, learners have access to the entire set of FCs (e.g. the Weak Continuity Hypothesis, cf. Clahsen, Eisenbeiss & Penke (1996), or the Modified

Structure Building Hypothesis, cf. Hawkins (2001), also Klein & Perdue (1997), arguing for the existence of FCs but that the features are weak).

In the comparison of first and second language acquisition, these models allow specific predictions as to the similarity or difference between the two situations. To simplify somewhat, we may propose:

- either that both L1 and L2 acquisition follow a Structure Building Model (= the Non- or Weak Continuity Hypothesis), i.e. that FCs are developed later than lexical categories, or
- that both L1 and L2 acquisition follow the Strong Continuity Hypothesis, i.e. that in both cases FCs are present from start, or
- that the two types of acquirers behave differently in this respect: the most natural assumption in this case would be that L1 acquisition follows the principles of the Non- or Weak Continuity Hypothesis, whereas L2 develops according to the Strong Continuity Hypothesis, i.e. the FCs are clearly present in the L2 learners' speech from the start, but not in the same way as with the L1 learners.

In the project DURS, of which the present study is a part, the above issues were among those addressed. The project has involved comparing bilingual Swedish-French children (= 2L1 acquisition) and adult Swedes acquiring French (= adult L2 acquisition). Earlier research on this corpus has revealed differences between the 2L1 and the adult L2 learners, concerning both the initial stage and further development. As regards the Determiner Phrase (articles, adjectives, agreement, etc., see Granfeldt, 2000), subject and object clitics (see Granfeldt & Schlyter, 2004), and verb morphology (see Schlyter, 2003), it seems that, for all the domains studied, the children gradually build up their syntactic structure (at least as far as is visible in their production), whereas the adult L2 learners already have access to greater parts of the structure and to the FCs, in the sense that these may be lexically instantiated, but have difficulties with the morphological realisations of them. This has led us to argue in favour of Weak Continuity in the case of the children and Strong Continuity in the adults, i.e. the third position among those presented above.

In the present study, another phenomenon will be studied in this framework: the appearance and acquisition of adverbs. Such a study has been made possible by the work of Cinque (1999). According to Cinque's very interesting and suggestive theory, adverbs are specifiers of the different FCs established for verbal categories such as mood, tense, aspect, etc. This means that, just as mood-tense-aspect-voice, etc., occur in a hierarchy, the adverbs are also subject to the same hierarchy. In applying this to acquisition, I will assume that if a learner uses adverbs from the higher levels of the hierarchy (e.g. adverbs of epistemic modality such as 'probablement'), he/she also has access to the FC in question, and to the FCs below it, since the categories are hierarchically organised.

In this chapter, we will show that the children, in their 2L1 acquisition, begin with the adverbs from the lower part of the hierarchy, and start using their higher-level adverbs clearly later on, which seems to support a Structure Building Model. Inversely, we will show that the adult L2 learners, even from the very earliest stages of acquisition, use the adverbs from the highest levels, which indicates that they have access to the entire set of FCs and seems to support the Strong Continuity Hypothesis.

FCs and Adverbs According to Cinque

Cinque (1999) developed the idea of Split Infl (Pollock, 1989), postulating a great number of clausal Functional Heads – supposedly universal – from which each language selects a certain set to mark morphologically. Whereas Pollock proposed to separate Tense Phrase (TP) and Agreement Phrase (AgrP), and others have proposed more categories such as Aspect Phrase (AspP) etc., Cinque proposed a great number of FCs representing different kinds of Mood, Tense and Aspect, based on evidence from verb morphology, auxiliaries, etc. Each of these Heads (represented by an auxiliary or verb affix) has as its specifier a certain type of adverb. Cinque argues, with the help of data from a great number of unrelated languages, for around 30 categories of this kind, which are universal and provide a possible site for adverbs, but not all of which are necessarily marked by verbal morphology in each specific language. Cinque postulates the hierarchical position of each adverb using evidence from data on word order and on scope: a higher adverb takes scope over a lower one (cf. also Schlyter, 1974, 1977 for a similar method although for a much simpler hierarchy). There are evidently problems with word order, due to factors such as information structure (cf. p. 1), more specifically the function of many time or place adverbs as 'setting', etc. (p. 15), which makes them figure not only inside the utterance, but also in initial position.

After having adjusted the Heads according to the adverbs studied, Cinque (1999: 106) arrives at the hierarchy presented below of Tense-Modal-Aspect Heads, with the corresponding adverbs in their Spec position. The corresponding French words are taken from Cinque, or are inspired by Schlyter (1974, 1977). The exact corresponding words are, however, not always quite clear, and this uncertainty is marked by a '?'. It is important to note that the same adverb can sometimes appear in different classes, depending on its position and interpretation (cf. also Schlyter, 1977). In order to refer more easily to the categories throughout the chapter,

I have numbered each, beginning with those highest in the syntactic structure and ending with the lowest.

(1)	frankly (Mood, speech act)	franchement
(2)	fortunately (Mood, evaluative)	heureusement
(3)	allegedly (Mood, evidential)	apparemment
(4)	probably (Mod, epistemic)	probablement
(5)	once (T, past)	une fois?
(6)	then (T, future)	alors? et puis?
(7)	perhaps (Mood, irrealis)	peut-être
(8)	necessarily (Mod, necessity)	nécessairement
(9)	possibly (Mod, possibility)	possiblement?
(10)	usually (Asp, habitual)	normalement, generalement
(11)	again (Asp, repetitiveI)	encore
(12)	often (Asp, frequentativeI)	souvent
(13)	intentionally (Mod, volitional)	intentionellement? (attentivement?)
(14)	quickly (Asp, celerativeI)	rapidement
(15)	already (T, anterior)	déjà
(16)	no longer (Asp, terminative)	ne . . . plus
(17)	still (Asp, continuative)	toujours / encore
(18)	always (Asp, perfect?)	toujours
(19)	just (Asp, retrospective)	juste(ment), ('vient de')
(20)	soon (Asp, proximative/Mod,root)	bientôt
(21)	briefly (Asp, durative)	?
(22)	characteristically(?) (Asp, generic/progressive)	?
(23)	almost (Asp, prospective)	presque
(24)	completely (Asp, sg-completiveI)	entièrement
(25)	tutto (Asp, pl-completive)	tou(te)s
(26)	well (Voice)	bien
(27)	fast/early (Asp, celerativeII)	vite
(28)	again (Asp, repetitive)	encore
(29)	often (Asp, frequentativeII)	souvent
(30)	completely (Asp, sg-completiveII)	complètement?

Cinque does not integrate AgrS or Neg in the hierarchy, since these have a problematic and non-systematic distribution in different languages. I suppose, however, along the lines of Schlyter (1974, 1977), that Negation in French is positioned somewhere in the middle of this hierarchy, lower than no. 9 and higher than no. 26. (For more details on the evidence used, etc., the reader is directed to Cinque's book.)

This list corresponds to a tree structure in which the first categories are at the top, roughly corresponding, in the Schlyter (1974, 1977) framework, to the sentence adverbs generated under S', and in which the lower ones correspond to the verb-modifying adverbs generated under VP. Here, the list will provide a basis for studying the appearance of the adverbs in L1 and L2 acquisition. If the acquirers build the syntactic structure from the bottom up, they should start with the lowest categories, i.e. those with the highest numbers. If they do not, but have access to all FCs from the outset, their first adverbs could represent any level of the hierarchy. Certain parallels will be drawn between adverbs and the development of Functional Heads, represented by verbal morphology (cf. the evidence for the FCs in question, Cinque 1999: 52) in the two categories of learners, but the study will focus on adverbs.

Previous Research on FCs in L1 and L2 as Regards Acquisition of Verbs

Before addressing the question of adverbs, we will briefly discuss some previous work on verbal FCs. Certain studies indicate structure building in children (e.g. Meisel, 1994, for finiteness, agreement and tense). Since the FCs proposed by Cinque (1999) should largely be interpreted as universal, semantic categories, it is also interesting to look briefly at previous work on the development of the semantic, formal and cognitive categories of TMA (tense-mood-aspect) in child language. Weist (1986), in his survey of the acquisition of TMA in many languages, proposes the following general development, building on the Reichenbachian categories: S (= Speech time), R (= Reference time) and E (= Event time):

(1)   the Speech Time system: E = R = S (Present);
(2)   the Event Time system: R = S, and E before, after or simultaneous with R (Perfect, Immediate Future or Present);
(3)   the Restricted Reference Time system: R not = S, and E = R (Past, Future);
(4)   the Free Reference Time system: R, E and S are independent of each other (e.g. Pluperfect, Futur Antérieur, etc.). (Cf. Weist 1986: 357.)

Schlyter (1990) shows, for children acquiring French and German, a development essentially along these lines. It is argued that the first concepts expressed by the children studied are an observed change of state (e.g. *cassé, parti*) and a wanted action (e.g. *boire*). It is also observed that this corresponds well to the first type of adverbs used: *encore* (wanted action), frequent in French, and *so* (observed change), frequent in German. In the next stage, these children refer to proximal past or future events, i.e. in which the event is closely related to the speech situation, such as: *est cassé, a trouvé, veux boire*, etc. (according to Weist, R is 'frozen at' S, but E can precede or follow R). Later, children can talk about events that occurred long ago and in another situation, i.e. remote events such as a visit to the grandparents the week before:

(1)   j'ai fait pipi, et après j'étais tout mouillé.

Such a development could probably be related to the FC hierarchy proposed by Cinque in the sense that the Event Time System seems to correspond to Asp-proximative and Asp-retrospective, nos. 19 and 20, and the Restricted Reference Time system to T-past and T-future, nos. 5 and 6, which would mean that lower FCs are acquired before higher ones. Moreover, Modal verbs (*peut, doit, faut*, etc.) are first used in a deontic sense by the children (*je ne peux pas faire cela; tu ne dois pas manger ça!*), thus they seem to correspond to Mod-root (= Asp-prospective, no. 23), and only much later function in an epistemic sense (*il doit être parti; elle peut bien avoir fait cela*), which would represent Mod-epistemic, no. 4. It is also well known that verb morphology representing Mood, such as subjunctive or conditional, appears considerably later, suggesting that Mod and Mood of lower categories are acquired before those of higher categories.

This shows that there are certain facts, of both a lexico-semantic (Schlyter, 1990) and a morpho-syntactic nature (Meisel, 1994), suggesting a development in child language that, assuming a Structure Building Model, is at least compatible with the FC hierarchy proposed by Cinque (1999).

As for adult L2 acquisition of these FCs, the facts are less clear. Structure Building Models and Continuity Models have been proposed (cf. above), but essentially on formal, rather than functional-semantic, grounds. As for semantic development, Dietrich, Klein and Noyau (1995) propose a morphologic development not very different from that proposed for children – the difference being that adult learners rely more on pragmatic processing and on lexical devices for expressing temporality, which suggests that temporal concepts are available to adult L2 learners before they are morphologically marked (cf. also Klein & Perdue, 1997).

The Corpus

In the project DURS, bilingual Swedish-French children are compared to adult Swedes acquiring French. The fact that the children are bilingual allows us to control for the possibility of transfer from Swedish and to concentrate on age differences.

The 2L1 acquirers are four bilingual Swedish-French children, growing up with both languages at home, and all living in Sweden: Jean, Anne, Dany and Mimi. The children are studied from the age of 1;10–2;0, when they have their first two-word utterances, to the age of about 4;0, when the entire syntactic system – including most tense oppositions, subordinations, etc. – has been acquired. Their two languages are not always quite in balance, one being somewhat weaker in periods, but this seems to have little influence on the data presented here.

The adult L2 learners in the project are 11 adult Swedes acquiring French, some in a formal setting (four years of French studies at school, about 500 hours), but most as naturalistic learners, i.e. acquiring French in France practically without language instruction, but instead via French input and interaction. The study is half longitudinal, half cross-sectional (due to the difficulty in finding enough informal L2 learners of French), and the proficiency of the learners varies from very simple first utterances (after about three months of residence) to very good mastery of French morphology and syntax, with tense oppositions, subordinations, clitic pronouns, etc. (cf. Schlyter, 2003; Granfeldt, 2000 etc.). The range of proficiency seems to be similar in children and adults – for both categories it would certainly be possible to find earlier stages, as well as later and more developed ones. For more information on these learners, see also Granfeldt, this volume.

In this adverb study, only the four most low-level L2 learners are analysed, since our essential interest is the initial stage, i.e. to what extent FCs are present from the outset of acquisition.

Adverbs in L1 French Acquisition

In this corpus, all adverbs produced by the children, those ending in -*ment* and others, have been sorted out from the database with their context. The adverb utterances have been classified into three groups that could represent developmental stages. Here attempts were made to classify the adverbs both independently of verb morphology and in accordance with the development of TMA semantics and verb morphology. The classification results in three levels regrouping adverbs, verb morphology and semantics, and age/MLU. An exhaustive list of all adverbs found (not a large number), both in the children and in the adults, has been established. For each of the three proposed developmental stages, the number of occurrences is indicated; see Tables A3-A6 in the Appendix.

The earliest adverbs

In the French child data from the earliest recordings, about age 2;0 up to about 2;6, we find the following adverbs (the letters J, A, D and M are the initials of Jean, Anne, Dany and Mimi):

Là! (J, A, M, and D, all recordings)
Encore (J2, M1, D2) *Aussi* (A2, M1)

Comme ça (J2, D2, M1)
Mal (J1), *Bien* (A3, J3), *Vite* (A2)
Ici (A2)
Dehors (J2), (en-) *dessous, là-haut* (A2),

This developmental stage corresponds to Jean 1–5 (1;10–2;6, MLU 1.3–2.0); Anne 1–3 (2;3–2;8, MLU 1.4–2.7); Dany 1–2 (2;2–2;6, MLU 1.2–1.8) and Mimi 1–2 (2;0–2;2, MLU 2.1–3.2), i.e. a MLU normally below 2.5 (counted in words). At this stage, the children produce very few grammatical morphemes, and auxiliaries and modals are not yet used systematically (see Appendix, Table A1, on IP/CP). For more details on the occurrences of the adverbs, see Table A3 in the Appendix.

Where are these adverbs in the hierarchy presented above?

'Là', the very first adverb to appear in all children, is not included in the hierarchy by Cinque, but if we consider it an adverb, it may be very low, having the possibility of following most others according to test sentences such as (2a–d). (The numbers after the adverbs indicate their position in the hierarchy.)

(2) (a) il est presque (23) là
    (b) il l'a déjà (15) mis là
    (c) il l'a toujours (18) mis là
        il l'a juste (19) mis là

'Encore', the next adverb to appear very frequently, is explicitly stated (p. 104) to be very low (repetitive, no. 29). In our data, this adverb first occurs in isolation – indicating a second appearance of an object, or the desire to repeat an action. Somewhat later these objects or actions are mentioned:

(3) (a) encore, pince le nez!   (Jean 2, 2;0)
    (b) petit chat encore   (Mimi 1, 2;0)

'Aussi', as a focusing adverb, is not considered by Cinque. We might consider it a variant of 'encore', indicating repetition:

(4) ça aussi   (Mimi 1, 2;0)

in which case it would be assigned number 29. (It is, however, less frequent than 'encore' and the occurrences appear somewhat later.)

Other low-level adverbs are also among those to appear early: 'mal', 'bien' (Jean, Anne) and 'vite' (Jean, Anne).

(5) aime bien   (Anne 3, 2;8)

In the adverb hierarchy, 'vite' has number 27, and 'bien' number 26, i.e. very low-level adverbs (verb-modifying and under the scope of negation, in Schlyter, 1977).

'Comme ça' is often used in isolation, accompanying an action, and sometimes the action is mentioned:

(6)   (a)   comme ça (ça marche)   (Mimi 1, 2;0)
      (b)   (on met) comme ça   (Dany 2, 2;6)

'Comme ça' is not mentioned by Cinque, but as a verb-modifying adverb of a similar type as 'bien', it probably comes near it in the hierarchy. In any case, it would seem to be rather low, at least below 'toujours', and probably also below 'bien', as seen in test sentences:

(7)   (a)   on a toujours (18) fait comme ça
      (b)   il a travaillé bien (26) comme ça.

The early adverbs 'ici', 'dehors', 'dessous' and 'là-haut' are not mentioned by Cinque. But if we apply the same criteria as for 'là', they should also have a low position in this hierarchy. If we use negation as a criterion for low-level adverbs (cf. Schlyter, 1974, 1977), we observe that these, as well as all the other adverbs used by the children at this level (with the exception of 'encore', it seems), are under the scope of the negation.

To summarise the first stage of adverbs in the children, we can observe that they all seem to be from no. 26 and lower (see further Table A3 in the Appendix). There are no occurrences of adverbs of a higher level, with the exception of one 'maintenant' in Mimi 2 (who is, however, somewhat more advanced than the other children at this stage, cf. Table A1 in the Appendix).

Adverbs used in the second stage

An intermediate stage has been established for the following recordings: Jean 6–8 (2;9–3;1, MLU around 3.0), Anne 4–6 (2;10–3;1, MLU around 3.0), Dany 3 (2;10, MLU 3.1), and Mimi 3 (2;6, MLU 3.5). This intermediate stage of L1 acquisition is, apart from adverbs, characterised by quite productive use of different subject clitics, and the appearance of auxiliaries and modals (see Table A1 in the Appendix). In contrast to later stages, Imperfect and reference to remote time is not yet used. As for CP, subordinates are not very productive at this point.

At this intermediate stage, certain temporal – or rather aspectual – adverbs start to appear in all children:

(situation: Jean tries to bring a toast)
(8) on boit maintenant. on dit 'santé!'   (Jean 6, 2;9)
(9) xx défaire maintenant?   (Mimi 2, 2;2)

The adverb 'maintenant' is here used, not for an ongoing event, but for one that is about to occur, i.e. soon after the actual situation, S. Reference Time is the same as Speech Time (S = R), and Event time follows it. The adverb apparently represents Asp-proximative, and has number 20, at this early stage.

In some children, a very similar function is represented by 'et puis',[1] or 'après':

(10) (a)   et puis – (D. want to see next picture)   (Dany 3, 2;10)
      (b)   (et puis) on va prendre (un autre), (un) livre   (Dany 3, 2;10)
(11) Mère: on va trouver après.
      Anne: ap-pé (= après)
      Mère: après. Voici il y a un coin.
      Anne: ap-pé!   (Anne 4, 2;10)
(12) après, il veut dormir   (Mimi 3, 2;6)

These adverbs, too, are used to refer to a point in time soon after the actual situation, and could therefore be considered, in the same way, as Asp-prospective, no. 20.

At this age, Anne also uses 'déjà':

(13) (a) a déjà mangé
      (b) a déjà tout mangé   (Anne 4, 2;10)

This adverb is analysed by Cinque as T-anterior, no. 15.

Other low-level adverbs are also used at this age (*souffler fort, j'aime bien, il vole bien; il va trop vite*), but since these are not of a higher level than those mentioned, they do not participate in the adverb progression we are aiming at here.

Thus far, these adverbs seem to be in good agreement with the adverb hierarchy proposed by Cinque (as well as with the TMA development reported in Weist, 1986).

A first step up in the hierarchy seems to be taken by Mimi in her use of 'et puis' as an adverb referring to a time point R_2 which immediately follows a time point R_1, both in the past (of a story shown in a picture book), since Mimi uses the past tense Passé Composé:

(14) et puis, il a fait pipi.   (Mimi 3, 2;6)

This seems to be a step in the direction of the types of adverbs used in the next stage, and may be due to the somewhat higher developmental level of Mimi.

One adverb, *peut-être*, causes a problem for our Structure-Building claim (or for the hierarchy proposed by Cinque?), since, according to Cinque, it is higher than the other adverbs used at this level: Mood-irrealis, no. 7 (or Mod-possibility, no. 9?). This adverb is used by the children when solving a puzzle, dressing a doll, etc.:

(15) (a) peut-être là?   (Anne 4, 2;10)
     (b) ça peut-être?   (Mimi 3, 2;6)

To summarise this stage, we can argue (in spite of some problems) that the children lexically and morphologically instantiate functional categories of aspect from about no. 20 to 15 in the hierarchy. Not only do they use the adverbs, analysed as Spec to these heads, but this is also the period in which they use auxiliaries and modals in the sense of immediate past, perfect, immediate future, and deontic modality (cf. also Schlyter, 1990). We can interpret the stage as one in which FCs of the highest type are not yet fully developed, but one in which those of the intermediate categories are.

Adverbs in the third stage

After about the age of three, the children start to use past tense to refer to remote past events, and they also use Imparfait (*était, avait, voulais* etc.; see Table A1 in the Appendix), and sometimes Futur Simple (*pourra*). There is, thus, evidence for T-past and T-future as regards verb forms. Here, they also regularly use different kinds of subordination, i.e. there is evidence for CP. We propose a third stage of development, comprising the Jean 9–12 recordings (age 3;3–3;9, MLU 3.0–4.5), Anne 7–13 (age 3;3–4;4, MLU 3.0–4.5), Dany 4–7 (age 3;2–4;2, MLU 3.2–4.4) and Mimi 5–8 (3;2–4;2, MLU 3.4–4.3).

Dany 4, age 3;2, had just spent the summer in France and spoke French very well. He was able to talk about what had happened during the day, which he did to a great extent. He frequently used 'et puis' as a text-cohesive device, to relate succeeding points of time in the past (i.e., R_2 after R_1, and both before S):

(16) (situation: Dany tells about his day at daycare)
     D: j'ai mangé des 'korv' avec du pain.
     M: tu as mangé des 'korv' avec du pain?
     D: et puis j'ai mangé –
        et puis Svenne a dit qu'il voulait manger quelque chose

The children also use 'd'abord' (Dany 4, Anne 7), 'juste avant' (Jean 10), 'après' (Jean 12), 'alors' (Jean 12) and rather often 'maintenant' – now more in order to contrast with later or earlier points in time (cf. the Free Reference Time of Weist, 1986).

Cinque (1999: 87) discusses temporal adverbs, which seem to be quite clearly related to the FCs T(past) and T(future). There are, however, problems in their distribution (they often function as 'setting'), and on distributional grounds he only admits adverbs such as 'allora' (then), 'un tempo', 'una volta' (once) and 'ora' (now) in this position. He proposes these as no. 5 and 6, slightly lower than epistemic adverbs (no. 4). They are consequently clearly higher than the different kinds of aspectual adverbs.

Most of the adverbs that the children start to use during this stage seem to be of this category, and in test sentences they can figure below an evaluative (no. 2) or epistemic (no. 4) adverb:

(17) heureusement / probablement il a ensuite mangé du pain
                              alors
                              d'abord

(The adverb 'et puis', vacillating between a time adverb and a discourse particle, is more difficult. It seems to precede all the other adverbs. For the moment, we cannot resolve this problem.)

We can then consider the time adverbs used by the children at this stage (and possibly also 'puis' in a clearly temporal function), as T-adverbs (no. 5 and 6) according to Cinque (1999: 87):

(18) on parle pas maintenant. on mange d'abord.   (Dany 4, 3;2)

We can observe that, at this age, the child was able to mark the relation between different reference times not identical to the speech time 'now' (= S). Both 'parle' and 'mange' refer to points in time after the Speech time, but the child expresses clearly that 'mange' should precede 'parle', i.e. two Rs related to each other independently of S. The child seems, therefore, to have attained the 'Free Reference Time System'.

This relation between two Rs that are not = S (but here following S) can also be observed clearly in the following sequences of Jean 12:

(19) (Situation: Jean's mother is telling him that they will have to put their furniture in the cellar, because of their imminent move)
      M: on va descendre les lits aussi, on va descendre ton lit.
      J: oh, mais je pourra pas dormir après!
      M: mais, pas maintenant, le jour où on va partir.
      J: et, où on va aller ben alors?   (Jean 12, 3;9)

The time relations indicated by these adverbs are clearly more advanced and of a higher level than those of the same adverbs in functions no. 15, 18, 20, and we consider them here as instances of T-past or T-future (no. 5,6).

Anne (rec. 10) begins to use 'alors' frequently. The adverb is often used in a sense near that of 'in that case'. It establishes a relationship between two events in an imagined situation – which can also be considered as 'R not = S':

(20) Mère: alors là on voit le wagon qui se casse.
      Anne: mais <u>alors</u> le train il va tomber.   (Anne 10, 3;9)

In the same way, such adverbs can be considered as being of type no. 5–6.

At this stage, the children also start to use more systematically different kinds of what is traditionally called 'sentence adverbs'. Jean 9 frequently uses 'peut-être' (no. 7), now in an entire, structured sentence:

(21) <u>peut-être</u> c'est bon programme   (Jean 9, 3;3)

The children also begin using a certain number of 'seulement', a type of adverb not observed in earlier stages:

(22) (a). elle <u>seulement</u> prend beaucoup   (Mimi 6, 3;7)
      (b)   le papa il veut couper, <u>seulement</u>   (Mimi 6, 3;7)
      (c)   il pensait <u>seulement</u>   (Dany 7, 4;2)

Such adverbs are analysed by Schlyter (1977) as somewhat similar to sentence adverbs, in the sense that they cannot be focalised, and they figure easily after the auxiliary, a very frequent position for sentence adverbs. They seem to take scope over manner and other lower adverbs.

In the last recording, Mimi 8, the child uses *quand-même*:

(23) Mimi: elle a dit qu'elle va enlever ma dent.
      Moth: tu vas avoir un trou pendant très longtemps, tu sais. (. . .)
      Mimi: on doit (l')enlever <u>quand-même</u>.

This adverb is not mentioned by Cinque. It seems, however, to be of a rather high level (similar to evaluative, no. 2), since such adverbs take scope over negation, and not vice versa, and over low-level adverbs, as seen in test sentences:

(24) il n'a quand-même pas travaillé très bien/vite.

To summarise this stage, we can observe that the children here use adverbs of a still higher position in the hierarchy than those used previously. Their development seems – as far as these rather few items indicate – to agree with the adverbial hierarchy proposed by Cinque (1999) and with a structure-building hypothesis.

Adverbs in L2 French Acquisition

The adults, on the other hand, do not seem to follow the same kind of progression. They use, from the very first recordings, adverbs located quite high in the hierarchy. Here, we will study only data from the least advanced informal learners, Henry (about three months of only partial, and passive, exposure to French), Björn and Sara (both three and five months of residence in France), and the least advanced formal learner, Lisa (about 500 hours of studying French at school, with very traditional methods).

The least advanced learner in the corpus is Henry. If we look at his general level of proficiency, we observe a pattern similar to the Nominal Utterance Organisation (NUO) of the stage named 'Pre-Basic' (Klein & Perdue, 1997): he uses almost no productive verb morphology, many verbless sentences (only about 30% of utterances contain verbs), many negations of the form Neg+X (or cop + Neg + X), SVO order with object pronouns, etc. In spite of this, I have argued (Schlyter, 2003) that he has access to Functional Categories such as AgrS, T and CP, since he sometimes inflects person (*comprez-vous*), sometimes uses '*était*', and several times uses subordinations (relative clauses, see Table A2 in the Appendix).

The adverbs used are the following are presented in Table 3.1 (exhaustive list from Henry 1 and from Henry 2 – both at the same level of development):

Table 3.1 The adverbs used by the L2 learner Henry

adverb	*hierar no*	*occ H1*	*occ H2*
naturellement	2	4	12
probablement	4	1	1
avant	?	2	–
après	5–6	5	–
peut-être	7	4	9
normalement	10	1	2
personnellement	13?	2	–
partiellement	?	1	–
très, trop	?	3	–
même	?	1	2
encore	29	–	2
aussi	29?	1	1

hierar no = number in the hierarchy presented in Section 2;
occ = number of occurrences; H1, H2 = 1st and 2nd recording of Henry

Very different from the case of the children at a correspondingly low level, the most frequent adverbs here are those located highest in the hierarchy. Henry sometimes uses them in isolation, but often in a grammatically constructed sentence:

(25) (a)   mais mais, naturellement, c′ c′ est très minimal   (Henry 1)
     (b)   mais peut-être c′est # meilleur # peut-être dans la pigeonnier
                                                              (Henry 2)
     (c)   il y a naturellement # beaucoup de soleil   (Henry 2)

We can see, also in the other L2 learners at a low level, that the adverbs used are spread across the entire adverb hierarchy; see Table 6 in the Appendix. The learners all have great problems with verb morphology, both for distinguishing +/- finiteness and for marking past tense (cf. Schlyter, 2003). Still they all use 'après', systematically, as the essential marking of two events in the past succeeding each other:

(26) taxi # # dans la # bois, # après: pluie pluie pluie.   (Henry 1)
     (= we took a taxi to the forest, but then it rained and rained)
(27) (telling the story of Little Red Riding Hood)
     Int: . . . il la mange.
     Bjö: aha xxx # oui et après, un # eh un homme qui (. . .)
     il tire le loup.   (Björn 1, 3 months)
(28) (Sara about her exposure to French during her courses)
     Sar: je je je écoute.
     et # je écoute et 'la tête' et après 'the head'.
     Int: aha!
     Sar: et après, je comprends.   (Sara 1, 3 months)

This is similar to the use by the children in stage three, except that the children produce correct verb morphology. It is often mentioned that adult learners use adverbs as a supplement to missing verb inflection (von Stutterheim, 1984; Dietrich *et al.*, 1995; Benazzo, 2003; and many others).
  'Avant' is often used, in many cases to signal past tense (R not = S) when the learner does not master the verb form:

(29) j'ai un ami,
     # # il joue la trompette aussi
     dans le même conservatoire.
     # pas maintenant, mais deux, deux ans avant.   (Martin 1, 9 months)

The possibility adverb '*peut-être*' is very frequently used, and very early, by the adult learners:

(30) (Situation: Björn discusses his chances of earning some money for his music studies by playing in restaurants)
Bjö: après nous jou, nous jouen, nous jouon, jouE.
Int: mhm.
Bjö: et après # oh, pas payer (laugh) <u>peut-être</u>.

The adults use 'seulement' in a way similar to the children of stage three:

(31) (a) C'est pas <u>seulement</u> eh mouvement de mon école,
c'est aussi mes idées. (Sara 2, 5 months)
(b) mais # (je) <u>seulement</u> eh habite # là par # une sem semaine
(Lisa 1)

In this way, we can observe that, at very early stages, the adult L2 learners, in spite of the fact that TMA morphology and subject or object cliticisation are far from developed, do not lack adverbs of a very high order. The adverbs used are specifying Functional Categories such as T-past or very high-level ones such as Mood-evaluative (no. 2, *naturellement*, *bien sûr*) or Mood-epistemic (no. 4, *probablement*). This means that the learners clearly have access to these very high-level Functional Categories, in the sense of lexical instantiation, and not only to the very lowest ones in the hierarchy. This is in sharp contrast with the children of the earliest stages.

Summary and Discussion

The hierarchy of Functional Categories originally proposed for sentence and verb (TMA) categories, but now extended by Cinque (1999) and proposed also as a site for adverbs, has been used here. The appearance of adverbs in L1 acquisition and in adult L2 acquisition was studied to elucidate to what extent both types of learners, from their initial stages, have or do not have access to FCs of these types. Using data from both children and adult learners from as early a stage as possible (practically from the first time they are able to produce simple utterances of more than one word), we have shown that there is a clear difference between children and adults. In the initial stages (MLU around 2) of the children (bilingual L1 acquirers), we do not find any evidence for adverbs other than the most low-level ones. In the next stage (MLU around 3), adverbs specifying inter-mediate categories – aspect of different kinds – appear, and later (MLU around 4), adverbs specifying still higher FCs, such as Tense, appear. The adverbs appear simultaneously with the corresponding evidence from verb morphology for the same categories. In the adult L2 learners, on the other hand, adverbs from the very highest categories, such as Mood-evaluative, Mood-epistemic and Tense, appear in the earliest recordings, from the lowest levels of proficiency. In contrast to the L1 learners, there is little morphologic evidence for the same categories, but adult learners have great problems with verb morphology.

This difference constitutes additional evidence supporting our claim that the adult learners have immediate access to the entire syntactic structure, i.e. to all Functional Categories (in the sense that these can be lexically instantiated), thereby supporting the Strong Continuity Hypothesis in adult L2 learners. The same conclusion cannot be drawn from the data of the L1 learners, who apparently develop their FCs over time, at roughly the age of 2;6 (with some variations). Before this age, we find no clear evidence of FCs of the type Asp or Tense, either in the form of verb morphology or of adverbs. We therefore consider this as evidence for some kind of Non-Continuity or Weak Continuity Hypothesis and, since the FCs seem to appear gradually, for a Structure-Building Model.

The adults' problems with verb morphology are related to the hypothesis of the Missing Inflection. Our learners do acquire inflectional verb morphology, but clearly later than syntactic phenomena such as postverbal negation, case oppositions (*moi / je*), etc. (see Schlyter, 2003), which suggests access to FCs in a syntactic sense, and a dissociation of the development of morphology and syntax. The presence of these high-level adverbs in the L2 learners constitutes additional evidence for such a position.

The difference observed here between lacking verb morphology and the presence of adverbs expressing more or less the same concepts is not empirically new. As mentioned above, many scholars have shown how adult L2 learners, as they expressed it, 'compensated' for missing tense morphology by using time adverbs 'instead'. What we have attempted here is to give such observations a place in a more developed syntactic theory.

Proponents of functional approaches to language acquisition may object that the phenomena presented here are not due to syntax, but to the cognitive knowledge of the adult learners in contrast with that of the children. However, in recent syntactic theory, as in that of Cinque (1999), the Functional Categories increasingly take on the status of universal, thus cognitive, categories (cf. the discussion in Cinque, 1999: 127–8). An analysis such as that presented here is, thus, quite compatible with studies indicating differences between L1 and adult L2 acquisition as a result of differences in cognitive development. The difference seems to reside in our proposal that this cognitive or semantic development is also related to syntactic facts. In their discussion on the basic variety, Klein and Perdue (1997: 337) conclude:

There is evidence for semantic features of the sort typically linked to functional categories, there is no evidence for phonological features (. . .), and there is no clear evidence for 'formal features' and their various structural consequences.

As I understand it, such structural consequences might be phenomena such as post-verbal negation and case marking, which have been argued for in earlier work on this data. But we can also argue that the adverbs represent phonological features, i.e. there is phonological material in the Specs of the high FCs in question. This seems consistent with what Cinque (1999: 106) points out for standard adult use:

> . . . if each adverb class indeed corresponds to a different functional head, then, we have evidence that the entire array of functional heads (and projections) is available even where there is no overt morphology corresponding to the heads, as the respective specifiers are available.

The analysis proposed here is also consistent with the claim of Granfeldt and Schlyter (2004), and Granfeldt (2003) that L1 learners (and possibly child learners in general) can easily move elements into functional <u>heads</u>, whereas this is difficult for adult learners. Adults initially prefer elements in other positions, where they have a lexical (i.e. XP) status – which is the case for the Spec positions, where the adverbs are.

There are, however, many problems with the claim proposed here, and studies suggesting a Structure-Building Model of adverbs in adult L2 acquisition provide counterevidence to our position (Benazzo, 2003; Starren & van Hout, 1996). Since adverbs are rather rare in spontaneous speech corpora such as ours, more studies are needed. My hope is to inspire other scholars to look at their corpora, for refutation, validation or adjustment of the claim advanced here.

Acknowledgements
We thank the audiences of the Euroslal1 French Workshop for valuable comments on the presentation of this work. Special thanks to Guglielmo Cinque, Verner Egerland and Jonas Granfeldt for discussing different versions of this article. The usual disclaimers apply. This research is supported by a grant from The Swedish Council for Research in the Humanities and Social Sciences (HSFR), grant number F0686/1998.

Notes
1. 'Et puis' can also be used as a discourse particle. It is not always easy to distinguish different uses in child language.
2. He also has 35 more negations, which are chunks, NegX or have incorrect positions.

3. These are not yet controlled for different uses.

References

Benazzo, S. (2003) The interaction of verb morphology and temporal adverbs of contrast. In Ch. Dimroth and M. Starren (eds) *Information Structure, Linguistic Structure, and the Dynamics of Learner Language* (pp. 187–210). Amsterdam: Benjamins.

Cinque, G. (1999) *Adverbs and Functional Heads. A Cross-Linguistic Perspective*. New York, Oxford: Oxford University Press.

Clahsen, H., Eisenbeiss, S. and Penke, M. (1996) Lexical learning in early syntactic development. In H. Clahsen (ed.) *Generative Perspectives on Language Acquisition: Empirical Findings, Theoretical Considerations, and Crosslinguistic Comparisons* (pp. 129–59). Amsterdam: Benjamins.

Dietrich, R., Klein, W., and Noyau, C. (1995) *The Acquisition of Temporality in a Second Language*. Amsterdam: Benjamins.

Granfeldt, J. (2000) The acquisition of the Determiner Phrase in bilingual and second language French. *Bilingualism: Language and Cognition* 3 (3), 263–80.

Granfeldt, J. (2003). L'acquisition des Catégories Fonctionnelles. Etude comparative du développement du DP français chez des enfants et des apprenants adultes. PhD thesis, University of Lund.

Granfeldt, J. and Schlyter, S. (2004) Cliticisation in the acquisition of French as L1 and L2. In P. Prévost and J. Paradis (eds) *Acquisition of French Grammar*. Amsterdam, Philadelphia: Benjamins.

Hawkins, R. (2001) *Second Language Syntax: A Generative Introduction*. Malden, MA: Blackwell.

Klein, W. and Perdue, C. (1997) The Basic Variety (or: Couldn't natural languages be much simpler?). *Second Language Research* 13 (4), 301–47.

Lardière, D. (1998) Case and tense in the 'fossilized' steady state. *Second Language Research* 14 (1), 359–75.

Meisel, J.M. (1994) Getting FAT: Finiteness, Agreement and Tense in early grammars. In J.M. Meisel (ed.) *Bilingual First Language Acquisition* (pp. 89–129). Amsterdam: Benjamins.

Noyau, C., Houdaifa, E., Vasseur, M.T., and Véronique, D. (1995) The acquisition of French. In R. Dietrich, W. Klein, W. and C. Noyau (eds) *The Acquisition of Temporality in a Second Language* (pp. 145–209). Amsterdam: Benjamins.

Poeppel, D. and Wexler, K. (1993) The full competence hypothesis of clause structure. *Language* 69, 1–33.

Pollock, J.-Y. (1989) Verb movement, universal grammar and the structure of IP. *Linguistic Inquiry* 20 (3), 365–424.

Prévost, P. and White, L. (2000) Missing surface inflection or impairment in Second Language Acquisition? Evidence from tense and agreement'. *Second Language Research* 16 (2), 103–33.

Radford, A. (1990) *Syntactic Theory and the Acquisition of English Syntax. The Nature of Early Child Grammars of English*. Oxford: Basil Blackwell.

Schlyter, S. (1974) Une hiérarchie d'adverbes et leurs distributions – par quelles transformations? In C. Rohrer and N. Ruwet (eds.) *Actes du Colloque Franco-Allemand de Grammaire Transformationnelle* (pp. 76–86). Tübingen: Max Niemeyer Verlag.

Schlyter, S. (1977) *La place des adverbes en -ment en français*. Doctoral dissertation, Konstanz University.

Schlyter, S. (1990) The acquisition of tense and aspect. In J.M. Meisel (ed.) *Two First Languages. Early Grammatical Development in Bilingual Children* (pp. 87–121). Dordrecht: Foris.

Schlyter, S. (2003) Development of verb morphology and finiteness in children and adults acquiring French. In Ch. Dimroth and M. Starren (eds) *Information Structure, Linguistic Structure, and the Dynamics of Learner Language* (pp. 15–44). Amsterdam: Benjamins.

Schwartz, B.D. and Sprouse, R. (1996) L2 cognitive states and the full transfer/full access model. *Second Language Research* 12, 40–72.

Starren, M. and van Hout, R. (1996) Temporality in learner discourse: What temporal adverbials can and what they cannot express. *LiLi* 26 (104), 35–50.

Vainikka, A. and Young-Scholten, M. (1996) Gradual development of L2 phrase structure. *Second Language Research* 12, 7–39.

Weist, R. (1986) Tense and aspect. In P. Fletcher and M. Garman (eds) *Language Acquisition. Studies in First Language Development* (pp. 356–74). Cambridge: Cambridge University Press.

von Stutterheim, C. (1984) Temporality in learner varieties. *Linguistische Berichte* 92, 31–45.

Appendix

Table A1 Evidence from syntax and verb morphology for IP and CP in bilingual children

ANNE	fV+Ng	Case	Ocl	C	Nonfin	Scl+V	Aux+V	Mod+V	Impf
A1 2;3					1				
A2 2;6	2				1	20	1		
A3 2;8	6	+			1	23		1	
A4 2;10	4	+	1		1	24	4	3	
A5 2;11	7	+	1			37	10	1	1
A6 3;1	7	+	1			58	15	8	
A7 3;3	4	+		1		65	5	7	1
A9 3;7	+	+	+	3		+		+	1
A11 4;0	+	+	+	9		+		+	12
A13 4;4	+	+	+	5		+		+	10
JEAN	fV+Ng	Case	Ocl	C	Nonfin	Scl+V	Aux+V	Mod+V	Impf
J2 2;0					12	1			
J3 2;2					6	1	1		
J4 2;4	1				1	8			
J5 2;6	3				1	6		1	
J6 2;9	7	+	9			92	6	32	
J7 2;11	6	+	6	2	4	74	3	23	3
J8 3;1	+	+	+	4		+	+	+	4
J10 3;5	+	+	+	5		+	+	+	3
J12 3;9	+	+	+	28		+	+	+	11
DANY	fV+Ng	Case	Ocl	C	Nonfn	Scl+V	Aux+V	Mod+V	Impf
D1 2;2					3	1			
D2 2;6					2	15	10	(1)	
D3 2;10	1	+				72	2	33	
D4 3;2	26	+	3	10		96	9	26	5
D5 3;6	8	+	3	8	2	71	19	32	1
D6 3;10	+	+	+	5		+	+	+	4
D7 4;2	+	+	+	3		+	+	+	4

Table A1 (*cont.*) Evidence from syntax and verb morphology for IP and CP in bilingual children

MIMI	fV+Ng	Case	Ocl	C	Nonfin	Scl+V	Aux+V	Mod+V	Impf
M1 2;0	–	–	–	–	–	13	–	3	–
M2 2;2	11	+	–	3	3	58	7	6	–
M3 2;6	6	+	3	1	–	67	15	12	–
M4 2;10	7	+	2	4	–	83	11	7	–
M5 3;2	6	+	2	4	–	104	10	11	6
M6 3;7	+	+	+	6		+	+	+	5
M7 3;10	+	+	+	8		+	+	+	5
M8 4;2	+	+	+	5		+	+	+	4

Legend: fV+Ng = finite Verb+Negation (*pas*); case = *je/moi* etc in opposition; ocl = object clitic, in preverbal position; C = Complementizer, i.e. subordination with subjunctions; 'nonfin' = infinitive- or participle-like forms, without auxiliary or preposition (here = root infinitives); scl+V = subject clitic + verb; Aux+V = auxiliary (*a/est* etc.)+Verb; Mod+V = Modal verb (including *vais/va*'etc) + Verb; Impf = Imparfait; a '+' indicates further regular occurrences. The intermediate line indicates the postulated limits between the stages.
There are about 200 utterances in each recording, which makes the numbers comparable.

Table A2 Evidence from syntax and verb morphology for IP and CP in adult L2 learners

Learner	fV+Ng	Case	Ocl	C	Nonfin	PsujV	Aux+V	Mod+V	Impf
Henry1	8	+	–	–	9	26	5	–	3
Henry 2	9[2]	+	–	4	6	+	5	–	4
Martin1	5	+	–	5	3	144	1	–	–
Martin2	11	+	1	7	7	156	20	16	3
Martin3	4	+	2	10	8	165	31	24	9
Petra1	18	+	3	4	7	205	3	20	1
Petra2	30	+	4	11	5	294	39	15	1
Sara1	15	+	4	10	6	277	6	10	2
Sara2	12	+	1	9	2*	154	5	9	1
Lisa1	2	+	–	6	11	128	15	–	5
Lisa2	11	+	1	21	11	244	10	2	6
Lisa4	6	+	3	32	20	194	9	4	2
Sama1	19	+	–	6	2	125	6	11	2
Sama2	7	+	3	16	10	98	7	4	9
Sama4	29	+	6	52	11	158	16	6	2

Legend: fV+Ng = finite Verb+Negation (*pas*); case = *je*/*moi* etc in opposition;
ocl = object clitic, in preverbal position; C = Complementiser, i.e. subordination with subjunctions;
'nonfin' = infinitive- or participle-like forms without auxiliary or preposition (= here normally in finite context);
Psuj+V = pronominal subject + verb; Aux+V = auxiliary (*a*/*est* etc.)+Verb;
Mod+V = Modal verb (including *vais*/*va*'etc) + Verb; Impf = Imparfait; a '+' indicates regular occurrences.
There are around 300 learner utterances in each recording, except for Henry 1 who has about 100.
*+4 finite forms in nonfinite function

Table A3 Adverbs in L1 learners (children), first stage

Adverb	*hierar no.*	*Jean 1–5*	*Anne 1–3*	*Dany 1–2*	*Mimi 1–2*
bien sûr	2				
naturellement	2				
probablement	4				
seulement	?				
vraiment	?				
maintenant	5 contr				
alors	5 contr				
après	5 contr				
d'abord	5 contr				
peut-être	7				
normalment	10				
parfois	12?				
souvent	12				
personnellement	13?				
avant	15? 5?				
déjà	15				
tout le temps	18?				
encore/toujours	17				
toujours	18–19				
après	20 im fut				
et puis	20 im fut				
maintenant	20 im fut			1	
bien	26	1	1		
comme ça	26?	3			26
vite	27	1	1		
aussi	29?		8		5
encore	29	4		1	7
là	?	22	48	2	36

Legend: hierar no = number in the hierarchy as presented here in Section 2;
contr = with temporal contrast; im fut = reference to immediate future

Table A4 Adverbs in L1 learners (children), second stage

Adverb	hierar no.	Jean 6–8	Anne 4–6	Dany 3	Mimi 3
bien sûr	2				
naturellement	2				
probablement	4				
seulement	?				
vraiment	?				
maintenant	5 contr				
alors	5 contr				
après	5 contr				
d'abord	5 contr				
peut-être	7		3		2
normalment	10				
parfois	12?				
souvent	12				
personnellement	13?				
avant	15? 5?				
déjà	15		2		
tout le temps	18?				
encore/toujours	17				
toujours	18–19				
après	20 im fut		1		1
(et) puis	20 im fut	2	1	3	2
maintenant	20 im fut	2			3
bien	26		still occurring		
comme ça	26?			+	
vite	27			+	
aussi	29?			+	
encore	29			+	
là	?			+	

Legend: see Table A2

Table A5 Adverbs in L1 learners (children), third stage

Adverb	hierar no.	Jean 9–12	Anne 7–13	Dany 4–7	Mimi 5–8
bien sûr	2				
naturellement	2				
probablement	4				
seulement	?			3	3
vraiment	?				
maintenant	5 contr		6	5	7
(et) puis	5	1	1	11	
alors	5 contr	2	9		6
après	5 contr	6	3	3	3
d'abord	5 contr		6	4	
peut-être	7	8			
normalment	10				
parfois	12?				
souvent	12				
personnellement	13?				
avant	15? 5?	1		1	
déjà	15				
tout le temps	18?				
encore / toujours	17		2		
toujours	18–19				
après	20 im fut				
et puis	20 im fut			6	
maintenant	20 im fut	2	1	4	6
bien	26				
comme ça	26?		+		
vite	27		+		
aussi	29?		+		
encore	29		+		
là	?		+		

Legend: see Table A3

Table A6 Adverbs in adult L2 learners, first stage

Adverb	hierar no.	Henry 1–2	Björn 1–2	Sara 1–2	Lisa 1
bien sûr	2				1
naturellement	2	16			
probablement	4	2			
seulement	?			2	3
vraiment	?		1		
maintenant	5 contr		2	4	3
alors	5 constr				
après	5 contr	5	9	15	2
d'abord	5 contr				
peut-être	7	13	11	16	5
normalment	10	3			
parfois	12?				3
souvent	12		1		
personnellement	13?	2			
avant	15? 5?	2	4	2	
déjà	15				
tout le temps	18?			1	
encore/toujours	17			3	
toujours	18–19			1	
après	20 im fut				
(et) puis	20 im fut				
maintenant	20 im fut				
bien	26			3	7
comme ça	26?			9	1
vite	27				
aussi	29?	2	1	13	10
encore	29	2	5	1	4
là	?		1	1	2

Legend: see Table A3 above

Chapter 4

The Emergence and Use of the Plus-Que-Parfait in Advanced French Interlanguage

MARTIN HOWARD

Introduction

In contrast with other areas of second language (L2) acquisition, our knowledge about how the L2 learner expresses temporality has been greatly enriched within the last 20 years, thanks to the veritable flourishing of studies in this area (for an overview of research on the acquisition of temporality, see Bardovi-Harlig, 1999, 2000). Such studies have provided a pivotal insight into the L2 learner's aspectuo-temporal system, both in the case where grammatical marking is not yet present in learner interlanguage (IL), and in the case of the learner's early development on use of grammatical markers for the marking of present and past time.

Studies have generally noted the late emergence of grammatical marking of temporality in learner IL. Before the emergence of such grammatical marking, temporal reference is largely established through the learner's use of pragmatic and lexical devices. For example, Dietrich *et al.*'s (1995) cross-linguistic investigation within the European Science Foundation (ESF) Project of the naturalistic acquisition of temporality by adult immigrant learners of a number of European languages has very clearly documented a range of pragmatic devices, including the learners' recourse to the principle of natural order, whereby the order in which events are recounted reflects their natural temporal order; reliance on the temporal framework established by the learner's interlocutor; and the implicit marking of aspectuo-temporal relations based on the inherent lexical properties of the verb used to refer to a particular event. In tandem with such implicit means, explicit marking through the early use of temporal adverbials has also been found to be highly characteristic. For example, within the framework of the ESF Project, Starren and Van Hout (1996) note the efficient use of temporal adverbials by the L2 learner to express complex aspectuo-temporal relations, which would otherwise be marked by grammatical morphology in the target language.

Similar findings have also been noted for the role of lexical and pragmatic devices in the expression of temporality by instructed learners during the early stages of the acquisition of L2 French and other target languages. For example, using similar task types as in the ESF Project, Brum de Paula (1998) and Paprocka-Piotrowska (2002) respectively document their Brazilian-Portuguese and Polish instructed learners' heavy reliance on pragmatic and lexical devices in French IL before grammatical marking gradually emerges. Harley (1992) also notes her learners' early reliance on such devices in her investigation of the acquisition of French within the Canadian immersion setting. A final study is that of Bardovi-Harlig (1992), who specifically considers the role of temporal adverbials in the expression of temporality by her learners of English following a course of instruction in the US. She also notes the very frequent use of such devices as a means of explicitly marking temporal relations.

Whilst pragmatic and lexical devices have specifically been considered in terms of the expression of temporality when grammatical markers are not yet present in learner IL, they have also been found to co-occur with the emergence of such grammatical markers. From this point of view, the L2 learner's use of grammatical markers has been typically investigated in relation to the expression of past time relations, with a view to firstly identifying the pattern of emergence of grammatical markers in past time contexts. In the case of French IL, the following pattern can be proposed, based on such studies as Devitt (1995), Dietrich *et al.* (1995), Noyau (1991), Schlyter (1990), and Véronique (1987): '*présent* > *passé composé* > *imparfait*', such that the learner firstly uses the present in both present and past time contexts. Subsequently, the *passé composé* is contrasted with the present in past time contexts. Finally, the *imparfait* is contrasted with the *passé composé*, although the present also co-occurs.

Studies have also focused on the characteristic under- and overuse of such markers in learner IL. The quest to identify the underlying system behind such under- and overuse has given rise to a large number of studies which have proposed that a range of contextual factors constrain the learner's use of past time morphology, factors which are not at work in the native speaker, giving rise therefore to the characteristic differences between native-speaker and learner use of such morphology. Such factors have been shown to be vast, including grammatical aspect, inherent lexical aspect, discourse grounding, and phonetic saliency.[1] For example, in the case of grammatical aspect, studies of French IL such as Bardovi-Harlig and Bergström (1996), Howard (2001a & b, 2003 to appear b), and Kaplan

(1987) have noted that use of the *passé composé* tends to be more advanced in perfective contexts than use of the *imparfait* in imperfective contexts, where there is notable overuse of the present. With regard to the other factors, the similar systematic co-occurrence of each past time marker has been noted. For example, in the case of inherent lexical aspect, use of each past time marker has been found to systematically vary with different verb types (see, for example, Bergström, 1997; Howard 2001a, 2002c; and Salaberry 1998 in the case of L2 French). Past time marking has also been found to systematically vary depending on the discourse ground to be marked in terms of the foreground / background distinction (for studies of French IL, see, for example Howard, 2001; Noyau, 1997; Véronique, 1987). Another important constraint on past time marking in learner IL concerns the phonetic saliency of the verb to be marked in terms of whether it is regularly or irregularly conjugated (see Devitt, 1995; Dietrich *et al.*, 1995; Howard, 2002b).

Whilst such vast research has provided an important insight into the learner's aspectuo-temporal system during the emergence of such morphological markers, our knowledge of that system is much more limited in the case of the more advanced learner who productively uses aspectuo-temporal marking. A number of questions arise concerning the specificity of the advanced learner's aspectuo-temporal system, at a stage when aspectuo-temporal morphology is typically considered to be less in the emerging stage than having already emerged. For example, although the learner productively uses the L2 aspectuo-temporal morphology, little is known about the characteristics that distinguish that use from that of the native speaker, in terms of the specificity of the development that remains to be made by the L2 learner to approach native-speaker norms. Indeed, aspectuo-temporal research is only just beginning to move its focus beyond the more traditional study of the emergence of aspectuo-temporal morphology to consider the question of how the learner ultimately adjusts his / her functional use of that morphology in line with native-speaker norms. From this point of view, studies of advanced French IL such as Howard (2002a, 2002b, to appear a) and Kihlstedt (1998) offer an analysis of the internal development demonstrated by the advanced learner on use of such forms as the *imparfait* at various stages within the advanced learner variety. Such findings are particularly important in the case of advanced French IL, as a means of characterising the specificity of aspectuo-temporal marking beyond the creative grammaticalisation stage which has already been tracked by investigations of the emergence of the *passé composé* and the *imparfait* in less advanced IL.

Of equal importance, however, is the need to extend the focus of investigation to the learner's acquisition of other aspectuo-temporal markers such as the *plus-que-parfait*, and, indeed, the expression of other conceptual entities apart from past time, such as futurity and modality. As Bardovi-Harlig (1999: 374) writes, 'on the level of description, we need to explore the hypothesized sequences for the spreading of morphology, for which only the earliest stages have been documented'. This is perhaps more true in the case of French IL, where the study of such issues is less advanced than in the case of other L2s, such as in the case of future-time reference in L2 English (see Bardovi-Harlig, 2002) and L2 Italian (see Wiberg, 1998), and also in the case of the expression of modality in L2 Italian thanks to work by Giacalone Ramat (1992), and in L2 German, such as in the work of Dittmar and Terborg (1991).

In the light of the limitations which this very brief overview has provided of the current state of tense-aspect SLA research, which are perhaps best summarised in Bardovi-Harlig's call for research that details the spread of aspectuo-temporal morphology beyond the earliest stages, the study presented here has as its general aim to provide a preliminary analysis of the acquisition and use of the *plus-que-parfait* (PQP) to express the meaning of reverse order in advanced French IL. Indeed, such a study involves an investigation of a form-function relation which has hitherto received little consideration in L2 research in general, and in L2 French research in particular. However, before considering the place of such a study in relation to current findings on the acquisition of this form by the L2 learner of French, and its equivalent in other target languages, the following section will firstly briefly outline a theoretical framework for the analysis of the aspectuo-temporal value of this form in Reichenbachian terms (see Reichenbach, 1947).

The Use of the *Plus-Que-Parfait* within an Aspectuo-Temporal Framework

In narrative discourse, the principle of chronological order (Bardovi-Harlig, 1994), whereby events are recounted in the temporal order in which they occurred, has been widely recognised as highly characteristic of learner IL, both before and during the grammaticalisation of past time marking. Such a principle, which states that 'unless mentioned otherwise, order of mention corresponds to order of events' (Klein, 1994: 231), is exemplified in the following:

(1)   Prendre le bus pour aller en ville. Rencontrer mes amis vers sept heures. Rentrer très tard.

In spite of the absence of aspectuo-temporal morphology in this example, it is generally to be inferred that the second event recounted in this narrative sequence occurred subsequently to the first, thanks to the inherent lexical properties of each event which implicitly imply completion and change. Such a temporal relation is further supplemented by the explicit establishment of the reference time 'vers sept heures' for this second event. Similarly, in spite of the absence of grammatical marking, it is also a logical conclusion that the temporal occurrence of the third event recounted is posterior to the second. Since the speaker does not indicate otherwise, the narrative sequence of events appears to reflect their actual temporal occurrence.

When morphological marking is not yet developed in learner IL, the principle of chronological order functions as a pragmatic strategy whereby it can be inferred in what temporal order events occurred in relation to each other. Such pragmatic marking of temporality has been noted, for example, by Clark (1971), who refers to the 'order of mention contract' in her work on first language acquisition; by Bardovi-Harlig (1994); by Klein (1986) and Dietrich *et al.* (1995) who refer to the principle of natural order; and by Schumann (1987) who speaks of serialisation. Such interpretation of the temporal relation holding between each event is naturally dependent on the correct inference strategy on the part of the learner's interlocutor. In contrast to such implicit marking of the temporal order of events, which has been found to be highly characteristic of the pre-grammaticalised stages of L2 acquisition, such a temporal relation is grammaticalised in target-language French through use of the *passé composé*, as exemplified in the following:

(2) J'ai pris le bus pour aller en ville. J'ai rencontré mes amis vers sept heures. Je suis rentré très tard.

Use of the *passé composé* implies temporal progression along the time axis, since this form autonomously establishes a new reference time in the case of each event. As such, it is understood that the second event does not occur simultaneously to the first, but rather a relation of posteriority is implied between the second and the first event, and between the third and the second event. The following aspectuo-temporal relation emerges in Reichenbachian terms for each event:

$$E/R < S.$$

Thus, in the case of the second event, a past time relation is first implied, since its event time (E: 'rencontrer mes amis') is anterior to the speech time (S: the time at which the event was recounted). Secondly, the aorist value of the *passé composé* is implied since the reference time (R: 'vers sept heures') coincides with the time of the event, such that both are anterior to the speech time.

Whilst such chronological marking of events through use of the *passé composé* has been found to be highly characteristic of learner narratives during the stage of IL grammaticalisation of aspectuo-temporal relations, the recounting of events in reverse order (in other words, out of their chronological sequence) has not been widely investigated. Such reverse-order reporting is exemplified in the following:[2]

(3)   J'ai pris le bus pour aller en ville. J'*avais* déjà *rencontré* mes amis vers sept heures.

In this case, thanks to use of the PQP, it is understood that the event 'rencontrer mes amis' occurred prior to the reference point 'prendre le bus' which functions as a temporal anchor from which this second event is viewed. This reference point is also anterior to the speech time. The following temporal relation therefore emerges for this second event:

$E < R < S.$

In target language French, such a functional value is grammaticalised through use of the PQP, which implies that the time of the event referred to is anterior to a reference time already established in context, which also precedes the speech time. The use of the adverb 'déjà' also serves as an explicit marker of this relation of anteriority in (3) above. In cognitive terms, the functional value of the PQP appears as more complex than in the case of chronological marking with the *passé composé*, since the speaker must distinguish between three temporal points, where $E < R < S$. In contrast, as noted earlier, the relation is simpler in the case of the *passé composé*, where $E/R < S$, such that there is an overlap between the event time and the reference time. However, in spite of such cognitive complexity, use of the PQP allows the speaker considerable discursive freedom, by allowing him/her to abstain from adherence to the principle of chronological order in narrative discourse. This is particularly important in the case where the speaker has omitted an event in a narrative sequence, and wishes to specify its temporal relation with previously recounted events, as exemplified in the following:

(4)   Prendre le bus pour aller en ville. Rentrer très tard. Rencontrer mes amis.

As noted previously, if he/she were relying on the principle of chronological order, the learner's interlocutor would infer that a relation of posteriority holds between the second and the first event, and similarly between the third and the second event. However, considerable confusion arises in the case where the actual order of events is such that 'rencontrer mes amis' occurred prior to 'rentrer très tard'. Indeed, even when the *passé composé* is part of the learner's aspectuo-temporal system, similar confusion arises, since this marker implicitly establishes a new reference time of itself. The principle of chronological order therefore emerges as a potentially very inefficient and awkward means of establishing temporal reference when it is found not to hold true. In view of the potential ambiguity arising, the study presented here is concerned with an investigation of the L2 learner's attempts to recount events out of chronological sequence, and his/her use of the PQP to do so in target language French.

Literature Review

As stated above, few previous studies in the area of temporality have focused on the expression of reverse order in learner IL. In the case of L2 French, however, an exception is Kihlstedt's (1998) comparative study of Swedish advanced learners of French and native French speakers. She investigates their use of the PQP in terms of the level to which they engage in expressing temporal movement along the time axis ('*va-et-vient*' in her terminology). Kihlstedt suggests that, owing to their use of the PQP, the native speakers are more adept at anaphoric reference by establishing temporal relations between events in the past in relation to each other. In contrast, the learners tend to relate events to the speech time. As such, due to their restricted use of the PQP, Kihlstedt notes that the internal temporal order of events is vaguer in the learners' production, such that they tend not to make explicit any deviations from the chronological order in which events occurred. Kihlstedt concludes that contexts where a chronological relation does not hold between events constitute an area of considerable 'morphological breakdown' for the L2 learner.

Such findings in French IL reflect the late emergence of the PQP in French L1 acquisition, as detailed by Labelle (1994) in her overview of the acquisition of past time marking by francophone children. She notes that the acquisition of the PQP constitutes the final stage in their acquisition of the past time markers: the *passé composé* is first produced before being contrasted with the *imparfait*. Only subsequently is a contrast made with the PQP. Citing Fayol (1982), Labelle notes that tokens of the PQP are not 'susceptibles de marquer à eux seuls l'antériorité d'un procès par rapport à un autre' until between the ages of nine and ten years in French children (Labelle, 1994: 117).

Apart from French IL, reverse-order reporting has also been specifically investigated in L2 English by Bardovi-Harlig (1994). Her study is based on an investigation of the written productions of learners of English in the US who had various different L1s. Similarly to Kihlstedt's results, Bardovi-Harlig notes the relatively late emergence of the English equivalent of the

PQP, namely the pluperfect. However, in the absence of the pluperfect in their IL, Bardovi-Harlig notes that the learners rely heavily on lexical and pragmatic devices such that the meaning of reverse order can be inferred thanks to the presence of temporal adverbials and other implicit clues such as markers of subordination.

The late emergence of the pluperfect in English IL has also been observed by Dietrich *et al.* (1995) in the case of their naturalistic informants on the ESF Project. They found that this form was produced only by 'exceptional' informants who demonstrated considerably more advanced development on aspectuo-temporal marking, such as in the case of Lavinia, as specifically profiled by Klein (1994).

In spite of the important insight that the studies reviewed offer concerning reverse-order marking, there remains a considerable dearth of studies on this issue. The study presented here has as its aim to complement existing findings on this subject by investigating reverse-order reporting in anglophone learners of French. Such a study is particularly interesting for a number of reasons, which we shall outline here.

Firstly, unlike use of the pluperfect in target language English, as studied by Bardovi-Harlig (1994), use of the PQP is considered to be more obligatory in target language French. For example, in the following, we note that the speaker of English has a choice in using the pluperfect, whereas this is less the case with regard to use of the PQP in target language French:

(5) I had to return home because I forgot / had forgotten my wallet.
    J'ai dû rentrer à la maison parce que j'avais oublié mon portefeuille.

Therefore, in the case of Bardovi-Harlig's learners of English detailed above, their limited use of the pluperfect may reflect a certain effect for the fact that use of this form is obligatory only in those cases where ambiguity would otherwise be implied, such as in the following:

(6) When I came home, my friends came over* / had come over.

In this case, use of the simple past does not allow the events to be interpreted as occurring in the reverse order to which they are recounted. Use of the pluperfect is therefore necessary in such contexts as a means of avoiding this confusion.

In view of such differences between the PQP in French and the pluperfect in English, a study of the use of the PQP in the French IL of anglophone learners allows for an interesting investigation of the potential effect of such obligatory use of the PQP on use of this form by L2 learners of French, in comparison with the findings concerning the somewhat more optional use of the pluperfect by L2 learners of English, as reported on by Bardovi-Harlig (1994).

Secondly, in view of the more obligatory contextual use of the PQP in target language French in comparison with use of the pluperfect in English, it is important to consider any differential effect on recourse to lexical and pragmatic devices in reverse-order contexts by the L2 learner of French in comparison with L2 learners of English. As noted previously, Bardovi-Harlig finds that her L2 learners of English rely heavily on such devices to compensate for the missing pluperfect in their productions. In view of such a finding, she concludes that, just as the learner in the pre-grammaticalisation stage of acquisition relies on such lexical and pragmatic devices, the advanced learner similarly reverts to such devices as a means of expressing a conceptual entity which is otherwise grammaticalised in the target language, but has not yet grammaticalised in the learner's IL. However, Bardovi-Harlig (1999: 374) particularly notes that 'additional studies are necessary' as a means of testing such a hypothesis predicting that the L2 learner traverses the 'pragmatic-lexical-grammatical path' a number of times during the acquisition of additional morphology, 'if not all the way through, at least from the lexical stage to the morphological'.

Thirdly, in view of Bardovi-Harlig's findings in the case of English that use of the pluperfect requires considerable stability on use of the other past time forms, a similar question arises in the case of learners of French as to how their use of other aspectuo-temporal markers such as the *passé composé* and the *imparfait* may affect the emergence of and subsequent use of the PQP in their French IL.

Finally, an investigation of use of the PQP in French IL allows an interesting analysis of the effect of formal complexity as opposed to cognitive complexity on the acquisition of a morphological marker. As we noted above, previous studies have generally pointed to the early emergence of the *passé composé* in French IL. This is in spite of the fact that this is a formally complex form, requiring an auxiliary verb and a past participle, just like the PQP. If formal complexity is not a factor in L2 acquisition, it could be expected that the PQP should similarly emerge early in learner IL. However, if this is not the case, the late emergence of the PQP may reflect an effect for the functional complexity of the PQP, whereby the distinction between three temporal points, namely $E < R < S$, poses considerable cognitive difficulty to the learner. In contrast, as noted above, the functional value of the *passé composé* is less complex, implying the relationship $E/R < S$.

With such questions in mind, the study presented here constitutes a preliminary attempt to expand our understanding of reverse-order marking by the L2 learner, by focusing on L2 learners of French.

Study

The study is based on a larger project investigating the acquisition of French by Irish university learners of French, as detailed in Howard (2002b). The learners are native speakers of English, who, at the time of the study, were specialising in French and one other subject as part of their university degree programme. Prior to their university studies, they had been learning French for between five and six years at school. All the informants had also learnt Irish at school, such that French was not their sole second language. The syllabus for modern language teaching in Irish schools prescribes a communicative approach, which integrates the four language skills as well as aiming to develop the learner's metalinguistic knowledge of formal aspects of the L2, cultural knowledge of the L2, and strategic competence in learning and using the L2.

In the case of their university programme of studies in French, the learners followed courses in French language, literature and culture, amounting to approximately 200 contact hours annually. Much of the teaching of the learners' courses was done through the medium of French. As part of the language component of the learners' course of study in French, the learners followed courses in both written and spoken French, where explicit focus on the learners' grammatical skills was balanced by use of authentic written and aural materials to stimulate communicative interaction.

Following Bartning's (1997) characterisation of the advanced learner variety, the informants squarely match the profile of the advanced instructed learner, given their learner characteristics, concerning such factors as the duration of their acquisition of French, their metalinguistic awareness, and their motivation, amongst others. Furthermore, in terms of their linguistic profiles, the various morpho-syntactic forms of the L2 were no longer emerging, but rather had emerged in the learners' IL system.[3]

The study presented here is based on a comparison of 18 learners who were grouped according to their level of classroom instruction and the duration of their previous residence in France. Thus, at the time of the study, the learners in group 1 had completed two years of their university degree programme. Although they were about to participate in a 'year abroad' programme at a host university in France, they had not previously resided in a francophone community. In contrast, although the learners in group 2 had similarly received two years of classroom instruction, at the time of the study they had just returned from France, where they had spent the previous academic year as part of an international exchange programme between their home university and a host university in France. During that time, the learners followed a number of academic courses through French with native French students, although they did not receive any formal instruction in French. Finally, at the time of the study, the learners in group 3 had not previously resided in France but rather had received an extra year of classroom instruction relative to the learners in the other groups. By making a comparison between the three groups, the study therefore allows an investigation of the relative effects of classroom instruction and residence in France on the learners' linguistic development in L2 French. As the study is cross-sectional, it was important that the learners in groups 2 and 3 were at the same general level of proficiency as group 1 before they respectively studied abroad and received further instruction. This was done by a comparison of results on a general test of linguistic proficiency completed by the learners after two years of instruction, when they were at the same stage of instruction as the learners in group 1.

For the purposes of data elicitation, the informants participated in a sociolinguistic interview following the conventions proposed by Labov (1984). Each interview lasted approximately one hour, and was carried out by the researcher who, although not a native speaker, nonetheless demonstrated near-native proficiency in French. Although each interview followed the same network of conversational modules developed by Labov for the elicitation of natural spoken data, the actual topics of conversation were adapted to best suit the specific interests of the informants, and included, amongst others, such subjects as their academic studies, career plans, visits to France, hobbies, the summer vacation, and Labov's famous 'danger of death' module. Although, in the case of this study, we are specifically concerned with an aspect of the learners' past time system, such conversational modules also obliged the informants to speak within present and future time frameworks. Following the data-elicitation stage, the interviews were transcribed into standard orthography following the transcription conventions proposed by Blanche-Benveniste and Jeanjean (1987).

Data Analysis

For the purposes of this analysis, we extracted from the data all tokens expressing reverse order, that is to say, where the narrative sequence of events did not match the temporal order in which they actually occurred. The identification of such tokens was not dependent in any way on the learner's use of the PQP to mark the reverse order, such that during the data-extraction stage we did not pay any attention to the morphological forms produced by the learners. Since tokens on which the analysis was based occurred in personal narratives, as opposed to fictional narratives or other narratives based on shared knowledge between the informant and the researcher, it was necessary to infer the temporal order pertaining between the events recounted. However, in those cases where the temporal order was ambiguous, such tokens were excluded from the analysis.

We subsequently coded the tokens included in the analysis for the morphological forms used to mark the reverse order, as well as a number of other contextual factors. In the case of morphological form, we coded the two clauses constituting the reverse order report, as exemplified in the following:[4]

(7)   Ils *sont arrivés* **2** en retard parce que leur vol *avait eu* **1** un retard
                                                              (Caroline 284)

As such, it was possible to consider the type of morphological contrast made by the learners to express reverse order in such contexts, with a view to identifying whether the learners' use of the PQP develops in tandem with the emergence of the functional context requiring this form, namely the reverse-order report. The coding of the data for other contextual factors was done with the aim of identifying the role of pragmatic and lexical devices in the expression of reverse order by the learners. Thus, we firstly coded for the presence / absence of temporal adverbials, as exemplified in the following:

(8) Je suis arrivée je savais **2** même pas que c'était un restaurant je je suis j'y suis allé **1** *la semaine avant*   (Debra 353)

We also coded the data for the presence / absence of syntactic subordinators, which, according to Bardovi-Harlig (1994), also serve to allow the meaning of reverse order to be inferred. Such subordinators are wide-ranging, and include the following:

Relative Pronouns

(9)   Après je pense **2** *que* j'ai fait **1** quelque chose stupide (Ken 367)

Causal Subordinators

(10) Ils ont gardé **2** l'argent *parce qu'*on [n']avait pas lu **1** les petits les petits lignes   (Ken 242)

Complements

(11) J'ai fait **2** un coup de téléphone pour faire savoir *si* quelqu'un a laissé **1** mon sac à la réception   (Caroline 477)

Unlike lexical devices such as the explicit use of temporal adverbials to mark the temporal order, such pragmatic devices are necessarily syntactic constituents of the utterance produced, and therefore serve as a more implicit clue to the temporal relation holding between events. In the case of some tokens, it happened that more than one type of device was present. That is to say, there were cases where temporal adverbials co-occurred with a syntactic device, as exemplified in the following:

(12)   Ils faisaient **2** les mêmes choses *que* on a fait **1** *en première année*
(Sylvia 107)

The analysis of the data concerning the function of pragmatic and lexical devices in reverse-order contexts specifically focuses on the question of how such devices might compensate for the loss in meaning in those contexts where the PQP is missing. Such a question relates to the more global question posed by Bardovi-Harlig (1999, 2000) concerning whether the advanced learner might retreat to a more pragmatic mode to express the meaning of a grammaticalised form which is not (fully) part of his/her linguistic repertoire. This is in spite of the fact that the advanced learner is nonetheless characterised by a high level of grammaticalisation on use of other morphological forms. Such an analysis also allows us to consider the role of functional constraints in the case of reverse-order marking by the advanced learner. For example, if such lexical and pragmatic devices allow the meaning of reverse order to be inferred, it may be the case that use of the PQP is hindered in those cases where such devices are present. In contrast, use of the PQP may be promoted in contexts where such devices are not present, given that the meaning of reverse order cannot be otherwise inferred. Indeed, such an analysis provides a useful means of testing the Functional Hypothesis in advanced learner IL.[5]

Results

The results will firstly be presented in relation to the learners' use of morphological marking in reverse-order contexts, before considering the role of lexical and pragmatic devices in such contexts. The results are presented comparatively for the three groups of learners we identified earlier, namely the second-year instructed learners in group 1; the learners in group 2 who had received a similar level of instruction, but who had also spent a year in France; and the learners in group 3 who had received an extra year of classroom instruction in lieu of spending a year in France.

Table 4.1 presents the results concerning the type of morphological contrast made by the learners in reverse-order contexts. The first line details the relative frequency of use of the PQP to express reverse order. The second line details the relative frequency of reports where another

Table 4.1 Tokens of different types of morphological contrasts occurring in reverse order contexts

	Group 1		Group 2		Group 3	
Contrast	*n*	%	*n*	%	*n*	%
With the PQP	3	9	25	35	28	31
Without the PQP	22	65	21	30	38	44
No contrast	9	26	26	35	22	25
Total	34	100	72	100	88	100

marker is used, and where such a marker contrasts with the marker produced in the first syntactic clause constituting the reverse-order report, as exemplified in the following:

(13)   Après je *pense* **2** que j'*ai fait* **1** quelque chose stupide   (Ken 367)

The final row concerns the relative frequency of those reports where the same morphological marker was produced in both clauses constituting the reverse-order report, as exemplified in the following:

(14)   Il *est allé* **2** après que deux trois personnes *sont descendues* **1**
                                                                      (Daniel 498)

The table should be read downwards, in order to compare the relative frequency of each type of contrast for each group of learners.

Before detailing the morphological contrasts produced by the learners to express reverse order, it is firstly necessary to consider to what extent the learners engage in such reporting. The final row in table 1 details the total number of reverse order reports produced by the learners. By comparing the groups, it becomes clear that the study abroad group (group 2) and the group receiving further instruction (group 3) engage in reverse order reporting to a far greater extent than the pre-study abroad learners of group 1. Indeed, the former groups produce at least twice as many reports as the latter group.

With regard to their use of the PQP to express reverse order, we also note a considerable difference between group 1 and the other groups. This group produces only three tokens of this form. In contrast, the other groups make more frequent use of the PQP, suggesting that the learners in groups 2 and 3 are more successful at grammatically marking the meaning of reverse order. However, it is nonetheless to be noted that their use of the PQP is restricted to approximately one third of all contexts where it could be produced, suggesting that considerable development remains to be made on use of this form by the learners.

In spite of the restricted use of the PQP by the learners, it is nevertheless to be noted across the groups that reverse-order contexts where a morphological contrast is made, be it with the PQP or another form, are more frequent than those contexts where no such contrast is made. Such a result correlates with Bardovi-Harlig's (1994) finding in the case of her L2 learners of English, who attempt to make a morphological distinction between the two events which are expressed in reverse-order. Given such similarities in findings, our results further corroborate Bardovi-Harlig's conclusion that the learner tends to distinguish between the two events constituting the reverse order report by means of a morphological contrast. However, in the case of our results, it should be noted that such a tendency is less true in the case of our study-abroad learners (group 2) than in the case of our instructed learners (groups 1 and 3): the occurrence of reports where no morphological contrast is made is more frequent in the study-abroad learners of group 2 (35%) than in the case of the instructed learners of groups 1 and 3 (26% and 25% respectively).

In those cases where the morphological contrast does not involve the PQP, it is interesting to note that reports involving an aspectual contrast dominate over those involving a temporal contrast. The following example in (15) shows an aspectual contrast, involving two different past time forms. The example in (16) shows a temporal contrast, where the contrast is between the unmarked present form and a past time form. Table 4.2 thereafter indicates the relative occurrence of tokens involving a temporal contrast:

(15) C'*était* **2** assez difficile parce que surtout au mois d'août parce que y avait la dame qui faisait la serveuse qui était là là normalement qui qui *est partie* **1** en vacances   (Debra 374)
(16) Ce n'*est* pas **2** trop difficile car je *faisais* **1** ce travail ici alors ce n'était pas nouveau pour moi   (Edith 298)

The tendency by the learners across the groups not to make a temporal contrast further correlates with Bardovi-Harlig's findings by indicating, on the one hand, that the learners tend to mark the past time meaning of both clauses. Indeed, in the case of group 1, we note that their use of the past time forms in reverse order contexts is more frequent than in other past time contexts, as presented in Howard (2002b). On the other hand, however, it also indicates that the learners do not attempt to distinguish between the two temporal points which constitute the reverse order by contrasting the present with a past tense. Rather, they make an aspectual distinction in the

Table 4.2 Tokens of reverse order reports involving a temporal contrast

Group 1		Group 2		Group 3	
n	%	*n*	%	*n*	%
4	12	4	6	7	8

Table 4.3 Tokens of other morphological forms in reverse order contexts

Form	Group 1		Group 2		Group 3	
	n	%	*n*	%	*n*	%
Present	6	19	2	4	2	4
Passé Composé	19	62	32	70	37	66
Imparfait	6	19	12	26	17	30

past, from which the meaning of reverse order must be inferred. Such an aspectual contrast leaves ambiguous the temporal relationship between the two events which constitute the reverse order, as exemplified in (15) above.

In view of our learners' restricted use of the PQP, it remains for us to consider their use of alternative morphological forms in reverse-order contexts. The learners made use of three other forms in such contexts, namely the present, the *passé composé*, and the *imparfait*, whose relative occurrence is presented in Table 4.3.

In particular, we note the highly frequent use of the *passé composé* in place of the PQP. Indeed, use of the *passé composé* is considerably more frequent in reverse-order contexts than in other past-time contexts, as investigated by Howard (2002b). We also note a corresponding lower rate of occurrence of the present in reverse-order contexts than in past time contexts in general, suggesting that the learners attempt to express the past time meaning of the reverse order, as already noted. In cases where the *imparfait* is used in place of the PQP, it is notable that this form predominantly occurs with stative verbs. Indeed, in reverse-order contexts, very few stative verbs are used with markers other than the *imparfait*, suggesting that these verbs are more resistant to the PQP than dynamic verbs. This reflects Zielonka's (1999) finding that her Polish learners of Swedish have more difficulty recalling the PQP equivalent with stative verbs than with other verb types.

Use of such other markers as the present, the *passé composé* and the *imparfait* in place of the PQP to express reverse order gives rise to potential ambiguity concerning the aspectuo-temporal relation holding between events. It remains for us to consider how the presence of lexical and pragmatic devices may compensate for the potential loss in meaning in such contexts. Following the approach adopted by Bardovi-Harlig (1994), we compared the role of such devices in contexts where the PQP co-occurred and in contexts where the PQP was absent. Such an analysis therefore allowed us to consider how such devices might be more frequent in contexts where the PQP was absent than when it co-occurred, as a means of compensating for the loss in meaning when the PQP is absent. Table 4.4 therefore presents, in the case of each group, the frequency of use of such devices in contexts where the PQP co-occurred, and also in contexts where the PQP was absent. As noted above, in the presentation of the data analysis, such devices were coded in terms of temporal adverbials and other pragmatic devices, namely syntactic subordinators, which allow the meaning of reverse order to be inferred. We also included in the analysis those cases where no such devices were present, such that the meaning of reverse order had to be inferred solely on the basis of the general background context. In Table 4.4, these tokens are classified under the heading of 'context alone'.

The results will firstly be discussed for those reports where the PQP is absent (column 1), and secondly for the reports where this form is present (column 2). The table should therefore be first read downwards, in order to compare the relative occurrence of each device across the groups. By reading across the table, we can see how use of such devices differs in reports where the PQP is present and absent.

By reading down column 1, one notes that reports where lexical and pragmatic devices are present are more frequent than reports which rely on context alone. Thus, in reports where the PQP is absent, the meaning of reverse order can more often than not be inferred, thanks to the presence of pragmatic devices and temporal adverbials. Furthermore, it is also to be noted that in a previous analysis which compared use of temporal adverbials in reverse-order contexts and in other past time contexts, Howard (2002b) found that the learners' use of temporal adverbials is more frequent in reverse-order contexts than in other past time contexts.

Taken together, these two findings, namely the relatively less frequent occurrence of reports which rely on context alone to express the meaning of reverse order, and the higher use of temporal adverbs in such reports than in other past time contexts, suggest that, in the absence of the PQP, the learners revert to a lexico-pragmatic mode which compensates for the absent PQP as a means of expressing the meaning of reverse order.

It remains for us to compare these results with those concerning those contexts where the PQP is present (column 2). Given that group 1 produces

Table 4.4 Tokens of reverse order reports involving lexical and pragmatic markers

Group 1				
Device	Reverse order reports without the PQP		Reverse order reports with the PQP	
	n	%	*n*	%
Context alone	13	37	1	33
Adverbials	9	26	–	–
Pragmatic devices	13	37	2	67
Group 2				
Device	Reverse order reports without the PQP		Reverse order reports with the PQP	
	n	%	*n*	%
Context alone	19	33	12	43
Adverbials	17	29	7	25
Pragmatic devices	22	38	9	32
Group 3				
Device	Reverse order reports without the PQP		Reverse order reports with the PQP	
	n	%	*n*	%
Context alone	22	31	12	40
Adverbials	21	30	8	27
Pragmatic devices	27	39	10	33

only three occurrences of the PQP, our analysis is restricted to groups 2 and 3. By reading across columns 1 and 2 in the case of these groups, we note that reverse-order reports where the PQP is produced without any other lexical or pragmatic device are more frequent than reports where this form is absent and where the meaning of reverse order must be inferred based on context alone. In view of such a finding, the learners in groups 2 and 3 seem to rely less on pragmatic devices and temporal adverbials to express the meaning of reverse order when the PQP is present in context than when it is absent. Put another way, taken together, the occurrence of lexical and pragmatic devices is more frequent in contexts where the PQP is absent than where it co-occurs. As such, it seems that, when the learners produce the PQP, this form might reduce the learners' reliance on more pragmatic devices to express the meaning of reverse order. However, such a conclusion must be purely tentative given that the raw number of tokens associated with these differences is quite small.

Discussion

The results presented point to the general difficulty that use of the PQP poses to our advanced learners of French. Although the functional context requiring the PQP is present in their production, the learners make restricted use of this form. This is particularly true in the case of group 1, where only three occurrences were found. The learners' limited development in the formal marking of reverse order contrasts with their more increased development in use of the other past time markers, namely the *passé composé* and, to a lesser extent, the *imparfait*, as previously detailed by Howard (2002b). Such differences in development on use of each past time form point to a limited effect for their programme of formal instruction in bringing about more equally balanced development in use of the past tenses. This is in spite of the fact that the past tenses occupied a pivotal place throughout the programme of instruction that the learners had followed. Rather, the learners' rate of development of use of each form differed considerably, such that their use of the PQP developed at a relatively later stage compared with the learners' earlier development on use of the *passé composé*, and, thereafter, in use of the *imparfait*. Thus, the learners demonstrate differential development of use of the past time forms, such that their programme of instruction does not seem to have influenced their relative pattern of development in use of the past-time forms. Furthermore, a restricted effect for classroom instruction is also evident insofar as the instructed learners of group 3 and the study-abroad learners of group 2 show relatively similar levels of development, albeit limited, in use of the PQP.

Given such similarities between groups 2 and 3 in terms of their more increased use of the PQP relative to group 1, it was therefore necessary to tease out how other conditioning factors may have promoted their development on use of the PQP. From this point of view, both groups 2 and 3 were characterised by increased stability in use of the other past time forms, relative to group 1. Such a finding in the case of our advanced learners of French corroborates findings in the case of the acquisition of the pluperfect by L2 learners of English, as described by Bardovi-Harlig (1994), who notes that high stability in use of the past tenses was evident in all her learners who made use of the pluperfect. Thus, in spite of the more 'obligatory' quality surrounding use of the PQP in French compared to its formal equivalent in English, as described previously, such differences do not render the PQP a more easily acquired form in L2 French relative to the other past time forms.

Thanks to such existing studies of reverse-order marking by learners of other target and source languages, it is possible to draw a number of preliminary conclusions concerning the expression of reverse order by the L2 learner, based on a simple cross-linguistic comparison of results. The other studies principally concern Bardovi-Harlig's (1994) investigation of learners of English who had various different L1s, and Kihlstedt's (1998) investigation of Swedish learners of French, as previously reviewed above. From this point of view, the results of these studies as well as those presented in this study here point to a number of similarities in the expression of reverse order by the L2 learner, irrespective of the target or source languages concerned. Such similarities afford an interesting insight into a number of questions surrounding the acquisition of the PQP and its formal equivalents in other L2s.

Such similarities firstly concern the general difficulty posed by the grammatical marking of reverse order in learner IL, such that, relative to other past time markers, the PQP and its formal equivalent in other L2s are late to emerge. This is in spite of the fact that, in terms of their formal make-up, certain other past time markers are equally complex, such as in the case of the composed forms of the *passé composé* and the PQP in French, as well as in the case of the present perfect and the pluperfect forms in English. In fact, in L2 French, it is noted that the *passé composé* is the first past time form to emerge. Thus, given such discrepancies in the order of emergence of the past time forms across L2s, it must be hypothesised that the functional complexity of the aspectual value of the PQP and its equivalent in other target languages is a more relevant explanation of its late emergence. Indeed, as we noted previously, in Reichenbachian terms, such a form implies the temporal distinction between three temporal points, such that the event time precedes the reference time, which, in turn, precedes the speech time. Given the difficulty posed by use of the PQP and its equivalents in other L2s, this relation appears to be cognitively more complex for the L2 learner than those aspectual relations expressed by other past time forms. As such, where development on use of the PQP is concerned, cognitive complexity appears to be a more important factor than formal complexity.

A further general similarity across studies, and not unrelated to the factor of functional complexity as a constraint on development in use of the PQP, is the finding that stability in use of the other past time forms appears to be a prerequisite for the emergence of this form in learner IL. All the studies concerned note that the PQP is only present in those learners who demonstrate a high level of proficiency on past time marking in general. This, however, is not to say that the functional context requiring the PQP is not present in their IL: across the studies, it has been seen that the learners engage in reverse-order reporting even before the PQP is present in their IL. It is only subsequently that the learners produce the appropriate grammatical form expressing the meaning of reverse order. Thus, where the PQP is concerned, it seems that the functional context emerges in the learner's IL before the formal marker of that function. Such common findings across the studies concerned thereby indicate that, where this conceptual entity is concerned at least, function precedes form.

Finally, similarities also emerge across studies in relation to the pragmatic and lexical characteristics of the L2 learner's marking of a conceptual entity which is otherwise grammaticalised in the target language. In spite of the small number of tokens concerned, our results tentatively point to the important role of lexical and pragmatic devices as a means of allowing the meaning of reverse order to be inferred when the formal marker of this meaning is missing. From this point of view, our findings correlate with those of Bardovi-Harlig, who similarly notes the important role of lexical and pragmatic devices in the expression of reverse order. In the light of such similarities across studies, our findings provide preliminary support for Bardovi-Harlig's conclusion that the advanced learner relies on pragmatic and lexical devices to express a functional value which is otherwise grammaticalised in the target language. As noted, this is in spite of the fact that the advanced learner demonstrates considerable stability in use of other L2 markers. Indeed, such pragmatic marking is not unlike that observed prior to, but also during, the emergence of earlier aspectuo-temporal markers in less advanced learners.

Conclusion

Given the preliminary insight that this study provides into an area of aspectuo-temporal underdevelopment in advanced French IL, the study points to a need to extend the agenda of research on the acquisition of temporality beyond the investigation of the emergence of aspectuo-temporal morphology during less advanced stages of acquisition, so as to identify remaining areas of linguistic development in more advanced learners. As we have seen in this study, the expression of reverse order constitutes one such area of particular underdevelopment in advanced French IL, which contrasts sharply with the more increased general development demonstrated by the learners in use of other forms of the L2, including the other past time markers.

Furthermore, the study presented here highlights the particular benefits of making a cross-linguistic comparison of different studies involving learners of different target and source languages, as a means of identifying the potential universality of findings across learners, irrespective of the target or source language concerned, or, indeed, as a means of distinguishing the specificity of findings as a function of the target or source language concerned. In the case of reverse-order reporting, as noted previously, our findings for anglophone learners of French point to a number of similarities with those findings reported for Swedish learners of French (Kihlstedt, 1998) and learners of English with different L1s (Bardovi-Harlig, 1994). Such similarities specifically concern the difficulty posed by the grammatical marking of reverse order in advanced learner IL, which contrasts with the L2 learner's increased development in use of the other past time forms, as well as the role of pragmatic and lexical devices in reverse-order contexts.

In conclusion, in view of the benefits of such a cross-linguistic approach to providing a useful insight into an area of particular underdevelopment in advanced learner IL, at a stage of development which has tended to be neglected in second language research, the study presented here points to the need for future research firstly to investigate other areas of aspectuo-temporal underdevelopment in advanced learner IL. Secondly, with a view to considering how the characteristics of such underdevelopment may differ across learners of different L2s, future investigations must also include L2s other than English (such as French), and thereby provide a more expansive insight into the universality / specificity of the process of L2 acquisition in the advanced learner.

Acknowledgments

The project on which this study is based was funded by the Irish Research Council for the Humanities and the Social Sciences (IRCHSS), and the Association for French Language Studies (AFLS), UK, whose support I gratefully acknowledge. I also wish to thank Maria Kihlstedt for her comments on an earlier draft of this chapter, which was presented as a paper at the 26th Annual Research Symposium of the Royal Irish Academy, Maynooth (Ireland). My thanks also go to the anonymous referees for their insightful comments. Naturally, any shortcomings remain my own.

Notes
1. For an overview of such factors in the acquisition of temporality, see Howard (2002b).
2. The term is borrowed from Bardovi-Harlig (1994).
3. For discussion of the advanced learner variety, see also Howard (1998, 1999).
4. The examples provided are extracted from the learner data. The numbers in bold refer to the actual temporal order in which events occurred in relation to each other, where **1** marks the temporally more distant event, and **2** the temporally nearer event.

5. For an overview of the Functional Hypothesis in relation to L2 acquisition, see Tomlin (1990). For specific investigations, see, for example, Bayley (1996) and Young (1991, 1993) who respectively consider the role of functional constraints on variable t/d deletion and '-s' plural marking in English IL.

References

Bardovi-Harlig, K. (1992) The use of adverbials and natural order in the development of temporal expression. *International Review of Applied Linguistics* 30 (4), 299–320.

Bardovi-Harlig, K. (1994) Reverse-order reports and the acquisition of tense: Beyond the principle of chronological order. *Language Learning* 44 (2), 243–82.

Bardovi-Harlig, K. (1999) From morpheme studies to temporal semantics. Tense-aspect research in SLA. *Studies in Second Language Acquisition* 21, 341–82.

Bardovi-Harlig, K. (2000) *Tense and Aspect in Second Language Acquisition: Form, Meaning, and Use.* Oxford: Blackwell [Language Learning Monographs 2].

Bardovi-Harlig, K. (2002) A new starting point? Investigating formulaic use and input in future expression. *Studies in Second Language Acquisition* 24, 189–198.

Bardovi-Harlig, K. and Bergström, A. (1996) Acquisition of tense and aspect in second language and foreign language learning: Learner narratives in ESL and FFL. *Canadian Modern Language Review* 52 (2), 308–330.

Bartning, I. (1997) L'apprenant dit avancé et son acquisition d'une langue étrangère. Tour d'horizon et esquisse de la variété avancée. *Acquisition et Interaction en Langue Etrangère (AILE). Numéro Spécial: Les Apprenants Avancés* 9, 9–50.

Bayley, R. (1996) Competing constraints on variation in the speech of adult Chinese learners of English. In R. Bayley and D. Preston (eds) *Second Language Acquisition and Linguistic Variation* (pp. 97–120). Amsterdam/Philadelphia: Benjamins.

Bergström, A. (1997) L'influence des distinctions aspectuelles sur l'acquisition des temps du passé en français langue étrangère. *Acquisition et Interaction en Langue Etrangère (AILE): Les Apprenants Avancés* 9, 52–82.

Blanche-Benveniste, C. and Jeanjean, C. (1986) *Le Français Parlé: Transcription et Edition.* Paris: Didier Erudition.

Brum de Paula, M. (1998) L'appropriation de la Temporalité Morphologique en Langue Étrangère: Contextes Linguistiques d'Émergence et de Structuration. Doctoral dissertation, Université de Paris X-Nanterre.

Clark, E. (1971) On the acquisition of the meaning of before and after. *Journal of Verbal Learning and Verbal Behaviour* 10, 266–75.

Devitt, S. (1995) *French – Its Acquisition as a Second Language.* Dublin: Authentik.

Dietrich, R., Klein, W. and Noyau C. (eds) (1995) *The Acquisition of Temporality in a Second Language.* Amsterdam, Philadelphia: Benjamins.

Dittmar, N. and Terborg, H. (1991) Modality and second language learning. In T. Huebner and C. Ferguson (eds) *Crosscurrents in Second Language Acquisition and Linguistic Theories* (pp. 347–384). Amsterdam, Philadelphia: Benjamins.

Fayol, M. (1982) Le plus-que-parfait. Etude génétique en compréhension et production chez l'enfant de quatre à dix ans. *Archives de Psychologie* 50, 261–83.

Giacalone Ramat, A. (1992) Grammaticalization processes in the area of temporal and modal relations. *Studies in Second Language Acquisition* 14 (3), 279–319.

Harley, B. (1992) Patterns of second language development in French immersion. *Journal of French Language Studies* 2, 159–83.

Howard, M. (1998) Quasi-bilingual?: The advanced learner in second language acquisition research. *PaGes* 5, 63–77.

Howard, M. (1999) The advanced learner: Poor relation of the second language acquisition family? *Cahiers AFLS* 5(1), 7–26.

Howard, M. (2001a) The effects of study abroad on the L2 learner's structural skills: Evidence from advanced learners of French. In S. Foster-Cohen and A. Nizigorodcew (eds) *EUROSLA Yearbook 1* (pp. 123–41). Amsterdam – Philadelphia: John Benjamins.

Howard, M. (2001b) Foreign language learners who venture abroad are better than those don't right?: On the role of study abroad in second language acquisition. *PaGes 7*, 75–87.

Howard, M. (2002a) L'acquisition des temps du passé par l'apprenant dit avancé: Une approche lexicale. In E. Labeau and P. Larrivée (eds) *Les Temps du Passé Français et leur Enseignement* (pp. 181–204). Amsterdam – New York: Rodopi [Cahiers Chronos 9].

Howard, M. (2002b) *The Effects of Study Abroad on the Variable Marking of Past Time by the Advanced Learner of French.* PhD Thesis, University College, Dublin.

Howard, M. (2002c) Prototypical and non-prototypical marking in the advanced learner's aspectuo-temporal system. In S. Foster-Cohen, T. Ruthenberg and M.-L. Poschen (eds) *EUROSLA Yearbook 2.* Amsterdam: John Benjamins.

Howard, M. (2003) Second language acquisition in a study abroad context: A comparative investigation of the effects of study abroad and foreign language instruction on the L2 learner's grammatical development. In A. Housen and M. Pierrard (eds) *Current Issues in Instructed Second Language Learning.* Berlin: Mouton deGruyter [Studies in Language Acquisition].

Howard, M. (to appear a) The effects of study abroad on the formal expression of past time by the advanced language learner. *Teangeolas, Journal of the Institute of Linguistics of Ireland.*

Howard, M. (to appear b) Les contextes prototypiques et marqués de l'emploi de l'imparfait par l'apprenant du français langue étrangère. In E. Labeau and P. Larrivée (eds) *Nouveaux Développements de l'Imparfait.* Amsterdam/New York: Rodopi [Cahiers Chronos].

Kaplan, M. (1987) Developmental patterns in of past tense acquisition among foreign language learners of French. In B. VanPatten, T. Dvorak and J. Lee (eds) *Foreign Language Learning: A Research Perspective* (pp. 52–60). Cambridge, MA: Newbury House.

Kihlstedt, M. (1998) *La Référence au Passé dans le Dialogue. Etude de l'Acquisition de la Temporalité chez des Apprenants dits Avancés de Français.* Doctoral dissertation, University of Stockholm, Akademitryk.

Klein, W. (1986) *Second Language Acquisition.* Cambridge: Cambridge University Press.

Klein, W. (1994) Learning how to express temporality in a second language. In A. Giacalone Ramat and M. Vedovelli (eds) *Italiano Lingua Seconda/Lingua Straniera* (pp. 227–248). Rome: Bulzoni.

Labelle, M. (1994) Acquisition de la valeur des temps du passé par les enfants francophones. *Revue Québécoise de Linguistique* 23 (1), 99–121.

Labov, W. (1984) Field methods of the project on linguistic change and variation. In J. Baugh and W. Sherzer (eds) *Language in Use: Readings in Sociolinguistics* (pp. 28–53). Englewood Cliffs, NJ: Prentice Hall.

Noyau, C. (1991) *La Temporalité dans le Discours Narratif: Construction du Récit, Construction de la Langue.* Thèse d'Habilitation, University of Paris VIII-St Denis-Vincennes.

Noyau, C. (1997) Processus de grammaticalisation dans l'acquisition de langues étrangères: La morphologie temporelle. In C. Martinot (ed.) *Actes du Colloque International sur l'Acquisition de la Syntaxe en Langue Maternelle et en Langue Etrangère* (pp. 223–52). Besançon: Université de Franche-Comté.

Paprocka-Piotrowska, U. (2002) *Mais dans ce moment le chien est venu. Ou comment les apprenants formels polonophones s'approprient le système temporel du français*. In E. Labeau and P. Larrivée (eds) *Les Temps du Passé et leur Enseignement* (pp. 205–29). Amsterdam, New York: Rodopi [Cahiers Chronos 9].

Reichenbach, H. (1947) *Elements of Symbolic Logic*. London: Macmillan.

Salaberry, R. (1998) The development of aspectual distinctions in academic L2 French. *Canadian Modern Language Review* 54, 508–42.

Schlyter, S. (1990) The acquisition of French temporal morphemes in adults and bilingual children. In G. Bernini and A. Giacalone Ramat (eds) *La Temporalità nell'Acquisizione di Lingue Seconde* (pp. 293–310). Milan: Franco Angeli.

Schumann, J. (1987) The expression of temporality in basilang speech. *Studies in Second Language Acquisition* 9, 21–41.

Starren, M. and Van Hout, R. (1996) The expression of temporality in a second language. *Zeitschrift für Literaturwissenschaft und Linguistik* 104, 35–50.

Tomlin, R. (1990) Functionalism in second language acquisition research. *Studies in Second Language Acquisition* 12 (2), 155–78.

Véronique, D. (1987) Reference to past events and actions in L2: Insights from North African Learners' French. In C. Pfaff (ed.) *First and Second Language Acquisition Processes* (pp. 252–272). Rowley, MA: Newbury House.

Wiberg, E. (1998) Reference to future in Italian dialogues with L2 learners, bilinguals and monolinguals: The connection between lexical aspect and information structure. Paper presented at the 2nd Euroconference 'The Structure of Learner Varieties', Acquafredda di Maratea (Italy), September 1998.

Young, R. (1991) *Variation in Interlanguage Morphology*. New York: Peter Lang.

Young, R. (1993) Functional constraints on variation in interlanguage morphology. *Applied Linguistics* 14 (1), 76–97.

Zielonka, B. (1999) The use of the pluperfect in recalled sentences in Polish learners of Swedish as a foreign language. Paper presented at the special workshop on temporality, EUROSLA 9, Lund (Sweden), June 1999.

Chapter 5

The Emergence of Morpho-syntactic Structure in French L2

FLORENCE MYLES

Introduction

The aim of this chapter is to examine the early stages in the emergence of morpho-syntactic structure in classroom learners of French. I will first present a broad-brush picture of the structure of early L2 classroom learners' utterances in French L2, before looking more specifically at the role of the Verb Phrase within early L2 development, and discussing the findings in the context of current debates on the role of Universal Grammar (UG) in Second Language Acquisition. A considerable amount has been written very recently on the significance of morphological variability in L2 learners for our understanding of the role of UG in the acquisition process, and of the Initial State of L2 learners, i.e. the mental grammar L2 learners have at the onset of the acquisition process (Franceschina, 2001; Hawkins, 2001a; Herschensohn, 2001; Paradis *et al.*, 1998; Parodi, 2000; Sorace, 1998, 2000). Most of this literature, however, investigates learners who have already gone beyond the first stages in the acquisition of their L2, and very little has been written on the first emergence of the verb phrase in beginners. I agree with Vainikka and Young-Scholten (1996b) when they review the literature on the emergence of the Verb Phrase and point out that many studies making claims about the initial state might in fact be missing the very first stages, which are crucial to this particular debate. As pointed out by Lakshmanan and Selinker (2001: 397), 'in many cases, the speech utterances in the earliest samples of speech gathered may not have been collected early enough and may, therefore, not necessarily be reflective of the L2 initial state'. The present chapter aims to bring new evidence to document early development of the verb phrase in French L2, in order to inform this debate further. It is based on a longitudinal study of 60 learners of French within the British education system who have been recorded at regular intervals over the course of their first two years of learning French. The particular study reported here analyses the emergence of syntactic structure in 14 of these learners who performed the same task twice at a yearly interval, after one year and two years of classroom tuition respectively.

Theoretical Framework

Many arguments have been put forward suggesting that Universal Grammar is still involved in the construction of second language grammars (e.g. Hawkins, 2001b), such as for example the developmental patterns common to L2 learners from various L1 backgrounds (e.g. Dulay *et al.*, 1982, for early studies), or L2 productions which do not seem to be consistently related to either L1 or L2 properties but are nonetheless UG constrained (e.g. Epstein *et al.*, 1996; Schwartz & Sprouse, 2000). The UG approach has given rise to a wealth of empirical studies which have enhanced our understanding of the mental representation underlying L2 competence. One topic among others which has led to much theoretical and empirical debate over the last decade is the issue of the Initial State in second language learners. What kind of knowledge L2 learners bring to the task facing them, and whether they have access to UG in the same way as L1 learners do or not, has been hotly debated, as has what shape this access might take in the L2 context. The various theoretical possibilities are being actively investigated, with new empirical evidence being put forward all the time, and no consensus has been reached. The seminal Second Language Research (SLR) 1996 issue on the Initial State is still a good example of the questions being asked, although some of these have been refined and others have since been reformulated within the Minimalist paradigm. The different hypotheses about the involvement of UG in SLA can be briefly summarised as follows:

- Full Transfer / Full Access (Epstein *et al.*, 1996; Grondin & White, 1996; Schwartz, 1998; Schwartz & Sprouse, 1996): in this view, L2 learners have full access to UG, but rely on their L1 instantiations of UG until they have encountered sufficient evidence to reset the relevant parameters.
- Minimal Trees (Vainikka & Young-Scholten, 1996a, 1998): only lexical categories are projected initially, which transfer from the L1. Functional categories develop later in succession, but are not transferred from the L1.
- Valueless Features Hypothesis (Eubank, 1996): both lexical and functional categories are transferred early on (with a short stage in which only lexical projections are present), but functional categories lack

values such as tense, agreement etc. . . . and are present as syntactic markers only.

- Modulated structure building (Hawkins, 2001a): learners start with 'minimal trees', i.e. lexical projections determined by the L1. Functional projections develop gradually, with L1 functional features transferring onto the L2, but only at points of development in which the relevant syntactic representation has been sufficiently elaborated to instantiate the property in question. Hawkins and Chan (1997) have argued that functional features are at the root of L2 problems as they cannot be reset in the L2.

Recent work has investigated the acquisition of verbal morphology in order to provide some answers to these questions. In L1 acquisition, there are clear patterns underlying the emergence of inflectional morphology; children show a preference for untensed verbs initially, and gradually introduce tensed forms in their grammar which will eventually replace the untensed forms in all appropriate contexts, after a somewhat lengthy period of optionality in which the two forms will both be present. The onset of verbal morphology and subsequent optionality has been linked in children to: the emergence of functional categories (Radford, 1996); the initial underspecification of functional features (Hyams, 1996; Wexler, 1998); or the Truncation Hypothesis (Rizzi, 1994) which claims that children sometimes project VP, sometimes IP and sometimes CP, with different consequences for morphological realisation. Herschensohn (2001: 275–6) writes:

> The realization or not of verbal inflection is not a random occurrence in early child language, but it is rather systematically linked to syntactic development. During this stage the child produces on the one hand, root infinitives, null and VP internal subjects, determinerless (bare) DPs, preverbal negation, lack of auxiliaries, and – in the appropriate languages – lack of verb raising. (Hyams, 1996; Ionin & Wexler, 2000; Wexler & Harris, 1996)

Below are examples of the Optional Infinitive (OI) stage in French L1 children, as quoted in Herschensohn (2001):

(1)   Child root infinitives; OI stage:
    (a)   Pas manger la poupée.
         not to eat the doll   Nath. 1;9;3 (Pierce, 1992: 64)
         'The doll isn't eating.'
    (b)   Lancer la balle.
         To throw the ball   Philippe 2;1;3; (Pierce, 1992: 109)
         '[Someone] throws the ball.'

On the other hand, during the same period the child also produces sentences containing inflected verbs, overt nominative subjects (raised, clitic, 2a-b), post-verbal negation (2a), auxiliaries and verb-raising. (In French the diagnostics for root infinitives are (1) null or tonic pronoun subject, (2) infinitival verb, (3) pre-verbal negation; raised verbs show (1) nominative clitic subjects, (2) inflected verb, (3) post-verbal negation.)

(2)   Child inflected sentences; OI stage:
    (a)   Il est pas là
           he is not there   Nath. 2;2;2; (Pierce, 1992: 94)
           'He is not there.'
    (b)   Moi, je tousse encore.
           Me I cough again   Philippe 2;2;2; (Pierce, 1992: 96).
    Herschensohn (2001: 276)

In other words, when children produce inflected forms, they also invariably raise the verb, as evidenced by post-verbal negation and the use of subject clitic pronouns.

In L2 acquisition, the evidence is somewhat less clear. Although there is also evidence that L2 learners can have optional infinitives in their ILGs for considerable periods of time, sometimes resulting in missing or faulty inflections on verbs even in stable grammars (Lardière, 1998b), it has been more difficult to find patterns of verbal morphology as clearly linked to the emergence of functional categories; much of L2 optionality has been claimed not to be structurally constrained (Sorace, 2000). Whereas children, when realising verbal morphology, also show evidence of having acquired IP by e.g. raising verbs when appropriate, links between the emergence of inflection and verb-raising have not been so clear in the context of L2 acquisition, with some researchers arguing for such links and others not (Franceschina, 2001; Herschensohn, 2001; Lardière, 1998b; Parodi, 2000; Prévost & White, 2000; Sorace, 2000; White, 1996). Rule (2001), for example, showed that L2 learners of French in early stages readily accept sentences in grammaticality judgement tests containing a tensed verb which has not been raised past the negator, e.g. *je ne pas mange*, showing a dissociation between verb morphology and verb-raising.

Recently, researchers have been discussing whether the fact that L2 learners seem to have problems reliably supplying verbal inflections even after prolonged exposure to the L2 is due to a surface problem – due to processing difficulties – or a syntactic problem linked to access to Universal Grammar. Some researchers (Lardière, 1998a; 1998b; Prévost & White, 2000) argue that it is not due to a syntactic impairment but that it is a surface problem in the morphological realisation of agreement, on the basis of the fact that finite verbs in interlanguages are consistently produced in finite positions. For example, finite verbs are raised past the negator in languages like French which have strong AGR and they do not appear in non-finite positions (e.g. after prepositions, auxiliaries etc.). Conversely, non-finite verbs consistently appear in non-finite positions, although they are also sometimes used as default forms in finite positions. Herschensohn (2001) agrees with this view, giving as one further piece of evidence that learners have acquired the L2 syntax but suffer from a morphological deficit, the fact that they use clitics with infinitives (e.g. *je ne continuer pas*) and are therefore projecting IP, failing to correctly supply a verbal inflection. As we have seen, L1 learners, on the other hand, seem always to supply finite verb forms when using clitics, and stressed forms when using non-finite verbs. Franceschina (Franceschina, 2001) disagrees with this analysis of L2 acquisition, claiming that if it is just a morphological deficit and not a syntactic one, it becomes difficult to explain the differential suppliance of different kinds of morphology. Lardière's subject Patty produces case marking on pronouns all the time but fails to produce verbal morphology most of the time. Franceschina argues that it is in fact a syntactic problem, convergent with her findings that L1 English learners of L2 Spanish supply gender consistently on nouns, but not on adjectives or determiners, a fact which is consistent with their English grammar, which has no uninterpretable gender feature on adjectives and determiners.

Hawkins (2001a: 64) suggests that learners first build projections of thematic verbs, without an IP projection. It is then the acquisition of free grammatical morphemes such as the copula or auxiliaries that makes learners project IP. The copula 'be' will appear first, because it is minimally specified with respect to the kind of complement it requires (any complement except VP). Auxiliary 'be', being a free grammatical morpheme, will appear early, but not as early as the copula, as its selectional requirements are more specific (a VP with a V-ing head describing an event in progress).

The studies on which these apparently conflicting findings and analyses are based have tended to investigate intermediate or advanced learners, or even in the case of Lardière, 'end-state' learners who have reached a stable grammar. This is in the context of current theoretical debates about the divergent outcomes of the L1 and L2 processes: whereas children might exhibit an interim grammar with optional infinitives, their stable grammar invariably eliminates them. This does not seem to happen consistently in L2 acquisition, and the reason is not clear at this stage. Looking at end-state grammars, or even fairly advanced grammars, however, can tell us something about the availability or not of (some) parameter settings of functional features to L2 learners, but it does not inform us about the initial state as such, or about the development of syntactic structure. It is only through a better understanding of the Initial State and of the way in which learners go through ALL stages, including the very first stages, in their acquisition of the L2 that we can compare the L1 and L2 processes, and see if both have access to UG in the same way or not (for a discussion of this, see Hawkins, 2001b). Looking at ILGs already a long way down the L2 continuum will give only a partial picture of the processes involved.

Moreover, current discussions seem to imply that L2 problems with morphology are EITHER a processing problem (reflecting defective acquisition of the morpholexicon) OR a syntactic problem (reflecting defective acquisition of the L2 syntax). There seems little doubt that the acquisition of morphological markings can represent a substantial difficulty for learners from a processing point of view. This does not exclude, however, those difficulties existing in parallel with developmental stages in the acquisition of the syntax underlying these morphological features.

The present study aims to investigate the early stages of French L2 acquisition in an instructional setting, and to trace longitudinally the emergence of verb phrases and their development in L2 learners of French over two years.

Research questions

(1)   Trace the emergence of the verb-phrase over time: when do verb-phrases first appear, what are they like, and what role do they play in sentence structure?

(2)   Is the development of the verb-phrase in L2 learners similar that of L1 learners of French? More specifically:
   • Is the use of finite / non-finite verbs also context-sensitive?
   • Does the use of subject clitics with finite vs. non-finite verb forms differ?

(3)   Does the appearance of free grammatical morphemes such as the French equivalent of copula 'be' and then auxiliaries trigger the projection of IP?

(4)   What do these findings tell us about the initial state of learners and their construction of morpho-syntax in the early stages of development?

The Study

As already mentioned, this chapter is based on a longitudinal study of English learners of French in the early stages of development within a classroom context. The test used in this particular investigation is an elicited narrative based on a cartoon story administered to the children after one year of classroom instruction in the British educational context, and subsequently a year later. A detailed analysis of a subset of 14 children is presented here, comparing their performance over time.

The task

Children were presented with a booklet containing a picture story entitled *Monstre du Loch Ness: vrai ou faux?* (Loch Ness monster: true or false?) comprising 12 text-free pictures. This is summarised in the Appendix. The children were told the story in French once by the researcher and then asked to retell the story in their own words. This story was chosen for a number of reasons. It was long enough for subjects not to be able to memorise the researcher's version; moreover, the storyline was not so complex that subjects would not be able to follow it, but it was rich enough for even beginners to be able to retell a version of the story in keeping with their ability. Given the focus of the analysis on the emergence of the verb phrase in this study, the picture-retelling task was also chosen for the following reasons:

- Children could not rely on rote-learned formulas that they used in classroom routines and on which they relied heavily in some of the other tasks we administered. As shown in Myles *et al.* (1998; 1999), early learners rely on chunks in order to overcome communicative difficulties. These chunks invariably contain tensed verb forms, and tend to concentrate on the exchange of information about personal and school life, typical examples being *comment t'appelles-tu? je m'appelle .., quel âge as-tu? j'ai 11 ans, j'aime le foot* etc. As the project involved classroom observation as well as analysis of the textbooks used, we were able to ensure as far as possible that learners could not rely on such formulas in the task described here, which furthermore required them to narrate in the third person, something they were not accustomed to doing. Moreover, in order to perform this task, children had to operate outside the discourse fields they were used to. A drawback of this of course is that some of the vocabulary necessary for performing the task was unknown to them, and we had to provide a small glossary of key terms (see Appendix). Because the story is built around 'people doing things', which they often talked about when exchanging personal information, however, retelling the story was not beyond their capabilities. This task in fact elicited very few chunks, as defined in the articles mentioned above (Myles *et al.*, 1998; 1999).
- Secondly, a narrative was chosen because it involves the construction of a story around key words including actions, which will typically include verbs. In other tasks in which learners had to elicit information for example, single-word or phrase answers were often pragmatically adequate. Such tasks therefore did not lend them-

selves to the study of emergent syntactic structure, and the verb phrase in particular.

The researcher's brief was to interfere as little as possible with each child's narrative, merely prompting and encouraging children when appropriate. Leaving a full year between the two administrations of this task enabled us to be confident that differences in performance were not due to familiarity with the task, which they were unlikely to remember so long after, given also that it was one task out of a large battery of oral tasks. When performing this particular task for the first time, learners had already experienced two previous rounds of four and three tasks respectively during the previous school year, with the same researchers. This task was one of three in this particular round of elicitation, and subjects performed six more unrelated tasks as part of this research in the year preceding the second administration of this task.

The subjects

The data from a subset of 14 children who completed both tasks is presented here. This subset consists of seven girls and seven boys, seven each from the two schools who took part in the project. All the children started learning French a year before the first elicitation of this task, in year 7 within the British education context (approximately 141 hours of tuition; age 12 to 13), and received a further 254 hours approximately before the second elicitation (age 13 to 14). None of them were exposed to French outside the classroom, except for short family holidays in the case of some of them. All children took part in a range of semi-spontaneous oral elicitation tasks at termly intervals throughout the three-year life of the project, 18 tasks in total. There is therefore a large amount of data for each child, which enables easy verification of hypotheses about the development of individual children.

The performance of each child was taped and later transcribed and the transcription double-checked by another researcher.

Results and Discussion

All utterances produced by the subjects were analysed in terms of the following variables:

- The syntactic structure of the utterance (presence or absence of verbs; role of verb).
- All VPs were analysed in detail (thematic verbs; copula 'be'; auxiliaries).
- Verb morphology (finite vs. non-finite; default forms).

- Context in which finite and non-finite forms are produced.
- Use of subject clitics.

This analysis will enable us to establish which syntactic categories are projected in the very early stages of acquisition (minimal trees debate), and will further inform the morpho-syntax interface debate by tracing the early development of verbal morphology and of subject clitics (syntactic vs. morpholexical problem).

The emergence of syntactic structure

Results

If we take the suppliance of the verb phrase as the first visible sign of emerging syntactic structure in our learners' sentences, a first comparative glance at the children's two performances after a year's interval on this task revealed a marked change in their interlanguage, especially in terms of the number of verb phrases present in contexts in which one would be expected. At the first elicitation, the children tended to rely on the juxtaposition of NPs with the occasional PPs, hoping their interlocutor would fill in the gaps. This tendency had decreased sharply in the second elicitation, with a much higher proportion of VPs being supplied, and their role becoming much more central in the architecture of the children's utterances.

An example illustrates the difference between the two rounds of elicitation; the extract on the following page is from pupil no. 2 and conveys largely the same information (where <s r> is the researcher, and <s 02> the pupil).

Quantitatively, Table 5.1 calculates, for each child, the proportion of VPs supplied in relation to the number of propositions in the narrative. For the purpose of this study, I define a proposition semantically, with the verb seen as a function, and its subject and any objects as arguments of the function (Saeed, 1997). Given the nature of the task, it is relatively easy to recover the learner's intended meaning. In practice, a proposition will be either a turn (excluding semantically empty turns, e.g. uhmm, as well as repeats of the researcher's utterance, or utterances in English) or a unit made up of a verb (overt or covert) and its arguments, within a longer turn. So, in the extract, there would be seven propositions at Time 1:

(1) une family Rochdale en va- va- [laughs] vacances / /
(2) /une, un/ Lochside holiday cottage
(3) et des grand-mères
(4) tro- .. trois petits enfants / /
(5) deux .. no /une, un/ fille / / and euh ..
(6) et /une, un/ maman

Excerpt 1 Subject no. 2

Time 1	Time 2
<s > très bien Helen alors maintenant je vais te raconter .. te raconter l'histoire [tells story] .. bon .. alors très bien .. alors Helen alors maintenant c'est à .. c'est à toi de raconter l'histoire alors vas-y <s 02> can I make up the name of the family? <s r> oui oui bien sûr .. oui oui <s 02> une family Rochdale en va- va- [laughs] vacances / <s r> oui mais mais oui .. mais où est-ce qu'ils vont en vacances? où? <s 02> / une, un/ Lochside holiday cottage <s r> oui oui oui dans une petite maison <s 02> umm .. et de .. <s r> oui?< s 02 > et des grand-mères <s r> oui <s 02> tro- .. trois petits enfants / / <s r> oui très bien< s 02 > deux .. no / une, un/ fille / / and euh ..< s r > et des garçons? <s 02> garçons <s r> oui .. bon très bien et après? <s 02> et /une, un/ maman <s r> oui <s 02> près de la mer	<s r> okay je parle avec Helen okay Helen monstre du Lac Ness vrai ou faux? [R tells story] .. okay? .. okay bon Helen tu vas me raconter l'histoire oui? ça va? <s 02> la famille arriver euh .. Loch umm en vacances .. umm la mère .. no umm .. yeah le mère et la grand-mère et le deux .. garçons et le une fille .. umm .. à côté .. à côté la maison est lac un grand lac euh .. lac de Loch Ness

Notes: * /une, un/: unclear pronunciation, / /: pauses

(7) près de la mer

and three propositions at Time 2:

(1)   la famille arriver euh .. Loch umm en vacances ..
(2)   umm la mère .. no umm .. yeah le mère et la grand-mère et le deux .. garçons et le une fille .. umm ..
(3)   à côté .. à côté la maison est lac un grand lac euh .. lac de Loch Ness

Table 5.1 shows, for each subject, the number of propositions and the number of verbs, as well as the verb / proposition ratio, for each elicitation.

As we can see from this table, the number of verbs produced increases sharply in the second narrative. In the first narrative task, learners supplied

Table 5.1 Number of propositions, number of verbs, and verb/proposition ratio for each elicitation

Pupil	Time 1			Time 2		
	Propositions	*No. of VPs*	*%*	*Propositions*	*No. of VPs*	*%*
2	63	19	30.2	33	32	97.0
3	36	13	36.1	33	20	60.6
9	68	57	83.8	43	43	100.0
12	20	9	45.0	30	28	93.3
24	33	23	69.7	36	36	100.0
26	32	20	62.5	33	22	66.7
27	27	22	81.5	25	23	92.0
38	25	20	80.0	28	24	85.7
43	28	8	28.6	27	14	51.9
45	22	7	31.8	28	15	53.6
51	34	10	29.4	40	10	25.0
52	40	15	37.5	34	19	55.9
57	46	37	80.4	48	41	85.4
60	37	25	67.6	38	35	92.1
Total	511	285		476	362	
Mean			54.6			75.7

VPs overtly around 55% of the time, and by the second elicitation, they were able to supply VPs 76% of the time. The difference is significant ($Z = -3.15$, $p < 0.002$), using a Wilcoxon Signed Ranks Test.

Figure 5.1 presents the same table visually.

Discussion

These findings would seem to suggest that learners first go through a stage of projecting single lexical phrases, usually noun phrases, with the occasional prepositional phrase, a view compatible with an initial lack of functional projections (Minimal Trees hypothesis). A verbless phase in L2 learners has been documented before (Lakshmanan, 1998). The reason why learners fail to systematically produce VPs initially, I would suggest, is because of the verb's role in the architecture of the sentence. The argument structure of the verb and the requirement that noun phrases be licensed by a verb through theta marking and Case assignment play a core role in parsing' (Juffs, 1998: 406). It would therefore not be surprising that, because

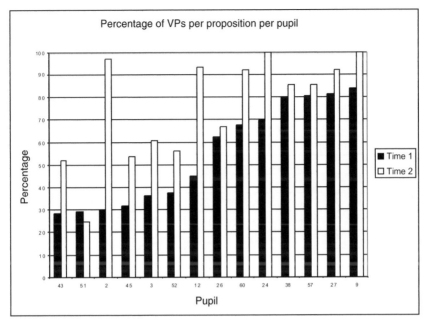

Figure 5.1 Percentage of VPs per proposition per pupil at Time 1 and Time 2

of these requirements, VPs present particular processing problems for learners in early stages. Not only do they have to acquire the relevant lexical item, but they also have to acquire its argument structure. Productions that require linking elements syntactically in a sentence have been shown to make heavy parsing demands on learners (Myles, 1995).

The relative lack of verbs might also be due to the artificiality of the task: as both the learner and the researcher are looking at the picture story, once the learner has identified the protagonists, the researcher can see what action is being described, making its description pragmatically superfluous. This does not explain, however, the significant difference in verb suppliance between Time 1 and Time 2, and the fact that this finding was replicated in other tasks throughout our data set generally (incidentally, one of the learners, no. 60, hesitates systematically before each verb, suggesting processing difficulties).

The development of verb morphology

We have seen in the theoretical discussion that there are clear patterns in the L1 acquisition of verbal morphology. In particular, children show a preference for untensed verbs initially, and gradually introduce tensed forms in their grammar which will eventually replace the infinitives, after a period of optionality.

Table 5.2 gives the number of finite and non-finite verbs in each elicitation, per pupil.

Table 5.2 No. of +fin/–fin verbs, per pupil, per test

Pupil	Time 1			Time 2		
	non-finite	*Finite*	*(%)*	*non-finite*	*Finite*	*(%)*
2	7	2	(22.2)	9	10	(52.6)
3	2	1	(33.3)	1	6	(85.7)
9	11	13	(54.2)	7	19	(73.1)
12	1	4	(80)	12	7	(36.8)
24	13	4	(23.5)	12	5	(29.4)
26	1	3	(75)	6	2	(25)
27	2	7	(77.8)	4	8	(66.7)
38	4	6	(60)	7	10	(58.8)
43	4	0	(0)	4	0	(0)
45	3	0	(0)	1	1	(50)
51	4	0	(0)	2	3	(60)
52	2	4	(66.7)	6	4	(40)
57	7	7	(50)	7	10	(58.9)
60	0	14	(100)	3	20	(87)
Total	61	65		81	105	
%	48.4	51.6		43.5	56.4	

We can see that the trend follows that observed in children learning their L1, with a decrease in the use of untensed verbs, and a corresponding increase in the use of tensed verbs, although it is not very marked. Using a Wilcoxon Signed Ranks Test, the difference between the proportion of non-finite verb forms at Time 1 and Time 2 respectively is not significant ($Z = -1.38$, p = ns). The difference between the proportion of finite verb forms produced at Time 1 and Time 2 is, however, significant ($Z = -2.88$, $p < 0.004$). The suppliance of verbal morphology is clearly still optional in our cohort at Time 2, although there is extensive variation from subject to subject.

Two points are worth mentioning at this stage. Firstly, whereas non-finite forms are regularly found in finite contexts, e.g. *ma mère regarder le magasin*, there are relatively few clearly non-finite contexts in our data to confirm findings that finite forms do or do not appear in such contexts

(Herschensohn, 2001; Lardière, 1998a; 1998b; Prévost & White, 2000). There are only three instances of verbs following prepositions in our corpus, all from the same learner, the most advanced in our cohort, in both rounds; two of them disconfirm the above claim: *un journaliste arriver pour parle avec grand-mère* (09, Time 1); *la famille quitte la maison quitte la ferme pour rentre à la maison* (09, Time 2), and the other one confirms it: *ils sont dans un bateau pour regarder le monstre dans le lac* (09, Time 1). However, there is a larger number of verb forms following auxiliaries, and we will return to this issue in the section on the use of *être* and *avoir*.

The second point I would like to make is that there is a large amount of variation across learners, with the following learners using substantially more tensed verbs in the second test (and fewer untensed ones) as can be seen in Table 5.3.

Table 5.3 Percentage of finite verbs for selected pupils

	Time 1 %	*Time 2 %*
02	22.2	52.6
03	33.3	85.7
09	54.2	73.1
57	50.0	58.8

Other learners make very limited use of any verbs at all by Time 2: subjects 43, 45 and 51 use fewer than five verb tokens in each elicitation. Let us classify learners into three groups (somewhat arbitrarily), according to the following criteria:

(a)   learners who make productive use of verbs (over 10 tokens) AND who use tensed verbs over 50% of the time by Time 2: subjects 2; 9; 27; 38; 57; 60;

(b)   learners who use few verbs (10 tokens or fewer) OR less than 50% finite verbs at Time 2: subjects 3; 12; 24; 26; 52;

(c)   learners who use very few verbs at all (fewer than 5 tokens per elicitation): subjects 43; 45; 51 (there are so few verb tokens that it renders the proportion of tensed forms meaningless).

It is interesting to note that these sets of learners correspond very closely to those we had previous identified as having made the most/least progress in their development of interrogatives, and in their analysis and creative use of chunks in earlier studies (Myles *et al.*, 1998; 1999). Myles *et al.* (1998: 352–3) summarise the results of their analysis of the breakdown of chunks in these very same learners as follows:

(1)   There is a clear developmental continuum among our learners as far
       as chunk breakdown is concerned, from those who started the break-
       down process early and who have gone a long way down the road of
       segmenting the subject pronoun from the verb, to those who do not
       seem to have even started the process.
(2)   The breakdown of the chunks under consideration was linked to the
       creative emergence of the subject pronoun system in non-formulaic
       contexts.
(3)   Within this continuum, our learners fell into three broad categories:
       (a)   learners who, by the end of our study, had analysed the
              chunks into their constituents, and freed the subject pronoun
              for use elsewhere (09, 27, 57; and 02, 60, although not so
              unequivocally; 31.25%);
       (b)   pupils who were at a later point of entry along this same
              developmental path by the end of the study, or, if their point
              of entry was as early, were progressing more slowly and ten-
              tatively along the continuum (03, 24, 26, 38 and 52 (31.25%);
       (c)   pupils who had made no progress along this developmental
              path after two years (34, 43, 45, 51, perhaps also 12, although
              less convincingly 37.5%; please note that no. 34 was not part
              of the present study).

The similarity in the stages of development assigned to these learners on
the basis of their use of finite forms on the one hand, and chunk breakdown
on the other, is striking.

We will turn to the relationship between the use of subject pronouns and
L2 development in the context of the present study in the next section.

Before this, a word of caution is needed: the results reported here have to
be interpreted with care. For obvious reasons, the analysis of early oral
interlanguage data is not unproblematic, and although we tried, through
double transcription, to be as consistent as possible, verb endings can be
particularly problematic to identify. Another point worth mentioning is
that at this early stage, verbs tend to be used in one default form only, and
there are very few verbs which appear with alternate forms in our data.
Moreover, the use of chunks or parts of chunks, even though the tasks did
not promote them, is nonetheless evident in places (e.g. *il y a, j'aime, je ne sais
pas; j'habite*). Claiming that one form is finite and another not can be
somewhat misleading, and we can only talk about broad developmental
trends. One verb, however, is used by all pupils in both untensed and
tensed forms, and it is therefore worth tracking its development over time;
this is the verb *regarder*. It must be noted, however, that the finite form of
this verb is produced repeatedly in the researcher's version of the story,

which the learner has listened to a few minutes previously (although we might therefore have expected ALL instances of this verb to be finite in the learners' productions, as they always are in the researcher's version, and this is clearly not the case) as can be seen in Table 5.4.

Table 5.4 Finite/non-finite forms of *regarder* at time 1 and time 2

Time 1		Time 2	
untensed	*tensed*	*untensed*	*tensed*
45	16	38	20
74%	26%	66%	34%

We can see that it follows the general pattern we have outlined above, with more tensed forms being produced at Time 2.

To conclude this section, our results clearly show that, in the same way as in L1 learners, L2 learners' use of finite forms is optional in the early stages of acquisition, but the use of finite verbs clearly increases over time, especially for some learners. The next sections will investigate in more detail the contexts in which +/- finite forms are used.

The emergence of clitic subject pronouns

There is remarkable consistency over time in the type of subject provided by learners, with lexical noun-phrases being preferred over pronouns, even though the task provided ample opportunity for pronominal reference (see Table 5.5).

What this table does not reveal, however, is the emergence of clitic (unstressed) subject pronouns in contexts other than that of chunks or impersonal formulaic expressions. The following table (5.6) includes all productions of subject pronouns, excluding repeats and chunks, e.g. *je m'appelle; je ne sais pas; j'habite; je ne comprends pas; j'aime; c'est; il y a.*

A number of interesting points emerge from Table 5.6. Firstly, we can see that clitic subject pronouns are not very frequent: 34 tokens across all learners, and across both elicitation tasks. Secondly, only eight out of the 14 learners make use of subject pronouns at all, with three of those using only one subject pronoun throughout both tasks, and only three pupils using five or more pronouns across both times (pupils 03, 09 and 26); student no. 09 is the only learner who can be said to be using a range of different pronouns productively (15 tokens). As we have said before, this learner is the most advanced by far in our cohort and is therefore somewhat atypical. If we now consider the context of use of these subject pronouns, it is very striking to note that they are almost exclusively used with tensed verbs,

Table 5.5 Subject types per learner

Pupil	Time 1			Time 2		
	φ	NP	Pro	φ	NP	Pro
2	2	10	2	2	20	5
3	3	6	5	11	13	2
9	0	27	25	0	22	21
12	0	6	2	3	22	1
24	2	16	2	0	19	13
26	7	11	1	3	14	6
27	0	13	5	1	13	3
38	1	14	2	2	18	2
43	3	7	0	0	14	1
45	2	6	0	2	7	0
51	1	5	2	1	7	1
52	1	11	1	4	11	1
57	2	19	11	1	21	17
60	3	19	2	4	23	4
Total	27	170	60	34	224	77
%	10.6	66.1	23.3	10.1	66.9	23

and this when we have already seen that tensed verbs are only used just over half of the time. Tables 5.7 and 5.8 quantify these results.

This result, showing that our learners use subject clitics with finite verb forms in over 91% of cases, is very similar to the patterns found in the first language acquisition of French. Pierce (1992: 86) reports that the children she studied use subject pronouns in finite contexts between 88% (Daniel) and 99 % (Philippe) of the time, and this, as in the present study, at a time when non-finite forms are frequent. The results reported here do not concur with the findings of Eubank and Beck (1998: 196) who report that Abdemalek uses subject pronouns 33.8 % of the time with non-finite verbs.

This would suggest that, at least for the learners in our cohort who have started making productive use of subject pronouns, an IP projection is present and that they therefore have gone beyond the Minimal Trees stage, having added functional projections to lexical projections. As argued in Pierce (1992: 92–3), 'this finding of a contingency between subject pronouns and finiteness is a very strong indication that the early grammar represents and projects Infl'. I would not want to claim, however, that this is the case

Table 5.6 Use of clitic subject pronouns

Time 1		Time 2	
– finite	*+ finite*	*– finite*	*+ finite*
• ils regarder le monstre 03 • elle peint les bouées parce que elle faire un monstre 09	• et deux enfants elles s'amusent 03 • il a à la maison 03 • il a le vrai monstre de Loch Ness 03 • elle peint le lac 09 • elle peint le lac 09 • elle regarde les jupes 09 • elle peint les bouées 09 • ils sont dans un bateau 09 • je suis désolée 09 • elle explique 09 • la bouée j'ai comprend pas 24 • grand-mère elle est .. bo.. what's string 51 • la mère et la petit garçon .. elle est allée en ville 57	• la mère faire des courses elle faire un promenade 09	• et la mère elle a regardé un livre 02 • il est en lac 03 • voilà une famille ils sont en vacances 09 • la fille et le petit garçon ils sont pêcher dans la lac 09 • elle peint un monstre 09 • elle crée un monstre 09 • il y a des touristes des journalistes et des enfants ils sont prener des photos 09 • je suis désolée dit grand-mère 09 • j'ai peint ça 09 • une jounaliste arriver at la lac .. il dit.. comment t'appelles-tu? 24 • j'ai .. how do you say made (R:fait) j'ai fait la Loch Ness monster.. 24 • en vacances la garçon et ma mère un grand-mère j'arrive à la maison .. en voiture 26 • le garçon il s'appelle Chip 26 • ma mère et le garçon j'arrive à la village 26 • la garçon la fille à ma mère j'ai regardé la lake 26 • ma mère et deux garçons une fille .. je .. dis au revoir 26 • je suis très .. (R: désolée) 27

Table 5.7 Use of clitic subject pronouns, across learners

Time 1		Time 2	
– finite	*+ finite*	*– finite*	*+finite*
2	13	1	18

Table 5.8 Use of subject pronouns in +/– finite contexts, both tasks

– finite	*+ finite*
3 (8.8 %)	31 (91.2 %)

for all our learners. Those who seem to be at a less developmentally advanced stage show little evidence of projecting anything other than lexical categories. Even for some of the learners presented in Table 5.6 as producing subject clitics (e.g. no. 24, 26), the status of their subject pronouns is somewhat debatable, as they do no agree with the referent, and they might be argued to be unanalysed chunks or part of chunks, typically involving first person pronouns frequent in classroom routines (e.g. *j'arrive, 26; j'ai, 26*).

To conclude this section, the development of morpho-syntax in French L1 and L2 acquisition as evidenced by the use of finite/non-finite verb forms and the use of clitics shows striking similarities (Pierce, 1992). In the data analysed here, there is evidence of the functional projection of IP, but only in some learners, and at Time 2, suggesting an earlier stage of Minimal Trees which most learners have not gone beyond. If it has not been documented before in the context of French L2 acquisition, I believe that it is because learners have been too advanced. Herschensohn (2001) is right in claiming that her learners clearly project the functional categories Tense and AGR, but they are a long way down the developmental route compared to the learners studied here.

A structure that would further help us inform this debate is the production of negatives. In French, the negative particle *pas* occurs before non-finite forms (*il n'a pas mangé*), and after finite forms (*il ne mange pas*). For finite forms to be able to be raised past the negator, learners have to project IP. We would therefore expect learners at the 'Minimal Trees' stage to produce utterances such as *le garçon ne pas mange*. There are 12 negatives in the stories produced by the learners, eight produced by subject no. 09, one by no. 24. one by no. 52, and one by no. 60, most of which are likely chunks (*je ne sais pas le mot* X 4; *je ne comprends pas* X 2; *ce n'est pas* X 3; *il n'y a pas; je ne sais pas; j'ai comprend pas*). It is therefore difficult to draw conclusions from so little evidence, and further research is needed in this area.

The development of *être* and *avoir*

Two issues will be addressed in this section. Firstly, we will look for evidence in our data supporting Hawkins' hypothesis about the way in which learners move from Minimal Trees to projecting functional categories in English L2:

> . . . after an initial stage of acquiring thematic verbs, when L2 learners first begin to acquire grammatical morphemes, they start with free morphemes which are minimally specified with respect to the kind of complement they require. Copula be is the least specified of morphemes which can appear under the category I in English. Learners will

only have to learn that it does not select a VP complement. Auxiliary *be*, by contrast, requires them to learn that it selects not only a VP, and no other type of complement, but a VP with a V-ing head describing an event in progress. Auxiliary *be* +V-ing, then, will appear early in learners' mental grammars because be is a free morpheme, but it will appear later than copula be because it has more complex selectional requirements. (Hawkins (2001a: 64)

Secondly, we will analyse in detail the use of *avoir* and *être* as auxiliaries to test further the view that there is no syntactic deficit in L2 grammars, and that what is faulty is the morphological realisation of agreement, on the basis that finite verbs do not appear in non-finite positions (Herschensohn, 2001; Lardière, 1998a; 1998b; Prévost & White, 2000).

Use of être

Table 5.9 shows the use of both copula and auxiliary *être* during both tests, for each learner.

We can see an increase in the use of *être* from Time 1 (75 occurrences) to Time 2 (107 occurrences). As suggested by Hawkins, *être* makes an early

Table 5.9 Use of *être*, per pupil

	Time 1		Time 2	
Pupil	*copula*	*auxiliary*	*copula*	*auxiliary*
2	3	1	10	5
3	1	0	15	3
9	17	0	10	2
12	1	0	0	0
24	1	2	8	0
26	5	2	1	0
27	8	0	3	0
38	3	0	2	0
43	1	0	9	1
45	1	0	0	0
51	2	0	0	0
52	1	1	0	0
57	14	6	20	9
60	4	1	8	1
Total	62	13	86	21

appearance as a free grammatical morpheme in our data, especially as a copula. Notice here again the variation across learners, with learners assigned to group (a) previously making more productive use of *être* than learners from groups (c) who do not seem to be using it at all.

It is also interesting to note in our data that, although *est* remains throughout the most common realisation of *être* by far, and it might be argued that it is often produced as a chunk, there are a few instances of *sont* and *suis* appearing at Time 2 in three of the learners (again, the most advanced of our subjects). Here are the instances of forms other than *est*:

Time 1:

- *Ils **sont** dans un bateau pour regarder le monstre dans le lac* (09).
- *Ils **sont** pêcher dans le lac* (09).
- *Pardon monsieur je **suis** désolée* (09).
- *Je **suis** désolée c'est* . . . (57).

Time 2:

- *Voilà une famille ils **sont** en vacances au bord du lac (09).*
- *Alors le grand-mère et les deux enfants ce **sont** dans le lac avec les bouées . . . le monstre **sont** . . . un monstre sont dans le lac . . . (09).*
- *Ils **sont** prener des photos (09).*
- *Je **suis** désolée dit grand-mère (09).*
- *Beaucoup de monde **sont** amusants (09).*
- *La Loch Ness monster . . . ils **sont** la télévision (26).*
- *Une journaliste arrive et . . . parler de le grand-mère . . . je **suis** très . . . désolée (27).*
- *Et le grand-mère dit euh excusez-moi je **suis** . . . oh . . . (57).*
- *Je **suis** désolée c'est une faux monstre . . . non le vrai (57).*

The number of subject clitics appearing with these forms is highly striking. If these forms are not part of chunks, and our previous analysis of chunks suggests that they are not, it would indeed appear that the acquisition of these free grammatical morphemes is linked to the appearance of subject clitics in our learners' grammar. In fact, over half (51.5%) of all subject clitics produced in these two tasks occur with *être* or *avoir*. If subject clitics can be linked to the projection of IP, as we have argued earlier, then it might well be the case that these forms of *être* and *avoir* trigger the move from lexical projections to functional projections, as suggested by Hawkins in his 'Modulated Structure Building' hypothesis. This hypothesis is also supported by the fact that many of our learners seem to transfer from English the complement selection requirement of 'be' to mark the progressive (e.g. *le frère est dessine le lac* (02); *et maman est regarder le livre* (03); *ils sont prener des photos* (09)). As the very common 'be + ING' does not exist in French, learners select a VP complement which is usually non-finite, if such a form is available to them.

The use of être and avoir as auxiliaries

As we discussed earlier, one test case for finding out whether the use of finite and non-finite forms is subject to syntactic constraints has been argued to be that finite forms do not occur in non-finite contexts, such as after prepositions or after auxiliaries. There were only three instances of verbs following prepositions in our data (two finite and one non-finite), which made it difficult to draw conclusions.

Verbs following auxiliaries are difficult to isolate, as the status of *a* or *est* in our data is often unclear. If we exclude ambiguous cases, where the form following the auxiliary could either be finite or non-finite (e.g. *est dit*, where *dit* can be finite as in *il dit* or non-finite as in *il a dit*; *est fini – il finit*, or *il a fini*), and also cases where the word following the auxiliary could be either a noun or a verb form, e.g. *est pêche (la pêche* or *il pêche)*, we are left with 15 instances of *être* and *avoir* followed by an unambiguous verb form. We have already seen many such forms with *être*; below are some examples of verb forms following *avoir*:[1]

> . . . *et la mère elle a regardé un livre (02)*
> *et . . . a fait des courses à magasin (26)*
> *un journaliste a parle de grand-mère (52)*
> *la garçon la fille à ma mère j'ai regardé la lake à Loch Ness (26)*

Out of these 15 verb forms following an auxiliary, 13 are non-finite (86.7%) and only two finite (13.3%), supporting the hypothesis that finite forms do not occur in non-finite contexts, and that the production of finite and non-finite forms in our learners is clearly syntactically constrained.

Conclusion

The investigation of the emergence of morpho-syntax in classroom learners of French can be summarised as follows:

(1)   Learners go through a verbless stage, which we suggest is due to processing difficulties linked to the central role of verbs in the architecture of sentences.

(2)   As in L1 acquisition, learners go through an Optional Infinitive stage in which verb forms are sometimes inflected in finite contexts and sometimes not.

(3)   As in L1 acquisition, the use of finite forms increases over time (and the use of non-finite forms decreases accordingly), for most of the learners in this study.

(4)   The appearance of subject clitics in the context of finite verbs only, bears striking similarities to developmental patterns found in French L1 acquisition (Pierce, 1992).

(5)   The appearance of free grammatical morphemes seems to be linked to the projection of IP, as suggested by the fact that clitic subjects occur predominantly with these forms.

(6)   The distribution of finite and non-finite forms seems to be syntactically constrained (as in L1, finite forms do not normally occur in non-finite contexts).

(7)   Developmental stages in the emergence of morpho-syntax in French L2 can be summarised as follows:

• A verbless stage, in which verbs are few, and lack a clear argument structure.

• A bare VP stage (Vainikka & Young-Scholten, 1996a: 16), characterised by its lack of: verb-raising; auxiliaries and modals; an agreement paradigm; complementisers; and wh-movement (as we showed for the same learners in Myles *et al.* 1999).

• An IP stage, characterised by an agreement paradigm; verb-raising; auxiliaries and modals; subject clitics. Free grammatical morphemes seem to be triggering the move from lexical to functional projections, as suggested by Hawkins' (2001a) Modulated Structure Building hypothesis.

To conclude, this longitudinal investigation into the early stages of morpho-syntactic development has brought new evidence about the Initial State and the syntactic constraints underlying early morpho-syntactic development, evidence which has been lacking previously because of a lack of data from beginners. Learners project lexical categories only initially, and their projection of functional categories is linked to the appearance of free grammatical morphemes and subject clitics. Early L2 development of verb morphology has also been shown to be similar in important ways to that of children learning French as a first language.

Acknowledgments

I would like to thank the Economic and Social Research Council in the UK, who funded the research project on which this study is based (grant no. R000234754), as well as the other team members (Rosamond Mitchell, Peter Dickson, Janet Hooper, Judy Hawker and Luciana O'Neill). I would also like to thank the teachers and children in the two schools which took part in the project. Thanks also to Emma Marsden for her help with the statistics.

Notes

1. Examples occurring with *peint*, which was given in the glossary (as *peint = paints*) were excluded. This makes this verb problematic to analyse, as no other forms of that verb would have been available to the learners; it often seems to be misanalysed, e.g. as a noun (*e.g. le grandma une peint, grandmère est la peint la bouée, le grand-mère est peint, les grand-mère euh le peint*).

References

Dulay, H., Burt, M. and Krashen, S. (1982) *Language Two*. New York: Oxford University Press.

Epstein, S., Flynn, S. and Martohardjono, G. (1996) Second language acquisition: Theoretical and experimental issues in contemporary research. *Brain and Behavioural Sciences* 19, 677–714.

Eubank, L. (1996) Negation in early German-English interlanguage: More Valueless Features in the L2 initial state. *Second Language Research* 12 (1), 73–106.

Eubank, L. and Beck, M.-L. (1998). OI-like effects in adult L2 acquisition. Paper presented at the 22nd Annual Boston University Conference on Language Development, Somerville, MA.

Franceschina, F. (2001) Morphological or syntactic deficits in near-native speakers? An assessment of some current proposals. *Second Language Research* 17 (3), 213–47.

Grondin, N. and White, L. (1996) Functional categories in child L2 acquisition of French. *Language Acquisition* 5, 1–34.

Hawkins, R. (2001a) *Second Language Syntax: A Generative Introduction*. Oxford: Blackwell.

Hawkins, R. (2001b) The theoretical significance of Universal Grammar in second language acquisition. *Second Language Research* 17 (4), 345–67.

Hawkins, R. and Chan, C. (1997) The partial availability of Universal Grammar in second language acquisition: the 'failed functional features hypothesis'. *Second Language Research* 13(3), 187–226.

Herschensohn, J. (2001) Missing inflection in L2 French: Accidental infinitives and other verbal deficits. *Second Language Research,* 17 (3), 273–305.

Hyams, N. (1996) The underspecification of functional categories in early grammar. In H. Clahsen (ed.) *Generative Perspectives on Language Acquisition* (pp. 91–128). Amsterdam: John Benjamins.

Ionin, T. and Wexler, K. (2000). Evidence for defaults in child L2 acquisition of finiteness. Unpublished manuscript, Cambridge, MA: MIT.

Juffs, A. (1998) Some effects of first language argument structure and morphosyntax on second language sentence processing. *Second Language Research* 14 (4), 406–24.

Lakshmanan, U. (1998) Functional categories and related mechanisms in child second language acquisition. In S. Flynn, G. Martohardjono and W. O'Neil (eds.) *The Generative Study of Second Language Acquisition* (pp. 3–16). New Jersey: Erlbaum.

Lakshmanan, U. and Selinker, L. (2001) Analysing interlanguage: How do we know what learners know? *Second Language Research* 17 (4), 393–420.

Lardière, D. (1998a) Case and Tense in the 'fossilized' steady state. *Second Language Research* 14 (1), 1–26.

Lardière, D. (1998b) Dissociating syntax from morphology in a divergent L2 end-state grammar. *Second Language Research* 14 (4), 359–75.

Myles, F. (1995) Interaction between linguistic theory and language processing in SLA. *Second Language Research* 11 (3), 235–66.

Myles, F., Hooper, J. and Mitchell, R. (1998) Rote or rule? Exploring the role of formulaic language in classroom foreign language learning. *Language Learning* 48 (3), 323–63.

Myles, F., Mitchell, R. and Hooper, J. (1999) Interrogative chunks in French L2: A basis for creative construction? *Studies in Second Language Acquisition,* 21 (1), 49–80.

Paradis, J., Corre, M. L. and Genesee, F. (1998) The emergence of tense and agreement in child L2 French. *Second Language Research* 14 (3), 227–56.

Parodi, T. (2000) Finiteness and verb placement in second language acquisition. *Second Language Research* 16 (4), 355–81.

Pierce, A. (1992) *Language Acquisition and Syntactic Theory: A Comparative Analysis of French and English Child Grammars.* London: Kluwer.

Prévost, P. and White, L. (2000) Missing Surface Inflection or Impairment in second language acquisition? Evidence from tense and agreement. *Second Language Research,* 16 (2), 103–33.

Radford, A. (1996) Towards a structure-building model of acquisition. In H. Clahsen (ed.) *Generative Perspectives on Language Acquisition* (pp. 43–90). Amsterdam: John Benjamins.

Rizzi, L. (1994) Early null subjects and root null subjects. In T. Hoekstra and B. Schwartz (eds) *Language Acquisition Studies in Generative Grammar* (pp. 151–76). Amsterdam: John Benjamins.

Rule, S. (2001) A cross-sectional study of French interlanguage in an instructional setting. PhD thesis, University of Southampton.

Saeed, J. (1997) *Semantics.* Oxford: Blackwell.

Schwartz, B. (1998) On two hypotheses of 'transfer' in L2A: Minimal trees and absolute L1 influence. In S. Flynn, G. Martohardjono and W. O'Neil (eds) *The Generative Study of Second Language Acquisition* (pp. 35–60). New Jersey: Erlbaum.

Schwartz, B. and Sprouse, R. (1996) L2 cognitive states and the Full Transfer/Full Access model. *Second Language Research* 12 (1), 40–72.

Schwartz, B. and Sprouse, R. (2000) When syntactic theories evolve: Consequences for L2 acquisition research. In J. Archibald (ed.) *Second Language Acquisition and Linguistic Theory* (pp. 56–86). Malden, MA: Blackwell.

Sorace, A. (1998) Residual L2 optionality and L1 attrition. Paper presented at the EUROSLA conference, Paris.

Sorace, A. (2000) Syntactic optionality in non-native grammars. *Second Language Research* 16 (2), 93–102.

Vainikka, A. and Young-Scholten, M. (1996a) Gradual development of L2 phrase structure. *Second Language Research* 12 (1), 7–39.

Vainikka, A. and Young-Scholten, M. (1996b) The early stages in adult L2 syntax: Additional evidence from Romance. *Second Language Research* 12 (2), 140–76.

Vainikka, A. and Young-Scholten, M. (1998) The initial state in the L2 acquisition of phrase structure. In S. Flynn, G. Martohardjono and W. O'Neil (eds) *The Generative Study of Second Language Acquisition* (pp. 17–34). New Jersey: Erlbaum.

Wexler, K. (1998) Very early parameter setting and the Unique Checking Constraint: A new explanation of the optional infinitive stage. *Lingua* 106, 23–79.

Wexler, K. and Harris, T. (1996) The optional infinitives, head movement and the economy of derivations. In H. Clahsen (ed.) *Generative Perspectives on Language Acquisition* (pp. 1–42). Amsterdam: John Benjamins.

White, L. (1996) Universal Grammar and second language acquisition: Current trends and new directions. In W. Ritchie and T. Bhatia (eds) *Handbook of Second Language Acquisition* (pp. 85–120). San Diego: Academic Press.

Appendix

Summary of the Loch Ness Story

A family: mother, grandmother and three children (two boys and a girl) arrive at a holiday cottage on the edge of Loch Ness. Two of the children start fishing; the grandmother starts painting the lake, and the other child starts drawing. The grandmother jokingly paints the Loch Ness monster on the lake. The mother leaves with the youngest boy by car to go shopping in the nearby town. Meanwhile, the grandmother makes a monster with tyres she paints and puts it in the middle of the lake, with the help of the children. On their return, the mother and little boy are very surprised to see a monster in the middle of the lake. Many people arrive and start taking pictures, and a journalist interviews the grandmother. She tries to explain that it is a joke and that the monster is fake. The last picture shows the family leaving for home, and the 'real' Loch Ness monster having appeared in the middle of the lake.

WORD LIST

en vacances	on holiday
peint	paints / is painting
dit	says
fait des courses	does some shopping / goes shopping
une bouée	a rubber ring
beaucoup de monde	a lot of people
un journaliste	a reporter
parle à	speaks to / is speaking to
prennent des photos	. . . are taking photographs
vrai	real

Chapter 6

Syntactic and Semantic Issues in the Acquisition of Negation in French

DANIEL VÉRONIQUE

Introduction

Since the early days of SLA research, the acquisition of negation has been a well-studied topic in relation to various theoretical issues. Hyltenstam (1977) examined cross-sectional data on the acquisition of negation in terms of markedness. Contradictory claims have been put forward as to the relation between the emergence of finiteness and the development of negation in L1 and L2. The sequence of development in the acquisition of negation in French L1 for instance, is the following: anaphoric negation (initially expressed by *non*, later by the same negator placed at the end or the beginning of minimal utterances) precedes non-anaphoric negation (inserted in complex utterances) and the use of *pas* (Meisel 1997a, b). Meisel (1997a, b) contends that, although there are remarkable similarities in the acquisitional sequences of surface patterns in L1 and L2, two properties of L1 acquisition cannot be observed during L2 acquisition: initial position of the negator in early phases of L2 acquisition and the existence of a correlation between the development of the syntax of negation and the movement of finite verbs. Meisel posits that, unlike first language acquisition where the acquisition of *Neg* is related to the development of the functional category of *Infl*, this category plays no role in the acquisition of *Neg* in L2.

Klein (1986) interprets L1 and L2 acquisitional data on negation differently from Meisel (1997a, b) (the L2s involved are English, German and Swedish). According to Klein's analysis, the rule to be acquired in the target languages (TLs) studied is 'Insert neg before the INF (infinitive) position'. The learners proceed in two stages: (i) Step 1: verb forms being non-finite in learner varieties, the rule applies in all contexts although it produces deviant TL utterances; (ii) Step 2: in the case of finite modal and auxiliary forms and non-finite verb forms, the learner is able to apply the TL rule for the placement of negation correctly; where only one lexical verb form is available (merging finite and infinitive according to Klein), the learner fails, at least temporarily. The major point of difference between Klein's analysis of negation in L2 (cf. Klein 1986/1989) and that of Meisel (1997a, b) lies in the assessment of the role played by finiteness and its syntactic implications in L2 acquisition. The relation between the syntactic position of negators and the development of verbal morphology has been much investigated in recent years (for example, Stoffel & Véronique, 1996; Meisel, 1997a, b; Giuliano, 2000; Bardel, 2000; Schlyter, 1998a, b, 1999).

The purpose of this chapter is twofold: (a) to describe the development of negation in the Moroccan Arabic (henceforth MA) 'learner varieties' (TL: French) compared to other learners of French as L2 (see Stoffel & Véronique, 1996; Giuliano & Véronique, 2003), (b) to examine the syntactic and semantic factors that account for the developmental sequences observed. The first section of the chapter is devoted to a contrast between negation in MA and in French. In the second section, hypotheses tested in this study are presented. The following section defines theoretical notions such as finiteness, inflection, topic and focus. The next section describes the informants and the data. Findings are presented in the following section and discussed in the last section.

Negation in Moroccan Arabic and French

Negation in Moroccan Arabic

According to Caubet (1996), in North African Arabic dialects, negation is mainly marked by preposing the marker *ma* to the inflected verb or to non-verbal predicates. In the course of linguistic evolution, a second item *Sa:j* (thing) has been added to *ma*, forming a discontinuous morph *ma . . . Si / Sa:j*, or a continuous item *maSi*. The other negator is *la* (no). Examples below are quoted after Adila (1996), Caubet (1996), Harrell (1962) and Marçais (1977). Some slight modifications have been introduced in the transcription of the examples.[1]

In the following, I shall first introduce some basic information about verb inflection, auxiliaries, modals and adverbials in Moroccan Arabic (henceforth MA) and then go on to specify various aspects of negation in MA.

MA verbs are inflected following two paradigms as in Table 6.1, the imperfective (or suffixed inflection) and the perfective (or prefixed inflection). A third form is the active participle (Caubet, 1996). MA combines inflection, pre-verbs, auxiliaries and adverbials to express various temporal and aspectual values in the following order:

Table 6.1 Moroccan Arabic verb morphology

Imperfective	Perfective
1. sg. ne- mʃ i (I leave)	mʃ iː-t (I left)
2. sg. te- mʃ i (you leave)	mʃ iː-ti (you left)
3. sg. masc. je-mʃ i (he leaves)	mʃ aː– ø (he left)
3. sg. fem. . te-mʃ i (she leaves)	mʃ aː– t (she left)
1. pl. ne-mʃ -u (we leave)	mʃ iː-na (we left)
2. pl. te-mʃ -u (you leave)	mʃ iː-tu (you left)
3. pl. je-mʃ - u (they leave)	mʃ aː-w (they left)

(2)   (Adv.) + (Auxiliary kaːn) + (preverb) + (Ka / Ø) + [(inflected (perfec-
       tive or imperfective) verb) + (active participle)] + (Adv.)
       (In the above, + expresses concatenation, ( ) optionality and [ ] that one
       of the items must be chosen.)

Pre-verbs include *Ghaːdi*, active participle of 'to go' expresses 'future',
bda (to begin) in the perfective and imperfective inflections, *baqi* (to stay)
inflected in the active participle form, *maːzaːl* (to stay) inflected in the active
participle form, etc.

Adverbials include *diːma* (always), *Ghədda* (to-morrow), *mən baÇd*
(after), *bəzzaːf* (often), *daba* (now), *l-baːraH* (yesterday).

Modal values are expressed through modal verbs such as *xəSS* (must),
bRa (wish / want) and connectors such as *kun / iːla* (if). Modal verbs, as well
as connectors (except for *kun / iːla.*), are followed by verbs in the perfective.

Different grammatical devices are used to express presentation, posses-
sion and identification in M. A as in (3):

(3)   Identification is marked by a specific form of *kan* (to be)
       Kayen wahed s-slugi l-l- biÇ temma
       'there's a greyhound for sale there'
       – possession is marked by preposition *Çand + pronoun*
       Çandi wahed d- dar kbira
       'I have one big house'
       – presentation is expressed by the specific form *ra*
       raːni ziːt
       'here I come'

The various forms of the negator in MA (*la, ma, ma . . . Si / Sa:j, la . . . S* and *maSi.*) are used in the following contexts.
    La is an anaphoric negator, as in (4):

(4)   [A: aZi] (= come) B: la (= no).

In purpose subordinate clauses and with certain psych-verbs expressing doubt or fear, the negator *la* has scope over the subordinated inflected verb.

(5)   [Sedd-u la iTiH] (catch imperative + him + neg. + to fall 3sg. imperfective = catch him so that he does not fall). The negator *ma* is used when the object NP bears generic referential value. It is a cate-gorical negative, negating the whole category referred to by the NP rather a specific member of the category (Harrell, 1962: 154):

(6)   [ma kla xobz] (neg. + to eat 3 sg. perfective+ bread) 'he did not eat bread'.

In MA, the partitive is marked in certain contexts by Si + plural NP – i.e. the same constituent that is found in discontinuous ma . . . Si – when the speaker wants to refer to a very limited amount of a given entity (cf. French peu de) (Caubet, 1983).

(7) [zi:d – ni Si be:Da:t]
            (Add + me + some + eggs (plural)) 'Add some eggs for me'.

However, in the context of a negative clause, Ø + singular NP may carry 'partitive' meaning, whether the NP is countable or not,

(8) [ma Sri:t Ø kta:b]
            (neg + buy (I) Perfective + Ø book) 'I bought no book';
(9) [ma ka:in Hli:b]
            (n0eg + existence + Ø milk) 'There is no milk'.

Hətta (up to, even, also) + singular NP (countable or non-countable) in a negative clause bears equally the same 'partitive' semantic value:

(10)   [ma Çandi Hətta kta:b]
            (neg + I have + neither + book) 'I have not one book';
(11)   [ma Çandi Hətta Xobz]
            (neg + I have + neither + bread) 'I have not one piece of bread'.

This can be further reinforced by recourse to Si, which adds qualitative information which can be translated by ' of a certain type'. Hence:

[12]   [ma Çandi Si H∂tta kta:b]
       (neg + I have + a small amount + neither + book) 'I have just / really
       not one book'.

ma is also used in the context of Çamm∂R (never):

(13)   [ma Çamm∂R-∂k tsni t∂mm]
       (neg. + never + you + to sign 2sg. imperfective + there) 'Never sign
       there'.

Discontinuous *ma . . . S* is used with finite verbs (including clitic pronouns
affixed to the inflected verb), either in the imperfective (suffixed inflection)
or in the perfective (prefixed inflection):

(14)   [ma ka-jakol S]
           (neg. + ka (durative marker) + to eat 3sg. imperfective + neg.) 'he
       does not eat'.
(15)   [ma kteb-hom-li S]
       (neg.+ to write 3 sg. perfective + them + prep. me + neg.) 'he has not
       written them for me'.

In the case of a complex VP (auxiliary / pre-verb / modal verb + inflected
main verb), the discontinuous negator is attached either to the inflected
auxiliary / pre-verb or modal verb which precedes the inflected verb:

(16)   [ma bRit S nddiha] (neg. + to want 1sg. perfective + neg. + to take 1 sg.
       imperfective + it / her) 'I did not want to take it'.

(Note that in a negative clause with a 'partitive' NP , *ma . . . S* may alternate
with *ma*, contrast (17) and (18) below with examples (8) to (11):

(17)   [ma Çandi S ∂l ktu:b]
       (Neg + I have + neg + the + books) 'I have no books';
(18)   [ma Çandi S ∂l Xobz]
       (neg + I have + neg + the + bread) 'I have no bread'.

The negator *la . . . S* is used with verbs in the imperfective (bearing prefixed
inflection),

(19)   [la t∂hD∂R S mÇa-h]
       (neg. + to talk 2sg. imperfective+ neg. + with / to him) 'Do not talk to
       him';

The negator *maSi* applies to non-verbal predicates, as *huwa* (him) in (11),

(20)   [maSi huwa lli ga:l li-ja ha:d ∂S-Sej]

(neg. + him + who + to tell 2 sg. perfective + to + me + this + the + thing) 'It's not him who told me that',

or when it has a negative verbal clause in its scope (Caubet, 1996),

(21) [maSi ma kan∂fh∂m S]
(neg. + neg. + auxiliary 1sg. imperfective + to understand 1sg. imperfective + neg.) 'It is not that I do not understand'.

To sum up, in MA negation is mainly expressed by ma in pre-verbal position. The distribution of the various negative morphs (except in contexts where la . . . [S], or ma . . . [S] and maSi could equally occur) depends on the type of predicate involved (verbal or non-verbal), on inflection if it is a verbal clause, on the semantics of the main verb and of the negated verb in the subordinate clause. There is interaction between the form of the clausal negator and the 'partitive' semantic value of the object NP.

Negation in French

The main morphemes of negation in French are *non* and *(ne) . . . pas*
Non is an holophrastic negator, with anaphoric function as in (22):

(22) Peut-il? Non
'Can he (do this)? No'.

However, it is also used in the negation of verbless clauses:

(23) Je prendrai le bus et non le métro
'I shall take the bus and not the subway'.

To negate verbless clauses, *pas*[2] may also be used. Blanche-Benveniste (1990) argues that there are two *pas* markers in French: *pas* in *ne . . . pas*, and *pas* which belongs to the same subsystem as *non* and *non pas*.

(24) Italien ou pas, il n'est pas élégant
'Italian or not, he is not elegant'.

(Ne) . . . pas is adjoined either to the finite verb and to its clitic object pronouns, or to the inflected auxiliary or to the inflected modal verb in a complex VP (Inflected Auxiliary + V in the past participle or Inflected modal + Infinite verb) (Arrivé, Gadet & Galmiche, 1986).

(25) Je (ne) lui en ai pas parlé
'I have not spoken to him about this'.

(Ne) pas is preposed to the non-finite verb as in (26), albeit never *ne* in isolation,

(26) Il a peur de (ne) pas s'en sortir
      'He is afraid of not being able to get out of this quandary'.

In spoken French, *pas* postposed to the inflected verb, or auxiliary or modal verb in a complex VP is the main negator.

Gadet (1992) mentions the development of double negatives (see also Harris, 1978) which bear no positive semantic value in spoken French as in (27) and (28):

(27) J'ai pas obtenu aucun résultat
      'I haven't obtained any result'
(28) C'est pas rien
      'It's not nothing'.

Commonalities and Differences Between the Source Languages and the Target Language's Negative Systems

With respect to the expression of negative functions, French and MA exhibit some similarities:

- both languages have a holophrastic negator distinct from the sentential negator;
- the discontinuous negators in both languages (*ne*) . . . *pas* and *ma/la* . . . *[S]* apply to the first or unique finite element of a complex VP and its clitics;
- *ne pas* precedes non-finite verbs and *maSi* non-verbal clauses.

The major difference between the two languages lies in the fact that in spoken French the negator is postposed to the finite element in a complex VP (since *ne* has lost its negative force) whereas in MA negation is preposed to the first finite element in a complex VP.

Hypotheses

Since MA is a Neg + V language, while French is a post-V language, it can be expected that Arabic-speaking learners will tend to favour pre-verbal negation before an inflected verb, auxiliary or modal because of transfer and for reasons of markedness (Hyltenstam, 1977). Nevertheless, the existence of the discontinuous negation *ma* . . . *S* could equally cause the MA speakers to become aware of French *(ne)* . . . *pas* construction. By the same token, MA speakers may be unable to parse such structures as *il n'a pas de, il n'y a pas de*, etc. (he hasn't, there isn't etc.) and negated clauses containing non-phonologically salient forms of the copula and of auxiliaries *être* (to be) and *avoir* (to have), given the manner in which 'partitive' meaning interacts with the form of the negator in MA.

Hence, the following predictions may be made:

(1)   Arabic-speaking learners will favour pre-verbal negation before an inflected verb, modal or auxiliary.

(2)   Arabic-speaking learners will be sensitive to the interplay between verb morphology and the placement of the negator.

(3)   Arabic speakers will fail to process negative partitive clauses and negated clauses comprising forms of the copula and of auxiliaries *être* (to be) and *avoir* (to have).

Definitions

Following the functional approach developed by Klein and Perdue (1992, 1997), a distinction shall be made in this contribution between *finiteness* and *inflection*. *Inflection* refers to the formal marking of tense, aspect and verb-subject agreement on the verb and *finiteness* to the abstract cognitive category of Assertion. However, in learner varieties, a non-inflected verb may bear finiteness. The emergence of verb inflection is not necessarily related to the expression of all the relational features (tense, aspect, agreement) associated with this category in TL. Learners may use L2 formal means to mark only part of the functions finiteness carries in TL.

Following Klein and Perdue (1992, 1997), *topic* and *focus* shall be used with the following meaning in the rest of this chapter. A *topic* defines the set of alternatives from which a choice must be made and the *focus* specifies the piece of information selected from the set of alternatives. In the following example (see also below):

(29)   Cycle 1 – Encounter 3
        IN: vous êtes mariée ou célibataire?
        'Are you married or single?'
        ZA: non < mariée > foc
        'no married'

The set of alternatives or topic is civil status (*mariée ou célibataire?*) and the focus is the alternative selected *mariée*).

Informants

The following informants have provided data:

For two speakers, Abdessamad and Malika H., only the first cycle of data collected has been analysed. As for Malika B., only six encounters of the first cycle of data collection were available, since she left the project after that period.

At the onset of investigation, the level of proficiency of the MA speakers

Table 6.2 Sociobiographical information on informants

	Abdelmalek (AE)	Abdessamad (AD)	Abderrahim (AB)	Zahra (Z)	Malika. H (MH)	Malika. B (MB)
Age (1983)	20	24	26	34	20	18
Civil Status	Bachelor	Bachelor	Bachelor	Married	Bachelor	Married
Education	Primary School	None	None	None	None	None
Date of arrival	Sept. 81	Oct. 81	Sept. 81	1981	Oct. 81	Oct. 82
French Courses	1h / week (7 months)	1h / week (7 months)	None	1h / week (4 months)	4h / week (7 months)	None
Other languages	Some written Arabic + some Spanish	None	Some Spanish	None	None	None
Occupation	Fisherman	Fisherman	Dishwasher	Cleaning lady	Cleaning lady	Bar maid

in French was not homogeneous. Malika B. was the least advanced, exhibiting a pre-basic variety (Perdue, 1996). Zahra and Abdelmalek used the basic variety at the start of the data-collection period. Although it is difficult to identify a clear boundary between one stage and another, their interlanguages evolved towards a post-basic variety from the second half of the second cycle onwards. This phase coincides with the emergence of auxiliaries and cases of subject-verb agreement. The identification of auxiliaries is easier in the case of Abdelmalek than in the case of Zahra. Malika H., as well as Abdessamad, was at a basic-post-basic stage at the beginning of the data-collection period

Data analysis

Malika B.

At the beginning of data collection, Malika B. makes use of only a few TL items such as *oui* (yes), *non* (no), *café* (coffee), *bar* (bar) etc. She produces mixed M. A and French utterances which are not fully understood by the investigator. After spending two months in Marseilles, Malika B. produces some simple TL strings without code mixing (*[se]* + SN/Adj; *moi* + V + SN, etc.). During this period, two negators are found in her utterances: *non*, by far the most productive item, and *pas* in some 'rote-learned' expressions such as *[se] pas* (know not) or *ça va pas* 'it's not OK'. Anaphoric *non* in focus position is often associated with a lexical topic as in (30):

(30) Cycle 1 – 3rd Encounter
       IN: oui? vous pouvez me l'écrire
       'Yes? Can you write this for me'
       MB (Produces a gesture of negation)
       IN non? 'no'
       MB non < français > top < non > foc
       'no French no'

From encounter 6 of cycle 1, when *N (V) N* strings tend to be more frequent, *pas* replaces *non* as clausal negator. In the examples below, *pas* either precedes the lexical topic in its scope (31) or follows the topical predicate (32). In both cases, it has focus status. Variation in placement of the negator seems to depend on the lexical and grammatical nature of the item under the scope of negation.

(31) M.B. [li] pas l'école
       'he / she no school'
(32) M.B. [jãnapa]
       'there is not'

To sum up, *non* is the main negator in Malika B.'s pre-basic variety. It is an external item, used anaphorically, often in focus position. The emergence of *pas* seems due to the learner's ability to identify the different functions fulfilled by *non* and *pas* in French (anaphoric negator *vs.* clausal negator). The extent to which the use of *pas* in Malika B's learner variety is related to the development of the verb phrase is hard to tell.

Zahra

Pas and *non* are found in the first encounters with Zahra. *Pas* is first observed in 'rote-learned' expressions purveying deontic modal meaning such as *je [kõprã] pas* 'I don't understand', *je [se] pas* 'I don't know', or in stereotyped presentational formulae like *[jãna] pas + X* 'there isn't X) et *[se] pas+ X* 'it isn't X' (Véronique, 1994). Gradually, the use of *pas* extends to the context of lexical verbs. *Non* is used by Zahra from the earliest data collected as an holophrastic negator:

(33) Cycle 1, Encounter 1
       IN: vous ne sortez pas?
       'you are not going out?'
       ZA: non 'no'
       IN: non? 'no?'
       ZA: non 'no'

Anaphoric *non* is also employed in external position with a nominal entity situated to the left of the negator, in answer to disjunctive questions.

(34) Cycle 1 – Encounter 3
      IN: vous êtes mariée ou célibataire?
      'Are you married or single?'
      ZA: non < mariée > foc
      'no married'

Although superficially identical, the negated clause in (30) is quite different from the clause in (34) in terms of topic-focus structure.
As for *pas*, Zahra makes early use of negative presentationals *[se] pas* and *[janapa]*:

(35) Cycle 1 – Encounter 2
      ZA: heureusement euh les enfants [jãna] pas de l'école aujourd'hui
      'Happily the kids do not have to attend school today'

As can be seen in (35), *[jana] pas* is used as a 'chunk', not necessarily analysed by the informant. The productive use of *pas* in that particular context may be questioned.

In Zahra's learner variety, *pas* follows lexical verbs (cf. *[ipart] pas*, 'he doesn't leave', in the first cycle of data collection, *[ipej] pas*, 'he doesn't pay' in the second cycle, etc.). These items formally resemble finite TL verbs. Incorrect segmentation of the TL VP leads the informant to produce utterances such as the following:

(36) Cycle 3- Encounter 2
      ZA: *[ilafe] pas* les chaussures
      'He has not made the shoes, cf. TL Il a pas fait les chaussures'

where the negator follows the lexical non-finite verb instead of the possible TL-like auxiliary *[a]*. In the course of linguistic development, *pas* is used with an increasing number of different lexical verbs.

Only one token of discontinuous negation has been observed in the whole data produced by Zahra.

(37) ZA: oui oui les femmes ne [travaj] pas
      'yes yes women do not work'

Table 6.3 illustrates all negative utterances with an explicit verb produced by Zahra along the three cycles of data collection.

Table 6.3 Zahra – Tokens of '*pas*'

	je /kõprã/–		*je /se/ –*		*/jãna/ – (X)*		*/se/ –(X)*		*Other Verbs*		*Total*
Cycle 1	53	(29.3%)	2	(1.1%)	7	(3.9%)	64	(35.4%)	55	(30.4%)	181
Cycle 2	39	(13.9%)	4	(1.4%)	14	(5%)	151	(53.9%)	70	(25%)	280
Cycle 3	30	(8%)	28	(7.4%)	23	(6.1%)	137	(36.3%)	158	(42%)	377
	122		34		44		352		283		828

Malika H. and Abdelmalek

In the first utterances of Malika H. and Abdelmalek, *non* and *pas* are both present. *Non* is used anaphorically, in question-answer sequences, and with a nominal or verbal item in topic or focus position, as has already been observed for other speakers.

(38)   Cycle 1, Encounter 6
    IN: c'est pas un tambour pour toi?
    'This is not a drum for you?'
    AE: < non > foc + < tambour > top
    'No drum'
(39)   Cycle 1, Encounter 1
    IN: vous faites un peu de couture + aussi?
    'Do you do some sewing also?'
    MH: < couture > top < non > foc
    'sewing no'

The position of the negator with respect to the element it accompanies is not strictly determined by the pragmatic organisation of the utterance since in *Neg + X* the item *X* can be either a focus (cf. ex. (34) in Zahra) or a topic (cf. ex. (38) above). Nevertheless, in *X + Neg*, *X* seems to always correspond to a topic (cf. ex. (30) in Malika B.'s data and ex. (39) above).

In example (40) below, it can be gathered from the preceding context that *non [se] possible* means ' it's impossible ', i.e. negator *non* has scope on the positive assertion *[se] possible*:

(40)   Cycle 1, Encounter 3
    IN: et oui c'est ça le problème + c'est pas possible?
    'oh yes this is the problem + it is not possible'
    M.H: < non > foc [se] < possible > top
    'no it's possible'.

In both Zahra and Abdelmalek, *pas* is found in formulaic modal expressions such as *[se] pas* (know not = 'don't know'), *[kõprã] pas* (understand not

= 'don't understand') as well as with presentationals *[jãnapa]* X (there isn't) and *[sepa]* X (it's not X). In contrast to Zahra, Abdelmalek places *pas* in preverbal position in the early phases of data collection except in 'rote-learned' expressions. However, as shown in Table 6.4 by the end of the data-collection period *pas* is placed in post-verbal position following TL norm.

Table 6.4 Abdelmalek: Tokens of *pas*

	X pas	*pas X*	*N pas X³*	*Aux. pas X*	*Other Verbs*
Cycle 1	246	64	18	2	39
Cycle 2	337	59	10	10	21
Cycle 3	347	28	3	9	31

A close inspection of Table 6.5 (Abdelmalek) shows that most verbs – other than those in formulaic expressions – exhibit preposed negation rather than postposed negation during the first cycle of data collection. Conformity to TL use starts towards the middle of cycle 2 in Abdelmalek's learner variety.

Table 6.5 Abdelmalek: Tokens of postposed *pas*

	(je)ʸ/kõprã–		*(je)/se/ –*		*/jãna/⁵–(X)*		*/se/ –(X)*		*Other Verbs*		*Total*
Cycle 1	14	(5.7%)	16	(6.5%)	111	(45.1%)	68	(27.6%)	37	(15.0%)	246
Cycle 2	27	(8.0%)	26	(7.7%)	68	(20.2%)	126	(37.4%)	90	(26.7%)	337
Cycle 3	38	(10,9%)	29	(8.4%)	46	(13.3%)	97	(27.9%)	137	(39.5%)	347
	74		71		225		290		264		930

One peculiarity of Abdelmalek's use of negator *pas* is the preposition of the negator to the verb where V is in topic position:

(41) AE Cycle 1, Encounter 1
      IN: Tu comprends?
      'You understand?'
      AE: non < pas > foc < [komprã] > top
      'no not understand = no I don't understand'

The preposition of *pas* to V seems also to be related to the absence of a grammatical subject, be it a clitic pronoun or a noun. Abdelmalek uses a fixed form *[nepa] / [napa]* preposed to V as in (42). (*Kõprã* in 40 and *kompriin* in (41) do exhibit some form of inflection, despite the fact that verbal alternation does not seem to be the carrier of specific meaning). The number of tokens

Table 6.6 Abdelmalek: Tokens of preposed *pas*

	(je) pas V		pas /kõprã/		pas /kompri/		Total
Cycle 1	49	(76.5%)	3	(4.6%)	12	(18.8%)	64
Cycle 2	54	(91.5%)	4	(6.7%)	1	(1.7%)	59
Cycle 3	28						28
	137		7		13		157

of this type of negator decreases during the data-collection period as can be seen from Table 6.5. Here is an example,

(42) AE Cycle 1, Encounter 2
AE:[saje] ça [napakompri] ça pas [kompri]
'OK that not understood that not understood' or 'OK that I have not understood that I have not understood)

As illustrated in (41), in the early stages of Abdelmalek's basic variety *[napa]* and *pas* seem to alternate freely.

In Abdelmalek's data the TL-like placement of *pas* is related to the analysis of the TL VP and to the development of verb inflection (in particular, the emergence of the pattern *V vs Aux + Vlex*, which is similar to the *présent/passé composé* opposition of the target language, and the subject-verb agreement marking, see Starren, 2001: 248–251) and clitic subject pronouns. This is well illustrated by one of the early examples of TL like placement of *pas* by Abdelmalek, where *parl* may be analysed as a proto-present tense,

(43) Cycle 1, Encounter 6
IN: oh mais tu vois des/tu parles français quelquefois . . .
'Oh but you see / you speak French sometimes'
AE: je [parl] avec toi le français [se] tout hein + les autres je [parl] pas
'I speak French with you that's all + (with) the others I don't speak'.

However, even when the use of the clitic subject pronoun tends to be generalized, some alternation in the placement of *pas* may still be observed.

(44) Cycle 2, Encounter 1
AE: ah moi je pas [ganje] trente dix mille par mois
'Oh me I not (= don't) earn thirty ten thousand per month'

Note that *je pas [ganje]* in (44) is ambiguous, given that *je* could be interpreted either as TL first person pronoun or first person pronoun + have (see (47) below for a clearer example).

In the course of the development of Abdelmalek's interim grammar, during cycles 2 and 3 of data collection, the following alternation may be observed: postposed *pas* co-occurs with the stem form of the verb (cf. *[sufl]* in (45) and *[part]* in (45)) whereas preposed *pas* is found in the context of the long form of the verb (cf. *[sufle]* in (45) and *[parte]* in (46)).

(45)   Cycle 2, Encounter 6
       AE: non non je [kraS] pas non
       'no no I do not spit no'
       non je [sufl] pas non
       no I am not breathless'
       non je pas [sufle]
       'no I am not breathless'
(46)   Cycle 2, Encounter 7
       AE: même euh je pas [parte] toujours hein une fois par semaine + chaque fois je [part] pas hein
       'even I not go always hey once a week + each time I do not go'.

V alternation in relation with the placement of Neg might result from an indirect influence of L1, which renders the L1 Arabic speaker sensitive to morphological variation on V (see examples 1 and 2 above). However, phonetic factors could equally explain this type of alternation. Obviously, it could also be the case that *sufl* for instance is interpreted as a finite form as compared to *sufle* interpreted as a non-finite form.

In the ultimate stage of development recorded, Abdelmalek resorts to the use of auxiliaries and places the negator, following TL norms, between the auxiliary and the non-finite verb:

(47)   Cycle 2, encounter 6
       AE: parce que [tu] la journée [Ze] pas [mõZi] alors parce que je [travaj] pas
       'because all the day I have not eaten then I do not work'

Table 6.7 Malika H. Tokens of *pas* (Cycle 1)

(je)/ sel–	(je)/ konel –	Other modals	/sel/ –	/ilja/ –	V–	Com- prendre–	+ small clause	– beau- coup	– + X	Other	Total
58	17	05	114	12	76	23	04	19	10	10	348

In early data from MH, *pas* is postposed to presentationals and verbs but is preposed to adjectives, small clauses and quantifiers.

(48) Cycle 1, Encounter 2
      [iparl] mais pas content
      'he speaks but (he is) not happy'
(49) Cycle 1, Encounter 4
      Meknes [setø] une ville pas grosse
      'Meknes was a town not big'
(50) Cycle 1, Encounter 4
      [jãna] mais pas comme là avec un djellaba
      'there exists but not like here with a djellaba'

Between cycle 1 and cycle 2 of data collection, MH develops verb morphology. Modal contexts and presentationals account for the largest number of tokens of *X + pas*. In Malika H.'s data, the placement of *pas*, though always post-verbal, varies as illustrated by examples (51), where the negator follows the whole verb phrase *[iladi],* and (52), where it follows the finite copula and the finite lexical verb according to TL norms.

(51) Cycle 1, Encounter 2
      MH: [iladi] pas hein?
      'he did not say it hey?'
(52) Cycle 1, Encounter 2
      MH: [ile] pas beau alors euh moi [fe] pas [zami]
      'he is not handsome so I do not make friends'

As soon as complex VPs are analysed and inflection on the verb emerges, *pas* is correctly postposed to the finite component. In (53), the copula *[ete]* is tensed following target norms as well as the modal verb *[vø]*, the placement of *pas* before non-finite *[rãtre]* is target-like. The broader context from which this excerpt is extracted clearly indicates that reference to past events is intended.

(53) Cycle 2, Encounter 9
      MH: je [lave] il [ete] maintenant trop petit il [vø] pas [rãtre]
      'I washed it was now too small it does not fit'.

(54) provides another example of postfinite *pas* in Malika H.'s learner variety,

(54) Cycle 3, Encounter 4
      MH: je [syi] pas [vy] des garçons ici beaucoup hein
      'I am not seen boys here many hey'

Examples (53) and (54) show that Malika contrasts a simple V, and AUX + V, whose functions seem to coincide, respectively, with those of *présent* and *passé composé* of the TL. In the case of the copula, Malika seems also to contrast TL *présent* and *imparfait*.

To sum up, the basic-post-basic varieties of Abdelmalek and Malika H. present both strong similarities and points of difference in the use of negator *pas*. In both varieties, *pas* is first found in the same 'rote-learned' expressions and presentationals as in the data from other informants. In non-stereotyped contexts, the same negator can either precede the still ambiguous lexical verb forms (cf. Abdelmalek) or follow Aux + VP (cf. Malika H.'s *[ilafe]* pas and Zahra's *[iladi] pas*). The segmentation of VP and the marking of inflection and finiteness on the verb lead informants to the target-like use of negation.

Summary

The data produced by the MA-speaking informants yield some common phenomena but also dissimilarities in the acquisitional paths of the four informants.

The negator *non* is in use since the pre-basic-basic variety. It is used both as an holophrastic negator and in small clauses with no fixed order of constituents. A focused element tends to follow negation *(Neg + < X > foc)*, while a topic precedes the negator that has focus status *(< X > top + < Neg > foc)* (cf. also Bernini, 1996; Giuliano, 2000, and Bardel, 2000).

Negator *pas* is first observed in formulaic modal expressions and with presentationals *[se]* and *[jāna]*; *pas* is always postposed in these contexts. The placement of *pas* is less clearly marked in the case of lexical verbs where informants vary.

The following developmental pattern emerges from the data:

(a)   the negator *pas* is always postposed to *être, avoir* and modals verbs *savoir* and *connaître* in the first instance and later *vouloir, falloir, pouvoir;*

(b)   more generally, when the TL non-thematic verbs (in particular copula and auxiliaries) become salient in learner varieties, *pas* is placed according to the TL use, namely after the finite component of VP.

Data from an advanced Moroccan Arabic speaker (Abdessamed) confirms this developmental trend. In formulaic modal expressions and with presentationals, Abdessamad uses post-verbal *pas*, hence *[janapa]* and *je [kōprā] pas*. Postposed *pas* is also used by this informant with thematic verbs as in (55):

(55)   Cycle 1, Encounter 2
       AB: je [Zue] pas parce que l'autre [ile Zue] à Mimoun
       'I played not because the other one he played with Mimoun'.

However, *pas* is also preposed to VP in clauses such as (56):

(56) Cycle 1, Encounter 1
AB: Je pas [travaj] comme aujourd'hui samedi
'I do not work since today (is) Saturday'.

Discussion

Of the predictions made initially on the basis of a comparison of MA and French negation, only the hypothesis relating to the perception of auxiliaries and copulas in negated clauses seems to be borne out by the data. Contrary to expectations, Moroccan informants do not exhibit marked preference for pre-verbal negation except in the case of Abdelmalek (but note that the latter has some rudimentary knowledge of Spanish). However, because of discontinuous MA negation *ma . . . Si*, MA speakers are able to notice TL post-verbal negation. This probably explains partly post-verbal placement of pas. L1 influence in the acquisition of negation is not absent from the MA data but it seems to be one factor in learner variety change as shown by the alternation of V morphology and the placement of the negator in (40).

The initial recourse to anaphoric *non* in the data seems to be related to a pragmatic principle (cf. also Bernini, 1996): when the negator is in focus position ([X]top + [Non]foc), it has the value of a prophrase. When the focus status is held by the item which is in the scope of the negator (Non + [X]foc), the negator can be regarded as having a neutral informational status (Giuliano & Véronique, 2003). The relationship between *non* and the constituent(/s) in the negated clause is both semantic, related to scope, and pragmatic (topic-focus relationship).

Modal formulae and presentationals play a major role in the TL-like placement of *pas*. This is due to the late development of the copula and the auxiliary in the MA data. The analysis of TL verb morphology paves the way for correct placement of the negator. Otherwise, some form of avoidance can be observed (see Malika H.'s [iladi] pas, Zahra's [ilafe] pas and the pre-verbal placement of negator in Abdelmalek).

Non-thematic verbs, possibly because of their 'lighter' character – they convey mainly relational information (tense, aspect, subject-verb agreement) following Parodi's analysis – play an important part in the TL placement of negation by the MA speakers. However, inflection is developed on non-thematic verbs at approximately the same time as the less numerous lexical verbs, at least in the earliest phase of data collection (Giuliano, 2000 and Starren 2001). One possible explanation for the placement of the negator after non-thematic verbs could be the role played by these items as relational predicates conveying assertion force, i.e. they mark the barrier between topic information and focus information and refer to the tense span to which an utterance is anchored and for which it is said to be valid or non-valid. The learner's perception that a negative utterance must necessarily be valid for a given Topic Time leads him/her to place the negator after the finite relational predicate (marking tense / aspect / agreement) but before the non-finite lexical predicate (marking only lexical information).

MA speakers develop along similar lines in their acquisition of the negation in French as the group of Spanish learners of French studied by Giuliano (2000). For both groups of informants, *pas* appears early in the context of the modal formulae *je (ne) sais pas* and *je (ne) comprends pas*. However, for MA speakers, presentationals play an equally important role while they play a minor role for Spanish-speaking informants. For most of the latter, [nepa(de)] (there isn't) is either the only form used for marking non-existence or is used in alternation with more target-like structures. Once utterances with an explicit lexical verb emerge, all Spanish-speaking informants mark a preference for the pre-verbal placement of negation, using the TL *ne* form. The explanation for this state of affairs may be transfer and convergence with 'natural' trends (cf. the Neg + V universal, discussed, for instance, in Bernini & Ramat, 1990).

The data from MA learners support Meisel's (1997a, b) claims as to the difference between the acquisition of negation in L1 and L2 on two counts:

(1)   non is never a 'grammaticalised' verbal negator,
(2)   *pas* develops as a negator before VP is fully analysed.

However, in contradistinction to Meisel (1997a, b), it can be observed in the MA data that, as the learners' repertoire of lexical verbs develop, TL VP undergoes analysis and the learners' VP and the placement of negation tend to become more target-like.

Acknowledgment

I would like to thank the anonymous reader and the editor for useful comments. Remaining mistakes are mine.

Notes
1. IPA has been used with some modifications. Emphatic consonants are transcribed with capital letters, hence R, D, L etc., [h] is transcribed by H, Ç stands for [ ] g, for [ ], and Z for [ ]. However, the manner in which each author transcribes oral Moroccan Arabic data has not been modified.
2. According to C. Blanche-Benveniste (1990), there exist two *pas* markers in French: *pas* in *ne . . . pas*, and *pas* which belongs to the same subsystem as *non* and *non pas*.

3. i.e /nepakompri/, /napakompri/ (not understand / understood) found in the first encounters with Abdelmalek.
4. ( ) mark the optional nature of the constituent.
5. This morpheme has various allomorphs: /jana/, /jan/, /jãna/ and /ja/.

References

Adila, A. (1996) La négation en arabe marocain (le parler de Casablanca). In S. Chaker and D. Caubet (eds.) *La négation en berbère et en arabe maghrébin. Bulletin des Etudes Africaines* 1, 99–116.

Arrivé, M., Gadet, F. and Galmiche, M. (1986) *La grammaire d'aujourd'hui. Guide alphabétique de linguistique française.* Paris: Flammarion.

Bardel, C. (2000) La negazione nell'italiano degli svedesi. Sequenze acquisizionali e influssi translinguistici. *Etudes Romanes de Lund* vol. 61, University of Lund, Sweden.

Bernini, G. and Giacalone Ramat, A. (eds) (1990) *La Temporalità nell'Acquisizione di Lingue Seconde.* Milan, Franco Angeli.

Bernini, G. (1996) Stadi di sviluppo della sintassi e della morfologia della negazione in Italiano L2. *Linguistica et Filologia III.*

Blanche-Benveniste, C. (1990) *Le français parlé. Etudes grammaticales.* Paris: Editions du CNRS.

Caubet, D. (1983) *La détermination en arabe marocain.* Paris: D.R.L.

Caubet, D. (1996) La négation en arabe maghrébin. In S. Chaker and D. Caubet (eds) *La négation en berbère et en arabe maghrébin. Bulletin des Etudes Africaines* 1, 79–97.

Gadet, F. (1992) *Le français populaire.* Paris: Presses Universitaires de France.

Giuliano, P. (2000) L'acquisition et l'expression des fonctions négatives en français et en anglais comme langues secondes. Confrontation d'études longitudinales et apports théoriques pour l'acquisition en milieu naturel. Unpublished Phd dissertation, University Paris 8 (France) and University of Pavia (Italy).

Giuliano, P. and Véronique, D. (2003) The acquisition of negation in French L2. An analysis of Moroccan Arabic and Spanish learner varieties. Unpublished manuscript.

Harrell, R.S. (1962) *A Short Reference Grammar of Moroccan Arabic.* Washington D.C: Georgetown University Press.

Harris, M. (1978) *The Evolution of French Syntax. A Comparative Approach.* London: Longman.

Hyltenstam, K. (1977) Implicational patterns in interlanguage syntax variation. *Language Learning* 27, 383–411.

Klein, W. and Perdue, C. (1992) *Utterance Structure (Developing Grammars Again).* Amsterdam: John Benjamins.

Klein, W. and Perdue, C. (1997) The Basic Variety. *Second Language Research* 13 (4), 301–347.

Klein, W. (1986 / 1989) *L'acquisition de langue étrangère.* Paris: Armand Colin.

Marçais, Ph. (1977) *Esquisse grammaticale de l'arabe maghrébin.* Paris: Maisonneuve.

Meisel, J. (1997a) L'acquisition de la négation en langue première. In C. Martinot (ed), *Actes du Colloque International sur l'acquisition de la syntaxe en langue maternelle et en langue étrangère,* (pp. 189–222). Besançon: Annales littéraires de l'Université de Franche-Comté.

Meisel, J. (1997b) The acquisition of the syntax of negation in French and German: Contrasting first and second language development. *Second Language Research* 13 (3), 227–263.

Parodi, T. (1998) Finiteness and Verb Movement in L2 Acquisition. A Correlation Revisited. Unpublished manuscript.

Schlyter, S. (1998a) Verbes et négation chez des apprenants suédophones de français. Paper presented at the European Conference on Language Acquisition, European Science Foundation, Maratea, Italy, 28 September–1 October.

Schlyter, S. (1998b) Négation et portée chez des apprenants suédophones de français. Unpublished manuscript.

Schlyter, S. (1999) Acquisition des formes verbales: temps, accord et finitude. Paper presented at the XI Colloque International sur l'Acquisition d'une Langue Etrangère: Perspectives et Recherches, Paris, 19–21 April.

Starren, M. (2001) *The Second Time. The Acquisition of Temporality in Dutch and French as a Second Language*. Utrecht: LOT.

Stoffel, H. and Véronique, D. (1996) L'acquisition de la négation en français par des adultes arabophones. Paper presented at the European Research Conference 'The Structure of Learner Language. Utterance and discourse structure in language acquisition', Espinho, Portugal, September 1996.

Chapter 7

Gender and Number in French L2: Can We Find Out More About the Constraints on Production in L2?

MIREILLE PRODEAU

Introduction

The use of the wrong gender is a key to finding the foreigner in a crowd of speakers of French. Moreover, this type of problem persists despite the effort of the bilingual speaker to sound native-like. Interestingly, the gender of the noun that is wrongly produced is usually known by L2 speakers. Why then are they unable to use this specific kind of knowledge when speaking? Is it because gender remains declarative in essence?

In French, gender is, like number, a diacritic feature of the nominal head. According to Corbett (1991), gender is used to mark the attitude of the speaker towards discourse referents but more so for referential tracking: gender is used to group words into phrases and, at the level of discourse, gender is a means of creating anaphoric or deictic referential constructions. To use gender is thus to link discourse and utterance organisation with grammatical organisation. Gender is above all language-specific. Comrie (1999) describes various systems of noun classes and shows that semantic principles are combined with formal ones to form rules of assignment.

According to the definition given by Matthews in the Concise Oxford Dictionary of Linguistics (1997), gender is also a system that shows which class the noun belongs to on related elements to the noun. If we take the example of German, which has a very opaque system, the gender of nouns such as *Messer*, *Löffel* or *Gabel* is generally to be discovered in the article which goes with the noun: *das* for neutral nominative, *der* for masculine nominative and *die* for feminine nominative. There is no semantic principle to explain how gender is assigned to each of these nouns and the formal one is hard to guess. The concept of agreement thus becomes crucial.

If the L2 speaker does not use a correct form, the question is whether the

135

problem is that of assignment or of agreement. This question has been addressed already (Carroll, 1989; Dewaele & Véronique, 2000, 2001; Hawkins, 1998) but the answers given are somewhat contradictory. To investigate the question, gender is compared with another relevant diacritic feature of the noun in French: number. Number is used only to mark the semantic concept of plurality. This direct mapping between plurality and number facilitates the processing of number by L2 speakers, who tend to use one form for one function. However, in French the difficulty of checking agreement between the head and its modifiers is the same for number and gender. The complexity increases even more when agreement is across phrases: from noun phrases to verb phrases (subject-verb agreement) for number and from head noun to predicative adjective for gender. This comparison should help us distinguish between what is related to assignment and what is related to agreement.

Previous Studies

These enquiries raise further questions about the architecture of the mental lexicon: how words are stored in memory and the various ways in which information is processed in production. Schriefers and Jescheniak (1999), who work on the basis of Levelt's model of production (1989), have shown that for L1 languages such as French, Dutch, German, etc., whose system includes gender, each lemma is associated with a gender node. This node would be used to speed up the word recognition in comprehension, according to the work done by Grosjean *et al.* (1994). More complex is the use of this node in production; once a lemma is selected, the gender node it is attached to is activated. This node is selected[1] only when it is necessary for the syntactic module to check the unification of features from the different elements of the NP.

Other studies in L1 were designed to discover how information about the features of gender and number is stored in the mental lexicon, how subjects have access to this stored information and how they process it. Dominguez, Cuetos and Segui (1999) for Spanish, and de Vincenzi for Italian (1999[2]), have shown that masculine and feminine forms are both stored in the mental lexicon. They report that the forms would be retrieved at a different speed depending on their frequency. Many lemmas are selected more frequently under their masculine form, which is the reason why masculine is called the default case. In the case of number, only the singular form is stored and the syntactic module will add the morpheme of plural when the semantic concept of plurality belongs to the pre-verbal message.

De Bot (1992), using Levelt's model (1989), designed a production model for bilinguals. In his view, the bilingual speaker needs to encode concepts lexically, grammatically and morpho-phonologically in both languages, and lexical information and procedures must thus be available in the for-mulator. He adds that the specific configuration depends on the level of competence and the specific links which exist between the two systems. For example, he suggests that for the most part a bilingual speaker whose L1 and L2 are close has one set of procedures. Pienemann (1998), who based his processability theory on the work done by Levelt and de Bot, discusses the various tasks the L2 speaker has to undertake in order to acquire the L2. One is to annotate the lexicon with features absent in L1. If features are similar in both languages, the task is simpler. Another one is to acquire specific procedures in relation to the new grammar. These procedures are supposed to be acquired in a specific order, from building a phrase to a complex sentence. This order is based on the hypothesis that the more distant the items whose features have to be unified, the heavier the load in the working memory. In the case of an overload, the L2 speaker would immediately resort to using a direct mapping between function and forms. Naturally, procedures that are similar in both languages have been automatised and thus use very little space in the working memory, so there is little risk of memory overload (cf. Towell & Dewaele, this volume).

De Bot (1992) and also Grosjean (1997) base their design of the mental lexicon on Paradis's neurolinguistic work (1987 for example) and talk of one system being organised into subsystems. Items inside one subsystem simply activate the other items inside the same subsystem, especially when the mode is monolingual.[3] They also believe that in bilingual mode, items between both subsystems can activate one another, especially when words or phonemes have a direct equivalent in the other subsystem. For both of them, the level of activation depends on the closeness between two items. Grosjean (1997), who works on comprehension, has looked at the role played by homophones. The closer one lexical entry is to its equivalent, the slower the lexical recognition. Gender being a feature specific to French should help the bilingual speaker to activate the French subsystem more than the English one. However, one should not neglect the fact that many lexemes are common to both languages.

This question of the influence of the specific L1/L2 configuration has been addressed by some. Bruhn de Garavito and White (2000), who have studied the acquisition of Spanish by French adults, have compared their results with those of Hawkins (1998) on the acquisition of French gender by English native speakers. The developmental pattern in both cases is similar, which would imply no direct and obvious effect of L1.

Research conducted by Parodi *et al.* (1997) deals with the effect specific L1/L2 configurations have on both storage and procedures. They have looked at how the L1 grammar influences the acquisition of nominal morpho-syntax in German L2, with the emphasis on number. They have compared speakers of Korean, Turkish and Romance languages. They conclude that there is no difference in the developmental patterns for the acquisition of number in German between the Korean and the Romance language L1 speakers. Even though Romance-language speakers use procedures of unification of the nominal diacritic features amongst the constituents of the NP, they do not systematically use these procedures in German. The Korean speakers, who do not have obligatory marking of number on the nominal head and have no procedures of agreement, perform the same in German as the Romance-language speakers. One may wonder if we cannot interpret the results of Parodi *et al.* (1997) in relation to the marking in German, even more so if we look at the results of Koehn (1990) and Müller (1990). They have looked at the acquisition of nominal features in the case of early bilinguals in French and German and found that when children acquire the marking of number in French and German, they mark it on the article in French and on the noun in German. The reason invoked by the authors is that there is one definite article in German to mark the plural and the feminine singular for the nominative and accusative case. Thus, the children keep *die* for the feminine gender and mark plurals with a morpheme added to the noun. This would then be interpreted as no agreement between the head and the determiner.

Another result common to studies in L2 and L1 acquisition concerns the difference between the articles: Bruhn de Garavito and White (2000) mention, too, that the marking of gender on the indefinite article poses problems for the adult L2 learners. For the bilingual French/German children of the Koehn and Müller studies (1990), gender appears later than number and first on the definite article. For Müller (1990), the indefinite article is above all a numeral and thus used essentially to mark one thing: the concept of singularity.

The question of what kind of errors L2 speakers make when solving a complex verbal task, assignment or agreement has to be examined slightly differently.

The emphasis in studies of a production model designed for bilingual speakers is mainly on the formulator and specifically on lexical storage, the grammatical encoder and its syntactic building procedures. Some also looked at the conceptualiser (see studies in the research programme 'The Structure of Learner Varieties' at the Max Planck Institut für Psycholinguistik, Nijmegen, The Netherlands). The idea of specific L1/L2 configurations and their impact on the phonological encoding and the articulator is very rarely envisaged. Yet gender in French is in many cases based on phonological distinctions, such as described by Carroll (1999). In the same study, Carroll shows that English L1 speakers who learn French are not very sensitive to these distinctions, contrary to children who learn French as an L1.

Hypothesis

To get back to the idea of a gender node, Guillelmon and Grosjean (2001) suggested that early French / English bilinguals store lemmas with features that include gender and are then capable of using gender to speed up word recognition. For the English native speakers who learn French after the so-called critical period, gender is no longer a systematic help. However, the role of the gender node in production would be linked to checking agreement, which leads us to more specific questions:

(1)   If we postulate the existence of gender nodes in French L2, the question is when and how they are activated. The hypothesis is that there is a link between using knowledge which could be declarative in essence and the position of the information in utterances and in discourse. Syntactic positions which claim room in the working memory or specific moments in discourse where retrieval from the mental lexicon has to be done concurrently with running the syntactic module and planning at both levels, utterance and discourse, may lead to choices where information from the context can supply the information otherwise given by the grammatical features.

(2)   If the gender node is activated properly as in the case of natural gender, the following question is about the potential influence of other levels than the grammatical encoder.

Data

The experiment was designed with two goals in mind: firstly, to find out more about knowledge and procedures relative to number and gender through a series of tests before looking at real-time production, and, secondly, to contrast the findings in various situations of production, from very constrained to freer but nonetheless complex verbal tasks. The experiment is thus in two parts (see Appendix for the lists of items and sentences used in the experimental tests). Half the informants did the test before the film retelling and before the descriptions, the other half the other way round.

Method

Experimental tests

All head nouns and adjectives used in the three experimental tests are extracted from the tables given in Le Goffic and Combe-McBride (1975).

Moreover, to check the impact of the task on production, native speakers were recorded performing the tests of repetition and replacement.

The first test is a simple task of gender assignment. As the participants hear a series of sound stimuli they have to choose, for each one, the correct form of determiner from a choice of two. The aim is to check declarative knowledge. The items chosen in this first task are used in both the second and third tasks, in which procedures are tested as well as storage in the lexicon.

The second task involves both comprehension and production: informants have to repeat sentences they hear twice in a given time slot calculated on the basis of a slow repetition by a native speaker. The goal is twofold: to compare the procedures used in marking gender and in marking number and to gain access to possible ways of storing forms in the mental lexicon. The hypothesis is that if one head noun appears with a different gender in the repetition, it reveals either that the form as such was not stored or that there was a more frequent one which was activated instead. The other interest of this task is to link erroneous inherent and derived gender and erroneous number-marking with syntactic positions in the sentence.

The third is a production task where informants have to transform sentences they hear and read from masculine into feminine. This task is also time-constrained, the time slot being calculated in the same way as in the second task. This third task is designed to check derived gender and link erroneous productions with syntactic positions.

Film retelling and descriptions

The other part of the data collection consists of a film retelling followed by several descriptions of the main characters in the film. Scenes from *West Side Story* were specifically chosen to stress concepts of plurality and/or differences in sex: for example when the two gangs fight each other, when male friends have a discussion over going to a dance, when female friends have a discussion over what to wear to the dance and when the male and the female main characters meet. All informants watch the first part of the film on their own, then retell what they have seen to an experimenter who needs to understand who the characters are because they will watch what comes after the first part.

After the narrative, the experimenter watches the second part of the film with the informant and asks questions about the identity of the characters based on what they both see and what the experimenter has been told. Questions in this descriptive part were designed to elicit answers about gender and number.

The discourse that results from the various questions such as: *what happened?* or *who is/are the character(s) we see on the screen?* is less constrained than the experimental tests, but the informant has to look for the form stored in memory while running the various procedures needed to create a series of sentences that are connected in a coherent way.

The Informants

The group of informants consists of British native speakers of English who, at the time of data collection, were studying French in an institutional setting. Their L1 is therefore dominant. They are considered as upper inter-mediate in French and all took part in undergraduate programmes. The age range is from 18 to 55. Their *'habitus'* (cf. Bourdieu) is therefore not the same. For example, younger students who haven't left the school system are more familiar with drills and tasks of a school type. In order to lessen the effect of the age factor, the group is divided in two. A first group (younger than 25) is made up of 13 students who started learning French in secondary school and have continued doing so at university. The average age is 23.7. A second group (older than 35) consists of 14 people who may have studied French when they were in secondary school but stopped and recently started learning the L2 at university while working. They attend evening classes either at Luton University or at Birkbeck College. Their average age is 41.8.

Experimental Tests

No statistics were run for the native speakers since only *hapax* (which are presented below) were found. Native speakers naturally do not hesitate when they assign gender to a noun and none experience any difficulty hearing the various items spoken. In the second test, that of repetition, one informant (Cedric) repeated the pronominal forms of sentences 4 and 14 leaving some ambiguity as to the vowel pronounced: in between [e] and [i].

For all, liaisons are made according to standard French:

(1)   Eric (NS)
      les petits_enfants attendent devant la télévision qui est_éteinte

In the third test, Eric once transforms the head noun from feminine into masculine but every modifier is thus masculine:

(2)   Eric (NS)
      le lion que j'ai acheté est gourmand

In the same test, another native speaker hesitates at the beginning:

(1)   Evelyne (NS)
      le le la chatte que j'ai achetée est mignonne

This seems to indicate that the model sentence they keep in front of them, which is in the masculine, activates the masculine gender. The attention required to deactivate the masculine node and to activate the feminine one takes time and explains the false start of Evelyne. However once it is done, the gender node helps to ensure that diacritic features are unified.

Assigning Gender to a Noun

Looking at global results, the non-native informants tend to know the gender of nouns frequently heard or seen.

The first test was specifically designed to check knowledge stored in the mental lexicon. Items on the list which are more frequently given the wrong gender are those which have an English equivalent, such as *lion, cat, cup, parent*. Taking the example of *lion*, the feminine phonic form in French [ljɔn] coincides with its English equivalent [lajən]. This either means that an English native speaker stores the two French forms, masculine and feminine, and accesses the feminine one more easily since the English cognate introduces a bias; or it means that the same speaker stores only one form, which would be the feminine one. The problem is similar with items ending in [ãt] [ãd].

One of the alternatives can be eliminated with the second task. In the second task, the informants hear a sound signal, which they need to store in memory to be able to repeat it afterwards. Items of proof are given that the informants attempt to associate a meaning with the sound signal to be able to reproduce it. When vocabulary is unknown to the speakers, they experience more difficulty in memorising the sound signal.

Calculations were made on the head nouns, independent of the satellites, whether determiners or adjectives. In the 15 sentences, 13 appear under a form which explicitly displays the inherent gender of the noun, of which seven are feminine: *étudiante* (×2), *danseuse* (×2), *couturière, coiffeuse, cliente*, and six masculine: *candidat, acteur, fermier, joueur, patron, ouvrier*. Masculine, which is the default case for the majority of French nouns, is better recovered than the feminine. Feminine forms which are transformed into masculine forms in the repetition are *étudiante* in the first sentence (43%

Table 7.1 Percentage of correct gender assignment

nouns	*X = 100%*	*90% < X < 100%*	*75% < X < 90%*	*50% < X < 75%*	*X < 50%*
groups					
less than 25	26%	16%	26%	23%	10%
more than 35	32%	16%	35%	13%	3%

Table 7.1b Items with lower and higher percentages

Nouns	less than 25	more than 35
menteuse	58%	100%
chatte	42%	71%
coupe	42%	50%
lionne	58%	29%
parente	33%	86%
artisan	100%	100%
danse	100%	100%
chien	100%	100%
coiffeuse	100%	100%
patron	100%	100%

Table 7.2 Correct restitution of gender

gender group	feminine	masculine
less than 25	59%	91%
more than 35	53%	78%

of correct answers, 46.5% of incorrect ones, and 10.5% of Ø) and *cliente* in the last one (28.5% correct, 68% incorrect, and 10.5% of Ø). It implies that for the words ending in either [ã] or [ãt], both forms are available. Note that the hypothesis about the informant being more prepared at the end of the test than at the beginning does not result in better accuracy: *cliente* is more often faulty than *étudiante*. *Etudiante* is also used in sentence XIV but contrary to the sentence I, it is preceded by an adjective, *bonne*, which already displays the feminine and the results are 64.5% correct occurrences and 35.5% incorrect ones.

  Danseuse (93% of correct answers in both sentences IV and X) and *coiffeuse* (sentence XI, 85.5% of correct answers, no wrong answers) offer no possible confusion for an English native speaker. Looking at *danseuse*, the English cognate *dancer* has a phonic form close to the masculine French form, *danseur*. However, both *danseuse* and *coiffeuse* are semantically associated more with the feminine sex than with the masculine one. *Acteur* in sentence III is repeated correctly by all the informants who could memorise the sentence.

  In summary, phonetics seems to play a disturbing role for the English native speakers who speak French, especially when it is not counterbalanced by semantics. In French, number and gender are not only phenomena of encoding on the nominal head but are used to group words together into phrases.

Agreement in Gender and Number

Agreement is both intra- and inter-phrastic. Gender is heard on the determiner when singular and many adjectives in attributive or predicative position. Number is heard on the determiner, sometimes on the adjective and in many cases on the verb form.

Looking at the agreement in gender between the nominal head and the adjectives, the results are higher for the masculine and that occurs in both groups.

Table 7.3a N-A agreement in a restitution task

groups	less than 25		more than 35	
	feminine	*masculine*	*feminine*	*masculine*
restitution				
correct	65%	91%	63%	83%
erroneous	19%	2%	14%	4%
ambiguous	7%	4%	5%	0%
Ø	10%	2%	18%	13%

Table 7.3b Restitution of gender

groups	less than 25	more than 35
restitution		
correct	74%	65%
erroneous	17%	20%
ambiguous	4%	3%
Ø	5%	12%

In other words, when the head is kept feminine, as it was in the original sentence, the adjective appears with the default case.

The percentages are not fundamentally different even though they are slightly higher when they concern agreement in number between the nominal head and the determiner. Few head nouns have a specific phonic plural form (except irregular cases such as *chevaux*), and the plural is essentially marked on determiners:

Table 7.4 Restitution of plural

groups	less than 25	more than 25
restitution		
correct	78%	78%
erroneous	10%	6%
ambiguous	0%	1%
Ø	12%	15%

The percentage of correct occurrences in S-V agreement is as high as that of correct occurrences in N-A agreement when N is masculine:

Table 7.5a S-V agreement in a restitution task

groups	less than 25		more than 35	
	plural	singular	plural	singular
restitution				
correct	85%	76%	80%	68%
erroneous	3%	8%	2%	9%
ambiguous	2%	8%	6%	9%
Ø	9%	7%	13%	15%

Note that results are in contradiction to the common hypothesis: singular is always the default case and should therefore be repeated in a higher proportion than plural. If ambiguous and Ø cases are not taken into consideration, the percentage of correct forms for the verbs when the subject is plural is respectively 96% for the younger group and 98% for the older group, while it is 90% and 89% when the subject is singular.

Table 7.5b Correct S-V agreement in a restitution task

groups	less than 25		more than 35	
	plural	singular	plural	singular
restitution				
correct	96%	90%	98%	89%

This can only be explained with the phenomenon of 'noise' which C. Carlo and I explain as follows: because informants have to produce speech in limited time periods, they have to anticipate and thus select characteristics according to their frequency. In this task, a third of the sentences have

NPs that are singular. Moreover, some NPs have the same heads: *étudiante*, *danseuse*. Memory seems to retain the category of number used in the previous sentences:

(1)   Arnold (younger than 25)
       les peintres <u>ont</u> parlé des villes qu'ils <u>ont</u> peintes
       les joueurs qui <u>ont</u> pris la balle <u>ont</u> gagné la bataille
       la danseuse qui vient **ont** été récompensées
       The 'noise' can affect more than just the last phrase:
(2)   Barbara (older than 35)
       <u>les</u> [p~et] les peintres <u>ont</u> parlé des villes [kizɔ̃] peintes
       <u>les</u> joueurs qui <u>ont</u> pris la la balle <u>ont</u> gagné la bataille
       les danseuses qui vient <u>ont</u> été récompensées

Besides this problem, which has something to do with the memorising of sound patterns, informants seem to experience less difficulty in making satellites agree with heads or heads together than reproducing the correct form of the nominal head.

Table 7.6 Gender assignment and agreement in a restitution task

groups	less than 25		more than 35	
	feminine	*masculine*	*feminine*	*masculine*
restitution				
correct gender assignment	59%	91%	53%	78%
correct N-A agreementt	77%	98%	82%	96%

Once the head is assigned a gender, whether it is the one given or the other one chosen, the informants tend to make the head agree with the satellites. In other words, informants transform the head noun from feminine into masculine more than they forget to dispatch the gender of the head to the satellites. It then seems that once a gender node is activated, it will be used to unify the diacritic features between the head noun and the satellites, which conforms to the results obtained on number and on S-V agreement. In both cases, it is no longer a question of lexicon but of procedures in the syntactic module.

The last interesting point is the relation between accuracy and syntactic positions: in the original sentences, I, II, IV and XI, several NPs appear with the plural definite article but they do not occupy the same syntactic position. Even if positions such as the beginning and end of a sentence are focal and thus better remembered, NPs in the subject position in the embedding clause are better processed than those in object or subject position in the embedded clause.

This influence of syntax on agreement can be better illustrated with the third test, where informants have to replace the masculine form of noun satellites by a feminine form. Comparing the various syntactic patterns given, we observe that agreement occurs not only according to gender itself but also to syntactic positions and frequency of occurrences.

Table 7.7 Gender in a substitution task

groups	less than 25		more than 35	
	feminine	masculine	feminine	masculine
noun and satellites				
head noun	79%	19% (= 98)	76%	18% (= 94)
article	60%	36% (= 96)	64%	27% (= 91)
adnominal adjective	31%	58%	33%	60%
predicative adjective	52%	37%	59%	37%
predicative NP	25%	53% (= 78)	31%	40% (= 71)

Table 7.8a Correct gender in a substitution task

	head	determiner	predicative adjective
groups			
less than 25	82%	79%	58%
more than 35	83%	83%	82%

Table 7.8b Correct gender in the second sentence

	head	determiner	predicative adjective
groups			
less than 25	84%	54%	68%
more than 35	67%	67%	82%

In sentence number 2, one attributive adjective precedes the head noun. In French, the most frequent position for this type of adjective is after the noun. For many of the informants, the syntactic module which checks that head and satellites are marked with the same gender was not run:

(3)   Zoe (younger than 25)
       c'est un beau danseuse qui est gourmande

When adjectives are predicative, marking varies: even if they tend to be marked with the default case, it also depends on the adjective itself. For example in sentence 1, *belle* is more easily accessed than *mignonne* (68% to 43%). Moreover when *belle* precedes the noun it sometimes triggers the feminine for the rest of the sentence: (79% for *belle* against 62% for *vieille*).

(4)   David (older than 35)
      c'est une c'est un vieux marchande qui est méchant
      c'est une belle danseuse qui est gourmande

There is a coalition of cues when the adjective 'belle' is combined with the head noun 'danseuse' and the link with the feminine node is more activated:

(5)   Tess (younger than 25)
      c'est un belle danseuse qui est gourmande
      c'est [un] bonne candidate qui est intelligent
      c'est [un] vieux marchand qui est méchante

Once again, as in the second test, because of semantic and pragmatic knowledge, the link between the word and the gender node is so strong that it enables the speaker to discard interference from possible English cognates or from complex syntactic structures.

What Can Be Deduced From the Experimental Tests?

Even if the gender of nouns is known, the information is not systematically available, more so when the constraints of the task imply too heavy a cognitive load.

In tests 2 and 3, gender is given, which makes it possible to find out when and how the syntactic module is run for both gender and number. The position of the item to be marked in the utterance influences the running of the syntactic module: for items after the head noun which require the use of the working memory, agreement varies proportionally to the distance between the head and the item to be agreed. The rule does not apply to attributive adjectives in pre-nominal position.

A closer examination of the errors leads us to the following hypothesis: independently of the storage in the mental lexicon and the syntactic module, the activation of a form, for the head noun or for any modifier, is caused by various factors at different levels of the production model:

- at the level of phonological encoding, when the closeness of an L1 form to a gender-marked L2 one influences the level of activation for the latter;

- at the level of semantics and pragmatics, when an item associated mentally with one sex influences the activation of the corresponding gender node.

In order to answer the question of storage and/or syntax raised by Carroll (1989), Dewaele and Véronique (2001) and Hawkins (1998), the filters given by the above hypothesis should enable us to analyse the informants' productions and eliminate what is related to the intrinsic diversity found in narration and description in order to focus on procedures used to solve the complex verbal task.

Narration and Description

Gender is not given in discourse production. Even if production is freer, it is linked to a multiplicity of operations which run simultaneously at various levels: planning at both levels utterance and discourse, accessing lemmas and their characteristics, running the syntactic module, and finding the sounds that correspond to what is obtained after the grammatical encoder. This should give us the opportunity to draw a map of resources in relation to discourse architecture.

Average numbers of occurrences[4] for each category in each group are compared in the following table:

Table 7.9 Average in narration and description

text type	group	masculine	feminine	plural	singular	S-V	N-A
narration	< 25	41.8%	35.7%	21%	56%	50.7%	15.7%
	> 35	51.2%	36.5%	28.2%	61.6%	54.2%	18%
description	< 25	36.4	23.3	12.3	47.6	36.2	13.3
	> 35	37.1	24.6	9.43	51.1	39.2	16

There are many more ambiguous cases in gender (assignment and agreement) than in number:

Table 7.10 Ambiguous cases in narration and description

text type	group	gender	number	S-V agreemt	N-A agreemt
narration	< 25	20%	5%	32%	48%
	> 35	23%	4%	37%	52%
description	< 25	21%	3%	31%	33%
	> 35	19%	3%	19%	56%

In all that follows, percentages of erroneous occurrences in both productions are calculated on the basis of evidence, which means first that ambiguous cases are not taken into account and second that the figures are calculated for gender on fewer occurrences than for number.

Table 7.11 Errors in narration and description

text type	group	masculine	feminine	number	S-V agreemt	N-A agreemt
narration	< 25	7.5%	18.5%	1.35%	3.1%	26.5%
	> 35	7%	15.5%	0.95%	3.5%	21.5%
description	< 25	7.75%	15.5%	0.5%	4.5%	22.25%
	> 35	8.5%	8.5%	0.3%	1.5%	32.5%

Assigning Gender to a Noun

Gender for many nouns in French is hard to guess; no semantic or formal principle such as those based on phonology are there to help. For example, *film* does not display its gender; there is no specific morpheme or end sound to reveal that it is masculine:

(6)   David (older than 35)
       c'est une film une série de petites films qui a commencé avec une
       scène dans une: une territoire pour le le basket ball . . .
       et les hommes [blõ/blã] a demandé des autres de l'autre groupe de
       donner le balle à l'autre groupe
       et puis la dernière scène était comme danse une le bal tu vois?

Matthews (1997) argues that if gender is not displayed on the head noun, the information is to be found in the determiner. Looking at *une film* (example 6), *film* would then be considered as feminine thanks to the fact that both determiner and modifier *petites (films)* are feminine. However, some may express doubts about why *petite* and not *petit* has been activated, especially in that pre-nominal position, and in the following example (7) both forms of the definite article, *le* and *la* are used with the same head noun.

More complex than *film* for an English native speaker is the French sound [bal]. David has problems with this sound. First, the same phonic form corresponds to two different referents in French and in English. Second, no obvious criterion could justify the fact that that sound is feminine when it means 'balloon' and turns masculine when it means 'dance', even more so when *ballon* is itself masculine and *danse* feminine.

David is so confused that he feels the need to ask the experimenter in the description:

(7) David (older than 35)
je crois que c'est le même homme qui qui est arrivé à l'appartement
avant de la bal pour eh [rãtr] cette fille
elle est l'étoile de la film le film
il est eh c'est c'est l'homme que le premier mec a invité au bal
< exp: d'accord >
c'est le bal ou la bal?

The same phenomenon already observed in the experimental tests, which we call 'contamination', can provide an explanation in some cases:

(8) William (younger than 25)
à la fin la robe était très jolie la jeune femme était très heureuse la robe était blanc eh blanche elle avait elle avait une centre rouge eh elle a dit magnifique

In a predominantly feminine surrounding, *centre* is assigned the same gender. The activated node remains activated for a while and thus contaminates the lemmas whose link with the masculine node is not strong. Agreement would thus be correct.

Agreement in Gender and Number

Running the syntactic module

Agreement in number and gender is not very different in narration and description from that in experimental tests. For example, when the referents are many, the informants mark the plurality with either a numeral or the plural definite article or both. When errors occur in discourse, it is on the pronominal forms, in other words when the distance between the head noun and the grammatical form is important:

(9) Elisa (younger than 25)
les jets eh cherchent des / je sais pas ce mot je connais pas ce mot ils veulent décider de eh d'avoir une bataille eh contre les sharks mais ils veulent d'accord avec [tut] le reste de la bande et c'est un conseil de guerre et **[il_esaj]** eh de décider leur le chose pour eh battre les couteaux etc.

The pronoun expected here is *ils* and the morpheme of plural should be heard with the liaison.

In most cases NP subjects agree with VP. When they don't, the NP subject is plural and the verb singular. In other words, the procedure to check unification between both heads has not been run:

(10)   Oprah (older than 35)
       le patron de cet groupe le chef eh il a voulu que **les** autres jeune_hommes eh **vient** avec lui pour prendre de la revanche contre l'autre groupe

The few cases found when the subject is singular and the verb plural has to do with the use of collectives:

(11)   Elisa (younger than 25)
       ce groupe sont les les [Zet] qui est le groupe américaine qui veut défendre le territoire contre les [Šark]

However, even though it was counted as incorrect, in the same context native speakers do not systematically know what to use after a collective.

A plural subject with a singular verb form is often observed when the context displays some syntactic complexity, i.e. when the verb form is in a different clause from the one where the lexical NP occurs:

(12)   Tess (younger than 25)
       ça te montre le [batr] la_haine [lamor] et l'amitié qui reste entre eh au moins les <u>deux filles qui</u> **vient** de les deux groupes: qui eh se détestent

The more distance there is between items sharing the same feature, the lower the rate of accuracy.

The rule applies for the agreement between head nouns and adjectives when, for example, the adjectives are in predicative position, in which case they are given the default value, which in many cases is the masculine one:

(13)   Irène (older than 35)
       l'histoire est bon la représentation est mauvais

In the first experimental test, Irène assigned the feminine gender to *histoire* and even if *représentation* was not part of the list in that test, it seems feminine too (definite article *la*).

In the experimental tests, when the adjective preceded the head noun, the informants seemed to forget to run the syntactic module:

Whatever the group, the result is identical in discourse. Taking away the ambiguous cases, the rate of accuracy follows a cline:

predicative NP > predicative Adjective > pre-nominal attributive adjective. When the informant uses a NP to predicate something about a referent, for example: *elle est la fille qui a fait la robe*, the second head noun is

Table 7.12 Rate of accuracy according to the position of the head modifier

groups	position and class	average per text	ambiguous %	correct %	erroneous %
< 25	prenominal adj	9.083	69%	17%	15%
	predicative adj	10.25	40%	40%	20%
	predicative NP	10.17	14%	78%	8%
> 35	prenominal adj	14.07	68%	22%	10%
	predicative adj	8.357	60%	32%	9%
	prenominal NP	8.643	9%	82%	9%

> 35 prenominal adjective: 68 + 22 + 10 = 100

what triggers the gender for the article or any other modifier in this second noun phrase.

Two reasons may be invoked to explain that in all kinds of production this pre-nominal position is more often erroneous than others. One is linked to the position itself: languages that have a [+strong] value of inflectional features also have their head move to a higher position to pick up inflection. This explains why in Romance languages most of the adjectives are in post-nominal position. The adjective is generated pre-nominally and its post-nominal position is derived from the movement of head over the adjective. Would the agreement be triggered by the move and percolate down to the adjectives over which the noun has been raised?

The other reason for erroneous production is linked to previous knowledge: attributive adjectives in English, which mostly appear in pre-nominal position, are invariable (English is characterised by having heads such as verbs and nouns with a [-strong] value). This position would then be more associated with the L1 than with the L2, and syntactic procedures associated with this position would be those of the L1.

Phonetics and semantics: which form is activated?

In some cases, the conclusion that the syntactic module has not been run is misleading. In example 8, note that William hesitates on the form to give to the adjective *blanc/blanche*. He finally opts for *blanche*. This could be because *blanche* is the default value like *belle* in the experimental tests. In example 17, Irène first chooses *blanche*. Two clues point to the masculine gender which ends up being selected, i.e. the referent to be qualified is male and the adjective is in predicative position (*il est blanche*), which is more often associated with the default case. Semantics obviously plays a role in how frequent a feminine or masculine form is selected.

The more frequently a form is selected, the higher its level of activation, and this applies to plural forms as well. These plural forms are replaced by singular ones when they differ from them:

(14)   Nelly (more than 35)
        la principale femme veut une robe magnifique . . .
        et l'homme et la femme principales se regardaient . . .

In the case of *principal*, the only form which combines masculine and plural ends in [o] and is therefore less often retrieved than the others. Furthermore, again the English equivalent introduces a noise into the search for the correct form and reinforces the access to the more frequent one. This influence of L1 is probably felt even more acutely for *important*:

(15)   Nelly (older than 35)
        je pense que dans la droite eh il y a peut-être un membre très importante de la groupe mais je ne sais pas qui est l'homme à gauche eh peut-être un ami

In this answer to a question about the two leaders of the groups, there is neither error about assignment, nor a lack of running the syntactic module since the head noun gets the masculine gender (default case) and the attributive adjective gets the feminine one (marked case). Wouldn't it be again a phonological problem? The closeness of the feminine form with the English cognate makes the feminine more easily accessible, being activated more often.

This problem is similar to the one found in the first experimental test with items ending in [ãt] or [ãd]:

(16)   Helen (younger than 25)
        et eh les mecs ils étaient assez jeunes mais ils étaient très violentes
        . . .
        je pense que les amis ben les le groupe de Maria était plus violente que l'autre groupe je pense

Looking at items ending in [ãt] or [ãd], and in [~e] or [yn], the rate of errors is above 20% in all cases:

When compared to the rate of errors in general (see Table 7.12) it is either equal or superior.

(17)   Irène (older than 35)
        la fille s'appelle Maria elle est blanche avec les cheveux eh pour une longue eh jusqu'aux ses épaules eh elle est jolie avec un eh une bouche généreuse et des des yeux [brn] je crois
        . . .

Table 7.13 Influence of phonetics on rate of errors

groups	sound	Average per text	correct %	erroneous %
< 25	[ã] / [ãt] or [ãd]	3.33	75%	25%
	[~e] / [yn]	6.17	80%	20%
> 35	[ã] / [ãt] or [ãd]	2.57	64%	28%
	[efi] / [yn]	4.64	66%	34%

> 35 [ã] / [ãt] or [ãd]: 64+28 = 92 (the remaining 8% are ambiguous cases).

le garçon est Tony le héros de ce film il est très blanche blanc il a les cheveux brunes.

In terms of pronunciation the indefinite article is like the pair *brun/brune*. The occurrences of the indefinite article have been contrasted with those of the definite article:

Table 7.14a Definite and indefinite articles in narration and description

groups	type of article	ambiguous		correct		erroneous	
		AV	%	AV	%	AV	%
< 25	definite	9.5	17%	38.2	70%	6.92	13%
	indefinite	1.75	7%	13.3	75%	3.33	19%
> 35	definite	9.71	17%	41.6	73%	5.29	9%
	indefinite	1.5	7%	14.8	72%	4.36	21%

AV = average of occurrences per text

Almost all the ambiguous occurrences of the definite article are due to the suppression of the vowel in the article when in front of a head noun or adjective starting with a vowel (see *l'homme* and *l'autre homme* in example 14).

The ambiguous cases for the indefinite article are due to pronunciation: [un], [n] are deviant forms which erase gender.

(18) Ruth (more than 35)
       c'est comme [un] danse comme [un] ballet c'est pas [real] la bagatelle c'est pas /
       E: et quand est-ce qu'ils se battent? (. . .) où où où est-ce / où et quand est-ce qu'ils se battent? au bal?
       une une pas le le l'homme [pr~esipo] mais je pense que l'autre homme dans le dans / une des autres deux autres hommes je ne sais pas comment dire dans des gangs

The sound [y] in *une* as in *une une pas le l'homme* is clearer than in [un] as in *[un] danse* or *[un] ballet*. Ruth, however, has one form for the indefinite article with various phonic output.

In total, the number of correct occurrences is three times as high for the definite article as for the indefinite and that in both groups.

Table 7.14b Rate of gender errors for the articles

groups		*definite*	*indefinite*
< 25	non ambiguous occurrences	45.12	16.63
	rate of errors	15%	20%
> 35	occurrences non ambiguous	46.89	19.16
	rate of errors	11%	23%

Even though the difference in percentage is not that high, especially in the younger group, the fact that the calculation is made on many more occurrences for the definite than for the indefinite is an indication that the indefinite article is erroneous more often than the definite article. We consider that phonetics is unlikely to be the sole cause of this difference. Both definite and indefinite articles are closely linked to the position of the NP in discourse. Another criterion, which could not be dealt with in the experimental tests, is the discourse structure.

Narrative structure and errors in gender

Narration, being less guided (for example, sometimes the experimenter even repeated erroneous items so as not to provide information about gender for example) and less constrained than description, offers interesting insights as to where the errors occur. To ensure that errors of assignment are not included, only items with semantically based gender are considered:

In the following example, gender is semantically based:

(19)   Ursula (less than 25)
         après on a vu un jeune fille avec sa mère

The choice of the most difficult form in terms of pronunciation for an English L1 speaker rules out phonetics as a reason for error in this case. This implies that the syntactic module was not run and that the article was given the default value, which may be explained in terms of resources: this is the beginning of a new episode, therefore the informant needs to give the new setting, new characters, and a new place. Planning activities are at their highest and the need for resources therefore is very high (Green, 1986).

Table 7.15 Natural gender agreement in narration

groups	less than 25		more than 35	
	right	*wrong*	*right*	*wrong*
discourse values				
specific indefinite	3	0.5	2.29	0.79
ambiguous [un]	0.33		0.07	
specific definite	20.08	1.08	13.71	0.29
ambiguous pronoun	0.08		0.14	
non referential	1.42	0.17	1.14	0.07
ambiguous l'	2		0.5	

All numbers correspond to an average per text.

When the referents are maintained, the encoding is either lexical with the definite article or pronominal:

(20) Lena (less than 25)
      il y a Ø autre fille dans un magasin différent avec un eh femme un peu
      vieux que elle qui a qui faire un robe robe pour le bal pour la la femme
      la femme est environ de dix huit ans je pense
      et elle a dit que le la robe est n'est pas bien pour elle c'est trop haut

Gender becomes crucial when it comes to anaphoric linkage.

Results found in Table 15 are confirmed: in both groups, rates of accuracy are higher with the definite article than with the indefinite (94.9% and 97.5% vs. 85.7% and 74.4%). When problems remain with the definite article, local elements might trigger the wrong gender, as in 21, where the masculine gender, the default case, is predominant in the first part of the utterance.

(21) Nelly (more than 35)
      il y a les deux groupes eh des amis eh qui sont rivaux et je pense que
      l'homme principal est du groupe des jet et le [pr~esipal] femme des
      shark

Moreover, the adjective modifying the head noun *femme* is in pre-nominal position, and adjectives in such position are more often kept invariable than in post-nominal positions.

Even though the extract of Krystin's text below (example 22) is the beginning of a new episode, which means that referents are newly introduced, Krystin is unable to assume that the experimenter she describes the film to does not know it:

(22) Krystin (less than 25)
      et après ça il y a la fille eh et je ne sais pas si c'était eh sa mère
      je crois pas je crois que c'était un ami eh qui a fini sa robe

As a result, she introduces new referents as if they were part of shared
knowledge, thus no error is found in the use of the definite article. As for
the NP with predicative value, *sa mère*, it is difficult to evaluate the possessive (it could be feminine because of the possessor and not because of the
possessed). For the other NP, *un ami*, the indefinite article is given the
default case, masculine.

At the beginning of a new episode, planning constrains the speaker to
say how many referents are introduced:

(23) Barbara (more than 35)
      puis on passe à une autre scène où on voit deux jeunes filles eh et eh il
      y a un qui qui eh <2s> elle a peut-être une aiguille pour réparer ou
      pour préparer une robe pour l'autre oui pour la danse

When they are of the same sex, the emphasis remains on number. As
soon as the emphasis switches to the referent and its essential feature in
order to create anaphoric linkage, no linguistic characteristic is
neglected:

(24) Tess (less than 25)
      et après ça eh il y a **une** des hommes qui va chez /
      . . .
      et puis après tu vois une fille en train de discuter avec une autre fille
      dans un autre endroit
      devant eh entre **eux** il y a un machine à coudre
      et eh il y a une fille qui est entrain de coudre une robe pour l'autre
      et puis **elles** sont entrain de discuter de l'homme d'un homme et puis
      eh qu'est-ce [ki] veut qu'est-ce [ki] veut
      et puis y a une fille qui sort avec l'homme qui arrive

Thus almost no errors are found on the pronominal forms except when
they combine gender and number. Plural seems to be a feature which
erases gender (see *eux* in example 25 and *ils* in 26)

(25) Elisa (less than 25)
      mais l'autre fille eh elle est une shark et elle veut que Maria sort avec
      Gino qui est un autre shark et c'est une discus / eh **ils_ont ils** discutent
      le bal etc.

When a L2 speaker is faced with a complex verbal task, where a multiplicity of information has to be encoded in one form, that speaker may be

forced to omit the marking of grammatical notions that require conscious-ness and attention. L2 speakers, like L1 speakers, usually choose to mark number at the expense of gender, which shows that knowledge relative to gender is for the L2 speakers not yet automatised.

What does the comparison between different tasks yield?

On storing and accessing lemmas:

Lemmas are not systematically stored with their gender, and accessing the form of the lemma differs depending on the strength of the link between the lemma and the corresponding gender node.

- For lemmas whose activation is frequent, or for those whose gender is semantically based, to postulate that there is a link with one gender node is not far-fetched.
- For all the others, there is probably no link and the speaker must attend to the characteristic of gender while speaking, which would explain the phenomenon of contamination inside one system or in between systems, when the L1 introduces a bias to one of the forms.

On Running the Syntactic Module

Pienemann's (1998) proposed order of acquisition of procedures corre-sponds only partially to our findings: phrasal procedures preceding sentence procedures with word-order rules when it comes to configura-tional languages. For example, when in French L2 the attributive adjective occupies the pre-nominal position, the standard position in English L1, speakers stop using procedures they have nonetheless acquired and used in other contexts, hence the lack of agreement in gender and sometimes in number. The same informant uses *les jeune_hommes, les_hommes* or *le jeune_homme*, thus the 'H' is not a barrier for the liaison.

Following Green (1986), Prodeau and Carlo (2000) have hypothesised that in complex verbal tasks, native and non-native speakers alike do not run the syntactic module when resources are lacking, a situation experi-enced due to syntactic and discourse complexity. Non-native speakers need more resources than native ones to attend to top and bottom opera-tions at the same time. The beginning of an episode appears to be one of those moments in text when discourse complexity is high. This accounts for the poorer results when the article is indefinite than when it is definite. L2 speakers select the grammatical notions they will encode, depending on global comprehension.

Conclusion

The fact that the informants chosen were not of the same age group did not affect the results. Even if differences between the two age groups are significant in some cases,[5] the general tendency is the same in both groups. There are indeed, as Carroll (1989) said, problems of storage but even when storage is correct, *i.e.* when the lemma is stored with all its features, and even when we have no doubt that there is a link between the lemma and the gender node, the running of the syntactic module to check agreement is not systematic (Hawkins, 1998). Syntactic procedures of the L1, when the L1 and L2 mental lexicon interpenetrate, are all factors that play a role when resources are insufficient. Gender is neglected when it is not fundamental for comprehension.

Various factors can explain errors in free production. They could be related to the kind of task the speaker is involved in and to previous knowledge such as the L1. Other L1/L2 configurations should therefore be scrutinised to examine how precisely this influence can be exerted.

Acknowledgment

I would like to thank J.-M. Dewaele of Birkbeck College, University of London and C. Lewis Villien of Luton University for their help in collecting the data. I would also like to thank A. E. J. Wolf of Cambridge University and the anonymous reviewers for their useful comments.

Notes

1. I refer to Green's definition of the different levels of activation (1986):
   (a) dormant: in the long term memory, no involvement with the production process;
   (b) active: plays a role in the production process;
   (c) selected: highest level of activation for words, phonemes . . .
2. Spanish, Italian and French have two genders, masculine and feminine. When the referent is human or animate with a clear distinction in terms of sex, gender is semantically founded. Otherwise, gender is formally based on quite regular phonetic patterns.
3. Grosjean (1997) defines monolingual and bilingual modes as ends of a continuum: on the one end, only one system is activated, on the other, both are equally activated.
4. The calculation was made as follows:
   Susan (older than 35)

   > la première scène est à New York où les deux groupes de de jeunes hommes eh sont en [piõ] pour se battre et eh il y a deux groupes opposés eh qui eh fait des [piõ] pour eh dans un cour de de basket ball les deux groupes s'appellent les [dZEts] et les [Šarks]

   The first NP is feminine (*la première scène*) and is considered correct. The two following ones are masculine: *groupe* and *homme*. However, if it seems obvious that *homme* is masculine, there is nothing to figure out the gender assigned to *groupe*. So it will be marked plural but with an unknown gender. As for *hommes*, the transcription made according to standard French does not preclude the analysis, which is unknown marking for number. Contrary to *hommes*, the presence of the numeral *deux* is sufficient to declare *groupes* in the NP, *deux groupes opposés*, plural. There are several cases of S-V agreement in that little extract: *la première scène est, les deux groupes sont, deux groupes opposés qui fait, les deux groupes s'appellent*. The agreement is marked correct for the first two, incorrect for the third and unknown for the fourth. Similarly three N-A agreements are to be found in this extract: *la première scène, jeunes hommes, deux groupes opposés*. Only the first is considered correct, the other two are marked unknown; there is no sound opposition to mark gender for both *opposé* and *jeune*. Moreover, the fact that Susan pauses between *jeunes* and *hommes* (no [Znom] or [Znzom]) does not enable the researcher to find out whether *jeunes* agrees with *hommes* in terms of number, it is thus marked unknown. The only NPs left are *un cour de basket ball, les jets et les sharks*. In terms of gender, *basket ball, jet* and *shark* are not counted because they are obviously borrowed from the original English version of the film. As for *cour*, feminine in standard French, it is marked incorrect. So in total there are: 4 masculine, 2 feminine, 5 plural, 2 singular, 4 S-V agreement and 3 N-A agreement.

5.   T-tests are needed to compare the results obtained in each group.

References

Bourdieu, P. (1991) *Language and Symbolic Power*. Cambridge: Polity Press.

Bruhn de Garavito, J. and White, L. (2000) L2 acquisition of Spanish DPs: The status of grammatical features. In A.T. Pérez-Leroux and J. Liceras (eds) *The Acquisition of Spanish Morphosyntax: The L1/L2 Connection*. Amsterdam: Kluwer.

Carroll, S. (1989) Second language acquisition and the computational paradigm. *Language Learning* 39 (3), 535–94.

Carroll, S. (1999) Input and SLA: Adults' sensitivity to different sorts of cues to French gender. *Language Learning* 49 (1), 37–92.

Comrie, B. (1999) Grammatical gender systems: A linguist's assessment. *Journal of Psycholinguistic Research* 28 (5), 457–66.

Concise Oxford Dictionary of Linguistics (1997).

Corbett, G. (1991) *Gender*. Cambridge: Cambridge University Press.

De Bot, K. (1992) A bilingual production model: Levelt's 'Speaking Model' adapted. *Applied Linguistics* 13 (1), 1–24.

DeVincenzi, M. (1999) Differences between the morphology of gender and number: evidence from establishing coreferences. *Journal of Psycholinguistic Research* 28 (5), 537–53.

Dewaele, J.-M . and Véronique, D. (2000) Relating gender errors to morphosyntax and lexicon in advanced French interlanguage. *Studia Linguistica* 54 (2), 212–24.

Dewaele, J.-M. and Véronique, D. (2001) Gender assignment and gender agreement in advanced French interlanguage: A cross-sectional study. *Bilingualism: Language and Cognition* 4 (3), 275–97.

Dominguez, A., Cuetos, F. and Segui, J. (1999) The processing of grammatical gender and number in Spanish. *Journal of Psycholinguistic Research* 28 (5), 485–98.

Green, D.W. (1986) Control, activation and resource: A framework and a model for the control of speech in bilinguals. *Brain and Language* 27, 210–23.

Grosjean, F. (1997) Processing mixed languages: issues, findings and models. In A.

M. D. de Groot and J. Kroll (eds.) *Tutorials in Bilingualism/ Psycholinguistic Perspective* (pp. 225–254). Hillsdale NJ: Lawrence Erlbaum.

Grosjean, F., Dommergues, J.Y., Cornu, E., Guillelmon, D. and Besson, C. (1994) The gender-marking effect in spoken word recognition. *Perception and Psychophysics* 56 (5), 590–98.

Guillelmon, D. and Grosjean, F. (2001) The gender marking effect in spoken word recognition: The case of bilinguals. *Memory and Cognition* 29 (3), 503–11.

Hawkins, R. (1998) Explaining the difficulty of gender attribution for speakers of English. Paper presented at Eurosla 8, Paris, September.

Koehn, C. (1990) The acquisition of gender and number within NP. In J.M. Meisel (ed.) *Two First Languages. Early Grammatical Development in Bilingual Children* (pp. 29–51). Dordrecht: Foris.

Le Goffic, P. and Combe-McBride, N. (1975) *Les constructions fondamentales du français*. Paris: Hachette, Larousse.

Levelt, W.J.M. (1989) *Speaking: From Intention to Articulation.* Cambridge, MA: MIT Press.

Mills, A.E. (1986) Acquisition of the natural gender rule in English and German. *Linguistics* 24 (1), 31–45.

Müller, N. (1990) Developing two gender assignment systems simultaneously. In J.M. Meisel (ed) *Two First Languages. Early Grammatical Development in Bilingual Children* (pp. 193–234). Dordrecht: Foris.

Paradis, M. (1987) *The Assessment of Bilingual Aphasia* Hillsdale, NY: Lawrence Erlbaum.

Parodi, T., Schwartz, B. and Clahsen, H. (1997) On the L2 acquisition of the morphosyntax of German nominals. *Essex Research Reports in Linguistics* 15, 1–43.

Pienemann, M. (1998) *Language Processing and Second Language Development: Processability Theory.* Amsterdam-Philadelphia: Benjamins.

Prodeau, M. and Carlo, C. (2000) Le genre et le nombre en français L2, traitement dans différentes tâches verbales. Paper presented at COFDELA IIIrd International Conference, Avignon, October.

Schriefers, H. and Jescheniak, J.D. (1999) Representation and processing of grammatical gender in language production: A review. *Journal of Psycholinguistic Research* 28 (6), 575–600.

Appendix

Task 1: List of items used

1: ce/cette (toile); 2: un/une (artisan); 3: un/une (menteuse); 4: ce/cet (acteur); 5: le/la (candidat); 6: un/une (histoire); 7: le/la (tableau); 8: un/une (chatte); 9: ce/cette (coupe); 10: un/une cuisinière; 11: ce/cette (charcutier); 12: un/une (lionne); 13: un/une (fermier); 14: un/une (parente); 15: un/une (marchande); 16: le/la (danse); 17: un/une (voisin); 18: un/une (cheval); 19: un/une étudiante; 20: le/la (groupe); 21: un/une (contrôleur); 22: un/une (conseiller); 23: un/une (infirmière); 24: ce/cette (chanson); 25: cet/cette (agriculteur); 26: un/une (chien); 27: ce/cette (cliente); 28: un/une (citoyen); 29: le/la (coiffeuse); 30: un/une (habitant); 31: le/la (travailleur); 32: un/une (cousine); 33: le/la (patron); 34: un/une (robe)

Task 2: List of sentences used

1   les jeunes étudiantes ont vu les toiles que les artistes ont peintes
2. Les nouvelles chansons ont été apprises par les jeunes candidats
3. L'acteur qui a remporté la coupe est chinois
4. Les nouvelles danseuses ont répété les danses qu'elles ont apprises
5. Les fermiers qui ramènent les chevaux sont récompensés
6. La belle couturière qui a fait la robe est blonde
7. De belles fleurs sont ouvertes après la pluie
8. Les peintres ont parlé des villes qu'ils ont peintes
9. Les joueurs qui ont pris la balle ont gagné la bataille
10. La danseuse qui vient a été récompensée
11. Les jeunes coiffeuses ont été soumises à des épreuves difficiles
12. Les petits enfants attendent devant la télévision qui est éteinte
13. Le patron qui a embauché l'ouvrier est roux
14. Ces bonnes étudiantes ont oublié les devoirs qu'elles ont faits
15. Les gentilles clientes qui étaient là sont parties

Task 3: List of sentences and items given

1. Le chien que j'ai acheté est malin
    chatte mignon, lionne gourmand, toile beau
2. C'est un petit bureau qui est ancien
    beau danseuse gourmand, bon candidate intelligent, vieux marchande méchant
3. Le frère qui est étudiant est beau
    copine contrôleur intelligent, cuisinière menteur petit, voisine jardinier content

Chapter 8

The Development of Gender Attribution and Gender Agreement in French: A Comparison of Bilingual First and Second Language Learners

JONAS GRANFELDT

Introduction

This chapter aims to explore the development in child and adult grammars of a noun-related feature in French, namely gender. In brief, previous research has shown that gender assignment and gender agreement in a language such as French is just as easy for the mono- or bilingual child (Carroll, 1989; Clark, 1985; Müller, 1990, 1994) as it is difficult for the (adult) L2 learner (Bartning, 2000; Carroll, 1989, 1999; Dewaele & Véronique, 2000, 2001; Harley, 1979; Hawkins, 1998, 2001). In their own right, these findings make it interesting to compare the development of gender in an age and/or an L1-L2 perspective, but to date few such comparative studies have been carried out (but see Andersson, 1992 on Swedish). Furthermore, since gender classification of individual nouns differs from one language to another, it must be learnt by exposure to input. Therefore, studying how gender is acquired might help to discover specific properties of different modes of acquisition.

In this study, a cross-learner perspective is adopted, comparing the acquisition of gender in two different modes of acquisition: the acquisition of French as a second language at an adult stage (L1 = Swedish) and the acquisition of French as one of two first languages where the other language is Swedish.

With respect to L2 acquisition of French gender, previous research has typically used cross-sectional data. This research has established the scope and the generality of the problem across (other) individual differences and across speakers' L1s (for example English, Flemish and Swedish). From this research we have substantial facts about 'the problem stage'. Much less seems to be known about whether and how adult second language learners can develop further with respect to gender.

In the present study, a longitudinal perspective on gender acquisition is therefore adopted. Previous cross-sectional research (Bartning, 2000) suggests that learners at lower levels of proficiency make more errors with respect to gender agreement than do advanced learners. The adult learners in this study have been subject to other studies of grammatical development concerning the clause and the noun phrase and have been found to develop in several areas (cf. Granfeldt, 2000a and b; Granfeldt & Schlyter, forthcoming; Schlyter, 1997, this volume and 2003). This study asks the question of whether a general development can be established within individual learners with respect to gender.

The longitudinal perspective also allows for a closer inspection of the different modes of acquisition. The chapter asks the question of whether there are qualitative differences between the way gender is acquired by the children and by the adults, and in particular how the development itself proceeds in the two cases. It will, in fact, be demonstrated that there are major differences in the way gender is acquired by the children and the adults.

Gender and Development

In the framework adopted here, the task of learning gender attribution can be represented in a highly simplified fashion as in Figure 8.1.

Figure 8.1 illustrates two simplified lexical entries for the French word *maison* at two different times. At Time$_x$, only the categorial features of the noun are specified ([–V], [+N]).[1] It is assumed for first language acquisition that all possible features of a natural language are provided from the outset

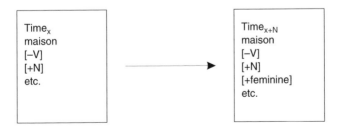

Figure 8.1 Development. Lexical entries for the word *maison* at two distinct times

of language acquisition (Chomsky, 1998). The task for the child is therefore that of selection, i.e. selection/activation of the features relevant to the language being acquired. Furthermore, it is possible that some features are universal and therefore not subject to selection whereas others are parameterised and acquired incrementally (Radford, 2000). Gender is not encoded in all languages and Figure 8.1 illustrates the hypothesis that there is a stage in acquisition where a French noun does not contain a gender feature.

At Time$_{x+N}$, the gender feature [+feminine] has been specified and integrated into the lexical entry. The attribution of [+feminine] to *maison* is of course learned by exposure to input. The task of the child is again that of selection, i.e. to decide whether a particular noun is [+feminine] or [-feminine]. But in a language such as French, where gender is predictable only in part of the inventory of nouns (cf. Corbett, 1991), this selection must be more inductive (i.e. more local) than selection of the gender feature itself.[2]

In the view of the lexicon-syntax interface adopted here, features of lexical entries project and depend on syntactic Functional Categories (FCs) for checking, deletion and ultimately for interpretation (Chomsky, 1995). It is a standard assumption that the features of the noun project an Extended Projection (EP) containing at least two FCs. The features of the noun will be checked (and deleted) against their copies on the FCs, before or after spell-out depending on feature strength.

Put simply, the addition (i.e. attribution) of a grammatical feature such as gender to the lexical entry of *maison* will in syntax produce an agreement effect on the word's satellites. In French, the agreement will be overtly marked on a subset of determiners and adjectives. But, as in the case of selection of the gender feature itself, the syntactic part of gender, of course, also affects the system globally.

Put this way, gender is present at three different levels in French: first as an abstract feature inherent to the class of nouns (Carroll, 1989); second as a (more) local choice of [+/- feminine]; and third, in syntax, as a grammatical feature triggering agreement between constituents.

Gender in Swedish and French

Both Swedish and French have binary grammatical gender systems. Modern-day Swedish distinguishes common from neuter gender (1a and 1b), whereas French has a grammaticalised feminine vs. masculine distinction (2a and 2b).[3] In both languages, the two genders are unequally distributed: about 70% of all French nouns are masculine and approximately 70–75% of all Swedish nouns have common gender (Andersson,

1992). This distribution will probably produce an overlap of masculine French nouns and common Swedish nouns, but apart from this frequency effect there seems to be no simple correspondences between the two lexicons, although such a correlation cannot be excluded.

(1)	a. en	gammal	bil
	a.indef.COMM.	*old.Sing.COMM*	*car:Sing.COMM.*
	b. ett	gammal-t	paraply
	a.indef.NEUTER	*old. Sing. NEUTER*	*umbrella:Sing.NEUTER*
(2)	a. une	vieille	voiture
	a.indef.FEM.	*old.Sing.FEM*	*car:Sing.FEM*
	b. un	vieux	parapluie
	a.indef.MASC	*old.Sing.MASC*	*umbrella:Sing.MASC*

As the above examples show, the gender feature produces an overt agreement effect on both the article and the adjective in both languages. The morphological gender distinction on the adjectives is lost in Swedish when the Noun Phrase is definite. In spoken French, only a third of all adjectives are gender-marked overtly (Riegel *et al.*, 1997), but the distinction is made on more than half of the adjectives in the register referred to as 'Français fondamental' (Surridge, 1993). In both languages, the overt gender agreement is lost in the plural, both on articles and adjectives.

Previous Studies

A number of scholars have asked somewhat different questions with respect to Figure 8.1, even though longitudinal studies in L2 are relatively scarce. In the following sections, the focus will be on research on French.

Triggering Assignment

One issue concerns possible triggers/cues for gender assignment. The impact of phonological, semantic and morphological properties of nouns is discussed in the literature. With respect to L1 acquisition, the well-known work of Karmiloff-Smith (1979) suggested that French children do have a creative assignment system based on formal properties. This confirmed the study by Tucker, Lambert and Rigault (1977) on adult native speakers (NS), who also demonstrated an ability to assign gender to novel nouns based on phonological properties. In an another study on 'French children', Surridge (1993) also found a primacy for phonological cues in gender assignment to simple nouns.

Carroll (1999), in a review of the literature, finds it settled that morphophonological cues are in fact the first to be considered by the child, whereas semantic cues only are learned relatively late. Müller (1999 and earlier studies) tries to show that French and German children draw on both formal (morphophonological) and semantic properties simultaneously (Müller, 1999: 352). Another perspective is offered by Carroll (1989), who points to the fact that gender is an inherent feature of the noun, but also a derivative property of determiners and adjectives. She argues that, for L1 acquisition: 'The clues for gender attribution for a word such as p ❑ m ❑ [. . .] are to be found rather in the syntactic context; namely in the words that agree with the noun' (Carroll, 1989: 551). At least for monosyllabic nouns, syntactic cues, i.e. structures where gender agreement is apparent, will act as a trigger for attribution.

With respect to L2 acquisition, Chini's (1995) work on L2 Italian provided support for a formal primacy, just as in L1 acquisition: 'D'après nos données, les critères d'attribution du G aux noms, semblent être d'abord phonologiques (terminaisons), puis sémantiques (sexe du référent) ou morphologiques (suffixes)' (Chini, 1995: 124–25). At least with respect to French, however, there seems to be general agreement that semantic cues (i.e. natural gender) are the first explored by the learner (Carroll, 1999; Harley, 1979; Surridge, 1993; cf. also Andersen, 1984 on L2 Spanish).

In order to investigate sensitivity to cue types, Carroll (1999) conducted an experiment with 88 speakers of English. Results indicated that generalisations are best / first / most easily made from semantics, i.e. natural gender is most likely to be acquired first (Carroll, 1999: 70).

Agreement D-N and D-A-N/D-N-A

Gender agreement in first language acquisition is often described as principled, and rapidly acquired without much error (Clark, 1985). Errors are nonetheless revealing. Müller (1990, 1994, 1995, and 1999), in her study of German-French bilinguals, found that, in the limited set of gender errors, the indefinite article was overrepresented. The children she studied had difficulties in acquiring the feminine indefinite article in French, *une*. Müller (1999) assumed that the indefinite article is first used as a numeral by the children and that once the feature [-definite] is associated with the indefinite article, gender agreement will be triggered.

As for L2 French, agreement has recently been discussed extensively (Bartning, 2000; Dewaele & Véronique, 2000, 2001; Hawkins, 1998, 2001; cf. also Chini, 1995 on L2 Italian). A common finding in these studies is that, in early L2, gender marking is more correct on determiners than on adjectives. Across learners' L1, this result emerges from two recent studies.

Bartning (2000), in a cross-sectional study, examined both advanced Swedish L2 learners (cf. Bartning, 1997) and pre-advanced L2 learners with respect to gender in French. Results indicated that the advanced learners scored significantly better than did the pre-advanced learners. Determiners were more correct than adjectives and it was more difficult for the learners to mark gender correctly on the indefinite article than on the definite article. Finally, both learner groups overgeneralised the masculine form.

Dewaele and Véronique (2000, 2001) applied the predictions of the *Processability Theory* (PT) (Pienemann, 1998) to the acquisition of gender assignment and gender agreement in French. Whereas the results did not support the predictions of PT, they confirmed previous findings that use of determiners is more correct than that of adjectives and that the masculine is overgeneralised. The authors proposed seven different scenarios, ranging from psycholinguistic to social factors, to account for the gender errors.

Looking only at articles, Hawkins (1998, unpublished but discussed in Hawkins, 2001b: 255–57) proposes a somewhat different interpretation of English speaking subjects' problems with French gender. Subjects were advanced university students of French in Canada and the UK. Hawkins found an effect of overgeneralising specific articles. The non-paradigmatic overgeneralisation was supported by the fact that the overgeneralised gender could be different with respect to definiteness, i.e. the overgeneralised definite article could be *le*, but *une* for indefiniteness. Hawkins also asked how learners come to use one article correctly with some nouns. He suggests that English learners, who have no grammatical gender feature in their L1, establish a set of exceptions to the default article without ever acquiring the gender feature itself.

Rationale and Research Questions

The cross-learner perspective adopted here allows for more general reflections on the properties of different modes of acquisition. Taking previous L1 and L2 studies into account, it has been suggested that gender is a candidate for being likely to be particularly affected by the acquirer's age, i.e. gender acquisition is subject to a critical age of onset. In an another framework, Andersson (1992, on Swedish) showed explicitly that, at least with respect to quantitative variables, gender is more a question of age of onset than of L1 and L2 acquisition: all the early L2 learners in his study performed better than the late and adult L2 learners (Andersson, 1992: 191). As expected, the L1 learners performed best, but were at the same time comparable to the early L2 learners (cf. also Möhring, 2001 on experimental data from early child L2 French).

But, on the other hand, there is no consensus with respect to the linguistic explanation for these facts. Carroll (1989) suggested that the anglophone learners of French had 'lost' the possibility of assigning gender and that determiners were learned through relexification. She also predicted that learners whose L1 include a grammatical gender feature will have few problems acquiring this aspect of French (Carroll, 1989: 573). Somewhat differently, but also for anglophones, Hawkins (1998 and also 2001) argued that the fossilisation is syntactic (see also Hawkins & Chan, 1997), in the sense that the relevant Functional Category (FC) (assumed to be NumP) will lack gender feature. One possible interpretation of Hawkins' proposal is that, even if learners are able to 'assign' a gender to the lexical entry, the feature will never be copied onto the relevant FC, since this would mean a resetting of a parametric choice of that particular FC (Tsimpli & Roussou, 1991 cited by Hawkins, 2001b: 206). Thus, there will be no syntactic 'reflex' of the, although possible, gender feature in the lexicon, resulting in the default system discussed in the previous section (cf. also Andersen (1984: 98) in a different framework).[4]

Now, if gender is subject to a critical period for acquisition, then one could expect the adult Swedish learners to remain at the same level of proficiency throughout development. In other words, we would expect them to develop in other areas but not with respect to gender, if not only at a surface level (e.g. becoming increasingly more proficient in handling a list of exceptions to a default, cf. Hawkins, 1998). On the other hand, theories like those of Carroll (1989) and Hawkins and Chan (1997) would seem to predict that since Swedish is a gendered language, this feature is acquirable also in their L2 French. Applying Carroll's relexification hypothesis to our case, we would expect the gender feature of Swedish determiners to carry over initially. On the other hand, Hawkins and Chan (1997) remain silent with respect to the initial stage but predict that, since the relevant FC contains a gender feature, gender will be acquired.

In the light of the above discussion, I propose the following research questions:

(A) Is gender attribution possible in adult L2 acquisition of French? If so, does it develop in individual learners, and how does it develop?

The second question deals with the possible differences between the adults and the bilingual children:

(B) If it is the case that the children and the adults differ in their performance on gender, how can this be accounted for (a) with respect to the type of knowledge that gender represents (cf. Section 1) and (b) with respect to the answer to question (A)?

In the following analysis these questions will be evaluated in Sections 5 and 6. The second question is discussed in relation to a case study on one adult learner and three children (Section 6). In this section the nature of the claimed development in the adults is also discussed. First, however, the data and the method used will be presented.

The Present Study

In this study, I will analyse gender assignment and gender agreement longitudinally in 2L1 and L2 French. The data have been taken from spontaneous speech (cf. also Schlyter, this volume). The children are bilingual from birth, having one French-speaking parent (here, the mother) and one Swedish-speaking parent (here, the father). The parents raised their children using the one-parent, one-language strategy. A research assistant made recordings at the children's home during spontaneous play and interaction between the child and the parent. Recordings started around the age of 2;0 (year; month) and continued regularly up to the age of four years (see also Schlyter, 1993, 1994).

Two groups of adult Swedish acquirers are considered: one group of five untutored (naturalistic) learners of French who, with one exception (Henry), lived for an extended period in Paris. These were different types of artist (musicians, painters, etc.) and one physicist, all of whom had received little or no instruction in French before or during their stay in France. The corpus is partly cross-sectional and partly longitudinal. It is cross-sectional in the sense that the time of exposure prior to the first recording range from the third month after arrival to (approx.) 20 months of immersion. The corpus is longitudinal in the sense that all learners were recorded at at least two distinct times of exposure. No learner, however, was studied for more than 15 months.

Recordings consist of spontaneous conversation about everyday life, future plans and past events, and include some guided tasks (narration, translation). With the exception of the translation task, which was excluded, all spontaneous production is considered independent of task production.

The second group of adult learners consists of tutored Swedish learners of French. Two learners are considered here, both first-semester students of French at Lund University, Sweden. They had not been to a French-speaking country for more than one week but had already received, at the beginning of the data-collection period, some 500 hours of French instruction in secondary school. The corpus is longitudinal and covers the first five months of studies.

Table 8.1 summarises the information on the child subjects and Tables 8.2 and 8.3 present the relevant information on the untutored and tutored adult learners.

Table 8.1 Information on 2L1 subjects

Child	Age	MLU	Files	French speaker
Jean	1;10–3;9	1.3–4.3	12	Mother
Anne	2;3–4;0	1.4–4.5	11	Mother
Mimi	2;0–4;2	2.1–4.3	8	Mother

Table 8.2 Information on L2 subjects – untutored learners

Learner	Occupation	Age	Files	Months after onset (1st recording)	Other language
Sara	Mime artist	22	2	3	English
Martin	Musician	19	3	7	English
Karl	Physicist	ca20	5	8	English
Knut	Painter	48	3	ca 20	?
Henry	Engineer	50+	2	< 3	English, German

Table 8.3 Information on L2 subjects – tutored learners

Learner	Occupation	Age	Files	Instruction before 1st rec.	Other language
Lisa	Student of French and economics	ca 20	4	ca 500 h	English
Sama	Student of French and mechanics	ca 20	4	ca 500 h	English

Method

I scrutinised the transcriptions for all unambiguous combinations of nouns, for gender-marked articles including the contracted masculine forms (*du /au*), and for attributive adjectives. Only attributive adjectives that have two orally distinguishable forms were considered. Possessive adjectives and demonstratives were excluded.

Calculations of incorrect and correct gender-marked articles and adjectives were made following the target language. The analysis distinguishes types from tokens. A separate category of 'Inconsistent gender marking' was created for noun types that, within the same recording, occur with both genders (i.e. *le* and/or *un bateau* and **la* and/or**une bateau*). There are three interpretations of this phenomenon: the strongest interpretation of types belonging to this category could imply that they are indicative of cases where assignment has not occurred. In a slightly less strong interpretation, one might say that they indicate cases where assignment is fluctuating. Third, the inconsistency could be due to a lack of control in speech production.

Analysis

Article agreement

Table 8.4 below reports on the agreement in gender between the article and the noun as produced by the bilingual children. Several data points have been collapsed into two groups in order to raise the number of types / tokens to a level comparable to that found in each recording with the adults. A first observation from Table 8.1 is the low number of incorrect types (24 out of 312, or 7.7%) and tokens (29 out of 475, or 5.9%).

A second observation is that the number of types occurring with both genders within the same recording (cf. 'Inconsistent gender marking') is very low during the whole data-collection period. In addition to their early acquisition of agreement, it also seems as though the children use gender markings consistently from early on. This might be indicative of early assignment. However, the overall analysis overlooks some properties of the early stages that could alter this picture. First, it should be noted that in the first time span there is also a substantial number of bare nouns (see Granfeldt, 2000b). Second, in at least one child (Jean), the form '*un*' is initially overgeneralised (see Section 6.3 below and Granfeldt, 2003). Finally, it is plausible that in some cases the articles are acquired as parts of nouns at this stage and subsequently reanalysed as independent grammatical morphemes (e.g. [$_N$lelait] > [$_{Art}$le [$_N$lait]]) (cf. Carroll, 1989; Granfeldt, 2000a; Sourdot, 1977). The unanalysed article-noun pairings in the first time span are probably responsible for the fourth observation from Table 8.1, namely that percentages of correct use are somewhat lower in the second time span.

Turning now to the adults, Table 8.2 reports the agreement between the

Table 8.4 Agreement in gender Article – Noun – 2L1

Name (age)	Types		Tokens		Inconsistent gender marking
	No.	% corr.	No.	% corr.	
Anne 1–7 (2;3 to 3;3)	49	90%	95	95%	1
Anne 8–13 (3;5 to 4;3)	135	92%	173	92%	3
Jean 1–7 (1;10 to 2;11)	49	96%	97	98%	3
Jean 8–12 (3;1 to 3;9)	79	94%	110	94%	1

Table 8.5 Agreement in gender Article-Noun – L2

UTLs	Months of stay	Types		Tokens		Inconsistent gender marking No.
		No.	%corr.	No.	%corr.	
Sara 1	3	36	69%	55	74%	13
Sara 2	5	30	70%	47	77%	4
Henry 1	< 3	32	78%	51	78%	6
Henry 2	< 3	41	66%	67	73%	2
Martin 1	7	34	71%	49	76%	2
Martin 2	14	41	80%	69	88%	4
Martin 3	16	36	86%	45	84%	2
Karl 1	8	69	67%	134	75%	9
Karl 2	10	60	62%	89	60%	18
Karl 3	12	107	77%	168	78%	25
Karl 4	14	34	94%	51	95%	9
Karl 5	16	61	87%	86	90%	9
Knut 1	ca 20	52	73%	77	74%	5
Knut 2	ca 22	32	75%	45	80%	–
Knut 3	ca 35	56	75%	97	90%	5
TLs of studies	*Months of studies*					
Lisa 1	1	64	73%	95	79%	4
Lisa 2	2	62	77%	92	78%	8
Lisa 3	3	48	75%	69	73%	6
Lisa 4	4	55	80%	65	78%	8
Sama 1	1	29	80%	39	82%	1
Sama 2	2	35	89%	49	90%	1
Sama 3	3	44	93%	63	92%	5
Sama 4	4	22	100%	39	100%	3

Legend: UTLs = Untutored Learners; TL = Tutored Learners

article and the noun. A number of observations can be made from Table 8.2. First, there is development as a function of time: all learners arguably perform better on gender agreement in later recordings. In some learners this is apparent both with respect to Types and with respect to Tokens (cf. Karl, Sama). In other learners it is most clear on the Types level (Lisa, Martin), and in others development is primarily on the level of Tokens

(Knut). Second, the number of 'Inconsistent gender markings' seems generally to be much higher in the adults than in the children. At later stages, at least in some learners (Sara, Knut), there is a drop in types appearing with two genders within the same recording.

The levels of performance of these learners correspond with those established by Bartning (2000) for other Swedish learners of French. Bartning divides her cross-sectional corpus into two groups: pre-advanced learners, for whom gender is correct on the article in about 80% of the tokens, and advanced learners, for whom gender is correct in about 90% of the tokens. Thus, the present longitudinal findings confirm that gender agreement is more correct in advanced learners, i.e. that a development in this area is indeed possible.

Adjectival agreement

Looking now at adjectival agreement, the differences between the bilingual children and the adult learners are strengthened. Table 6 shows that when the adjectives begin to appear in the children's production they agree in gender with the noun and with the article.[5] A third child, Mimi, was included in this count since the number of tokens was low in the child Anne.

Table 8.6 Adjectival agreement – 2L1

	Agreement Art-A-N (Correct tokens/Total tokens)
Anne 3–13	7/7
Jean 3–12	37/38
Mimi 1–10	24/26
Total:	68/71 (96% corr.)

The results in Table 8.6 differ from those in Table 8.7 where the same analysis is carried out in the adult learners. The adult learners generally perform less well on adjectival agreement than on article agreement, whereas there is no such difference in the children. The finding that adjectival agreement is more difficult than agreement on determiners has been reported several times (Bartning, 2000; Chini, 1995; Dewaele & Véronique, 2000, 2001).

At least in some learners, however, a development is attested. Karl again provides a good example of at least pre-nominal adjectival agreement developing over time. The same development can be argued for Martin and Sama, and possibly also for Knut. Owing to the few tokens of postnominal adjectives, it is not possible to establish any relation between the position of the adjective and agreement. It has been suggested previously

Table 8.7 Adjectival agreement – L2

UTLs	Months of stay	Agreement Art-A-N (Tokens)		Agreement Art-N-A (Tokens)	
		No.	*%corr.*	*No.*	*No. corr.*
Sara 1	3	16	17%	–	–
Sara 2	5	12	32%	7	1
Henry 1	< 3	9	78%	1	1
Henry 2	< 3	5	60%	1	1
Martin 1	7	4	75%	–	–
Martin 2	14	9	78%	6	6
Martin 3	16	3	100%	–	–
Karl 1	8	9	22%	5	4
Karl 2	10	24	46%	2	-
Karl 3	12	22	59%	5	5
Karl 4	14	7	29%	1	–
Karl 5	16	23	65%	4	4
Knut 1	ca 20	22	64%	2	2
Knut 2	ca 22	2	100%	2	–
Knut 3	ca 35	10	80%	1	–
Tls of studies	*Months of studies*				
Lisa 1	1	2	50%	3	1
Lisa 2	2	8	50%	12	6
Lisa 3	3	9	22%	7	3
Lisa 4	4	6	33%	8	6
Sama 1	1	–	–	3	2
Sama 2	2	6	50%	1	1
Sama 3	3	2	50%	1	–
Sama 4	4	2	100%	1	1

Legend: UTLs = Untutored Learners; TL = Tutored Learners

(see Bartning, 2000; Granfeldt, 2000b on some other L2 learners) that post-nominal adjectives are, in fact, more correct in agreement.

Summary

Summing up so far, we have seen that the children rapidly acquire a general mastery of agreement irrespective of whether this concerns articles or adjectives. Furthermore, the phenomenon of 'Inconsistent gender marking' is not a characteristic in these children, even if such productions do occur occasionally. From this information we can infer that attribution and agreement are acquired at an early stage in the children. This confirms previous studies on L1 monolingual French and L1 bilingual French (cf. above).

With respect to the adults, an increase in agreement on the articles and possibly also on the adjectives has been attested. Furthermore, Table 8.5 suggests that, at least in some learners, the phenomenon of 'Inconsistent gender marking' decreases over time. The problem is that these results are compatible with two types of explanation: on the one hand, they might reflect a development of the capacity to assign gender at the lexical level, and, on the other, they might reflect a development of the capacity to produce agreement within the Noun Phrase.[6]

It is a crucial problem to the study of gender that, at least in production data, attribution can be observed only from the syntactic side of the coin, namely from the perspective of agreement.[7] In an attempt to advance the study of attribution/agreement, I will in the following section describe in some detail the gender system of one adult learner. A smaller set of data will be chosen in order to place the analysis on the level of individual nouns. I will also provide some observations on the three bilingual children.

Case Study: An Analysis of Gender Development in One Adult Learner of French and Notes on Three Bilingual Children

Gender system in Karl (L2)

In this section a qualitative analysis of the development of gender marking on articles in the learner Karl is presented. In the quantitative analysis, presented in Table 8.5 above, it was shown that Karl develops with respect to gender marking. This section addresses the nature of this development.

Table 8.8 presents the use of articles in Karl's spontaneous production.

In his first two recordings, two articles, namely *le* and *une*, are overused by Karl. It is important to note that it is not a particular gender that is overgeneralised, but two articles of *different* genders. This is reminiscent both of Hawkins (1998, 2001) and of Andersen (1984).

But interestingly, Table 8.8 shows that a third article *la* is, compared to *le*, increasingly used incorrectly (i.e. overused) in the third and fourth recordings, but that in the fifth recording there are so few errors of gender marking that it is in fact difficult to establish any overused article at this point. It seems reasonable to assume that Karl knows the difference

Table 8.8 The use of articles in Karl (L2)

	Month of stay		le	la	un	une	Overgeneralised articles
Karl 1	8	m.	77	–	10	8**	le +une
		f.	38*	10	3	11	
Karl 2	10	m.	52	11	10	22	le + une
		f.	40	12	3	17	
Karl 3	12	m.	88	20	18	24	le/la +une
		f.	31	39	2	28	
Karl 4	14	m.	41	6	–	3	le/la + une
		f.	10	10	–	10	
Karl 5	16	m.	39	7	5	8	?
		f.	2	29	–	19	

* ex: le chambre; ** ex: une bateau

between definite and indefinite even though this has not yet been controlled for the entire corpus.[8] So the addition of a form of overgeneralised article is probably not caused by the fact that a definite feature is introduced/acquired.

The dynamics of Table 8.8 suggests instead that Karl's gender system changes over time. The following hypothesis captures the inherent mechanisms of development:

(3) In L2, whenever a new type is acquired, unless there is evidence to the contrary, it receives default marking at the level of syntax: one article for definite contexts and one article for indefinite contexts. The default marking can be subsequently specified.[9]

Applying the hypothesis in (3) to Karl's system, we can say that the default markings of definiteness and indefiniteness are *le* and *une*, respectively. The initial marking might be altered over time, which is revealed in the quantitative analysis as a development towards more correct gender marking (cf. Table 8.5).

How can a hypothesis such as (3) be verified? My suggestion is to look longitudinally at types that occur in more than one recording. The hypothesis would be supported if there was systematicity in the way 'new' types were marked initially and if their gender marking developed in a specific way. The hypothesis would be falsified if there was no systematicity in the way new types were introduced and if there was no developmental pattern to be found. In what follows I will show that, of the 73 types in Karl's corpus that occur spontaneously in more than one recording, the hypothesis is correct in 65 cases. Table 8.9 lists the 73 types occurring in more than one recording in Karl's corpus:

Table 8.9 Noun types with token ratio > 2 (N = 73)

aimant	chemin	fuseau	maison	semaine	voix
atome	chien	gardien	mère	soir	voiture
bateau	chose	gaz	mois	soleil	week-end
bidon	côte	grand-mère	moment	source	
bobine	coude	gens	monde	Suède	
bois	courant	nucléon	mot	surface	
boîte	cuisine	homme	neige	tension	
camp	eau	huit	nom	tente	
canon	église	île	lac	tempête	
carte	escalier	jardin	ligne	température	
chambre	femme	jour	pièce	temps	
champ	fil	lit	place	tissu	
chaperon	fois	loup	porte	truc	
château	froid	machine	salle	ville	

Looking now at the marking of gender on these types in their first, second, etc. occurrences, some patterns are distinguishable.

A first set of examples is given below. The number in parentheses refers to the recording (1–5, see Table 8.8 above for 'the months of stay' for each recording) from which the noun is sampled and the arrow (>) represents the temporal sequence. Importantly, all the following examples are target-like with respect to the definite/indefinite distinction:

(4)   (a) **une** champ (1) > le/**une** champ (3)
      (b) **une** nucléon (2) > le nucléon (3)
(5)   (a) une chambre (1) > **le** chambre (4)
      (b) une température (3) > **le** température (4)
(6)   (a) **le** place (2,3) > une place (4)
      (b) le château (1) > le/**une** château (3)

The types *champ* and *nucléon* in (4a and b) are incorrectly marked (bold characters) by *une* the first time they appear in the corpus (in recordings 1 and 2). The second time they appear they are marked correctly by *le*. In the case of *maison*, Karl also uses this type with *une* the second time. The examples in (5a and b) are, inversely, first marked with *une* correctly and then with *le* (incorrect). Yet another set of types in (6a and b) is first marked with *le* and second with *une*.

These types are indicative of default marking of the definite/indefinite features (cf. Table 8.11, in the Appendix, for the other types of this sort). They do not appear with any variation within the definite and indefinite paradigm, not within one and the same recording and not over time (cf. Andersen, 1984). It can be assumed that the articles appearing with these noun types do not encode any gender feature. Therefore, it seems reasonable to conclude that, contra Carroll (1989), Karl is not transferring all his lexical specifications from Swedish.

A second set of examples shows types for which there is a change in the form encoding definiteness or indefiniteness. Typically, the change is not within the same recording but occurs across recordings after the type has gone through the 'default stage' (cf. examples 4 to 6 above).

(7)   (a) **le** porte (1) > une porte (2,3,4) > (6x) la porte (5)
       (b) **le**/une pièce (1) > la pièce (5)
       (c) une source (1) > **le** source (3) > la source (5)
       (d) le /**une** bateau (2) > le/un bateau (3)
(8)   (a) **le** mère (1) > la mère (3)
(9)   (a) le/**une** atome (2) > **la** atome (3)
       (b) le/**une** courant (1) > un/le/**la** courant (3) > **la** courante10 (3)
       (c) le fuseau (1) > le/**une** fuseau (2) > une/le/**la** fuseau (3)

The examples under (7) show an interesting development on the level of types. Starting out as default-marked (*le*/*une*) for in/definiteness, later the articles appearing with these types have altered in form for expressing either definiteness (a, b, c) or indefiniteness (d). Interestingly enough, this development also applies to one case of semantic gender (cf. example 8a) that underlines Karl's initial marking of definiteness with *le* as a default strategy, not encoding any gender feature. The last set of developing types in (9) reinforces the idea that gender encoding actually emerges at some point. The development of marking of these types follows the same pattern as the examples in (7), with the sole difference that they end up being marked incorrectly with *la*. Arguably, it is not the case in this Swedish learner, then, as suggested by Hawkins (1998) for English learners, that the later appearance of *la* in combination with a particular type is rote-learned as an 'exception' to the default strategy. Rather, it seems as if the first default-marking system, at some point in time, is revised and expanded to include a gender feature as well. Following this line of reasoning, the examples in (9) show a development in which a gender feature is assigned over time, but incorrectly.[11] It should be noted that, according to the hypothesis, the point in time at which gender is assigned is specific to each and every noun type, at least at this level of general development/proficiency. For the three types *atome*, *courant* and *fuseau* this is possibly captured in the third recording.[12]

This last claim is, in fact, supported by noun types that at first seem to contradict the general hypothesis in (3). There is a smaller set of types for which the first occurrence is not determined by *le* or *une*. These are given below in (10):

(10)   (a) la femme (3) > la / une femme (5)
      (b) **la** escalier (2) > la / le escalier (5)
      (c) un coude (1) > **une** coude (2) > **une** coude (5)
      (d) un week-end (1) > le week-end (3)
      (e) un / le bois (3) > le bois (5)13
      (f) la boîte (2) > une boîte (5)
      (g) la voix (2) > une voix (5)
      (h) la voiture (2) > une voiture (3)
      (i) un truc (1,2) > le truc (3)

Apart from two examples (10b and c), these types are not only correct but also completely 'stable' in their gender marking *across* the definiteness/indefiniteness distinction, i.e. indicative of a gender paradigm (in contrast to examples under (4), (5) and (6)). Arguably, the existence of these types shows two things: first, that the development of correct gender marking on a particular noun type follows an individual timetable, and, second, that when gender is acquired, the establishment of stable paradigms is possible also in L2.

The second point, that the end stage for these types is characterised by a certain degree of stability, is partially confirmed by yet another set of types. These are 20 types that only occur with the same article in all occurrences. Examples are given below:

(11)   (a) le aimant (1,3)
      (b) le bidon (1,5)
      (c) le fil (1,3)
      (d) une fois (2,3,5)
      (e) **le** eau (1,3)
      (f) le froid (3,4)
      (g) le gaz (1,3)

Seventeen of these types are only determined with *le* in all occurrences, two only with *une* and one with *la*. More importantly, only two of them are incorrect (*le île* and *le eau*, both vowel initial), i.e. 90% of these types agree in gender with the preceding article. Now, Table 8.5 above showed that Karl does not generally perform at this level of correctness until the very last recording, making it plausible that many of these 20 types are what I refer to as end-stage types, i.e. types for which a gender feature has been integrated into the lexical entry. In any case, the initial default stage and the end stage for a particular noun type are probably the most stable stages.

This leaves us with a limited set of eight counter-examples to the hypothesis presented above. These are types for which the first occurrence is determined by either *la* or *un* and for which there is a subsequent development/change in the form of conveying in/definiteness. These are listed below, but will not be discussed further:

(12) (a) la ligne (1) > **le**/une ligne (4)
      (b) **la** lac (2) > **la**/le lac (3) > le lac (4)
      (c) le jour (1) > **la** jour (3) > **une**/le jour (4,5)
      (d) le/**la** chemin (2) > le/**une** chemin (3) > le/**la** chemin (5)
      (e) **la** chien (3) > un/le/**une**/**la** chien (5)
      (f) un/**une** camp (2) > le/un/**une** camp (3) > **une** campe[14] (3)
      (g) la neige (3) > **le** neige (4) > la neige (5)
      (i) un coude (1) > **une** coude (2) > **une** coude (5)

Summary

In this section I have tried to detail the quantitative figures in Table 8.5, suggesting that a development in gender marking is indeed possible in second language French. The qualitative analysis has revealed systematicity at the level of types and indicated how the gender feature comes to be integrated into the lexical entry of a particular noun. Previous studies (Andersen, 1984; Hawkins, 2001) have claimed the existence of an initial stage in which the gender feature is absent in English-speaking adult learners of a Romance language. I have argued, somewhat differently, for the existence of such a stage in Karl's data, but only on the level of individual nouns. More importantly, the analysis shows that some types develop into an establishment of stable paradigms, suggesting that it is indeed a feature that is acquired and not the acquisition of an exception rule. This is further supported by the fact that some types develop incorrectly.

Some Notes on the Bilingual Children

Table 8.10, below, reports the children's use of articles. Although errors are rare, it can be noted that more errors are made with the indefinite article, at least in Jean and Mimi (cf. Granfeldt, 2003 for a more detailed discussion).

With respect to first, second, etc. occurrence, contrary to Karl, there appear to be no restrictions in the children's data: any particular noun can appear for the first time with any one of the four articles:

Table 8.10 Use of articles in 2L1

		le	*la*	*un*	*une*
Jean 1–12	m.	59	1	53	5
	f.	2	34	4	15
Anne 1–13	m.	70	3	77	1
	f.	4	35	4	32
Mimi 1–9	m.	43	1	45	2
	f.	3	26	8+1?	35

(13) (a) le livre (C3) > un livre (C5)
  (b) le manteau (A1) > le manteau (A8) > un manteau (A12)
(14) (a) un livre (J2) > le livre (J3)
  (b) un chat (C1) > un / le chat (C5)
  (c) un monsieur (C2) > le monsieur (C3)
(15) (a) la pelle (A6) > une pelle (A7)
  (b) la plage (A11) > une plage (A12)
(16) (a) une maison (C6) > la maison (C7)
  (b) une maison (A4) > une maison (A6) > la maison (A9)

There are also types that first appear with contracted articles and subsequently develop into a marking with a non-contracted article, as in (17) below:

(17) au lait (J1) > du lait (J2) > le lait (J8)

These few examples might show two things, both contrasting with Karl's system: first, with the possible exception of early '*un*', there seems to be no clear default stage characterised by an absence of gender feature, in these children, i.e. a stage in which analysed articles do not encode gender.[15] Second, the few errors and rapid establishment of paradigms also suggest that the gender feature is activated initially.[16] If we accept the methodology chosen here, the fact that any type of initial marking can constitute the basis of a potential establishment of paradigms appears to indicate that the children both have access to and apply the abstract category GENDER itself from early on (cf. Section 1).

Summary and Discussion

In this chapter, I have argued that the grammars of L2 learners of French do develop with respect to the gender feature. A quantitative analysis showed that all the Swedish learners considered here mastered with increasing correctness the agreement between article and noun over time. At least in some learners a similar development was found in adjectival agreement. However, the study confirmed the finding of previous studies that adjectival agreement is harder for L2 learners than agreement between the article and the noun (Bartning, 2000; Dewaele & Véronique, 2000, 2002). The quantitative analysis also revealed sharp differences between the adult L2 learners and the bilingual children; when the children started to use articles and, later, attributive adjectives, they predominantly mastered agreement. This confirms findings reported from monolingual French children (Clark, 1985) and other bilingual children acquiring French (Müller, 1999).

The last part of the chapter asks the questions of whether there are also qualitative differences in the way the 2L1 children and the L2 adults develop, and especially of how to account for the adult's acquisition. In a case study on one adult learner, Karl, a systematic pattern on the level of types was found. A smaller set of data was chosen, consisting of noun types with a token ratio above 2 over the data-collection period. Looking only at articles at this point, it was found that Karl initially marked noun types only with respect to definiteness (*le / une*). Some noun types developed over time in the sense that one of the two articles changed in form (*le > la* or *une > un*), thus establishing a gender paradigm. This was interpreted as the addition of a gender feature to the lexical entry of a particular noun (i.e. assignment). Interestingly, the change in form of the definite or indefinite article did not always result in correct gender paradigms, but for a certain number of types, an incorrect paradigm emerged at a later point in time. I interpreted this as evidence against the learning of an exception rule and in favour of the hypothesis that, indeed, assignment and agreement are possible to acquire in L2.

Again, a differentiated pattern was found in the children. At the stage in which analysed articles are produced, gender paradigms were established rather quickly and, importantly, without passing through any clear default stage in which individual articles were overgeneralised. Rather it seems that the children are indifferent to the local article-noun combination and 'know' that gender is a possible feature of French. This interpretation would, therefore, confirm two hypotheses in the literature: (a) that abstract grammatical features are available to the child from the outset (UG) (Chomsky, 1998), and, (b) that the selection of the 'local' feature [+/− feminine] for an individual noun is triggered by properties of the noun (certainly formal, but possibly also semantic) (cf. Karmiloff-Smith, 1979; Müller, 1999).

With respect to the specific questions posed here (cf. Section 3), it has been confirmed that the Swedish L2 learners of French studied here were able to assign a gender feature to a particular noun, i.e. the gender feature can become a part of the lexical entry (Question A). Accepting this, both the qualitative and the quantitative differences between the children and the adults could emerge from the initial application of the abstract category GENDER. Here I have tried to argue that the high level of correctness in the acquisition of gender agreement in the children is at least partially the result of the selection and activation of this category. It could be, then, that the adults are initially unable to draw on the properties of this category when acquiring French, which, in turn, leads to a different pattern of acquisition occurring primarily on the level of individual types.

One interesting comparison can be explored in relation to this last question. Do Swedish learners differ from anglophone learners with respect to (French) gender? Recall that both Carroll and Hawkins seemed to argue that anglophones 'never' acquire gender (assignment or agreement). It follows from both Carroll (1989) and Hawkins and Chan (1997) that Swedish learners should be able to draw on their L1 knowledge of gender. So, if the L2 learners do not at first apply the abstract UG feature GENDER as the children do, does the gender feature from their L1 make a difference, perhaps, at a later stage? While it is clear that this property is not relexified to early articles in French L2, it is not quite clear whether there is a longitudinal difference between anglophones and Swedish learners such that only the latter will develop both an assignment and an agreement system for French gender at all. However, the fact that the Swedish learners incrementally move towards the French system, as I understand it, provides some support for the hypothesis put forward by Hawkins and Chan (1997).

Acknowledgements

I would like to thank Inge Bartning, Petra Bernardini, Susanne Carroll, Verner Egerland, Roger Hawkins and Suzanne Schlyter for commenting on or discussing (parts of) this chapter with me. I also gratefully acknowledge the comments of one reviewer. All errors remain of course my own. This research is supported by a grant from The Swedish Council for Research in the Humanities and Social Sciences (HSFR) to the DURS-project directed by Suzanne Schlyter, grant number F0686/1998.

Notes
1. In the framework of generative grammar, four lexical categories are traditionally distinguished: Noun [+N, -V], Verb [-N, +V], Adjective [+N, +V], Preposition [-N, -V].
2. In terms of input, the difference is easily understood. All strings involving gender-marking are relevant to the child when acquiring the gender feature itself.

This can be described as a 'global' parameter setting, affecting every lexical entry of nouns. It is still a matter of debate whether the word *maison* is assigned gender 'locally' from determiner-noun pairings or whether gender is assigned through inductive generalisation to a class of nouns, triggered by phonological, semantic or morphological properties of a particular noun class (see the review of the literature, section 2.1 below).

3. There are of course many differences between the two systems. For instance *common* refers to the gender which combines the earlier masculine and feminine distinction. Other differences relate to the basis of classification (see Corbett, 1991: 57–61 on French and Andersson, 1992: 35–39 on Swedish).

4. A possible third position, though not worked out for gender, is proposed by Lardière (1998, 2000). She claims a fossilisation with respect to the mapping of formal features onto morphological forms in adult L2. This last proposal shares much with other theories of morphology in L2 (e.g. Missing Surface Inflection Hypothesis, Prevost & White, 2000) and appears to predict that inflectional morphology is generally not acquired even in advanced end-state grammars (see Franceschina, 2001 for an opposing view).

5. Only pre-nominal adjectives are considered here, since there was not a sufficient number of post-nominal adjectives with audible gender distinction in the corpus.

6. One persistent difficulty, discussed by Dewaele and Véronique (2001), is to decide 'post-facto' the source of a particular gender error. Therefore, these authors introduced a definition of gender assignment errors: 'when a particular lexical item was used in two different utterances with a determiner of the wrong gender we assumed that it was wrongly assigned' [...] 'However, many nouns appear only once in the speakers' extracts preceded by an article in the wrong gender. These gender errors were also attributed to assignment problems'. The implication of assignment is the presence of stability: A noun can be assigned the wrong gender, but if it is truly assigned a particular gender, one expects it to appear repeatedly with that same gender. This is captured by the first set of error types in the definition by Dewaele and Véronique, but not in the second; a single isolated occurrence of an article-noun combination cannot, in fact, be more than suggestive with respect to assignment. Agreement errors were defined by Dewaele and Véronique as: 'For an error to be classified as an agreement problem, we needed to have at least one modifier agreeing correctly in gender with the head, for example: une affaire religieux (a religious affair (+fem)'.

7. I agree with the conclusion of one reviewer that another desirable consequence of this problem is to make more use of experimental data.

8. Bartning (2000: 230), discussing other Swedish L2 learners of French, says that: 'In our data the AL [Advanced Learner] has no difficulty in choosing the right determiner as far as the definiteness distinction between *le* and *un* is concerned. Interestingly, there are almost no cases of omission of the determiner [...] The advanced learner already knows the fundamental referential functions of the indefinite and definite determiner'.

9. One reviewer asks what determines the choice of the default. Whereas it could be the case that learners generally start out with a default system, it is not necessarily the case that they all pick the same formative to express in/definiteness.

10. Pronounced /korant/

11. This might correspond to the emergency of *la* as a third overgeneralised article as noted in Table 8.8 above.
12. It would require much more space to seriously address the issue of the cues to this development. Here, I will only note one tendency pointing to an influence of formal properties at an intermediate stage. In Karl 2 and 3, where his system seems to be under development there are signs indicating an assignment of [+feminine] to CVC-structures. Interlanguage forms like in 9b (see also 12f) are interesting in this respect. See Granfeldt (2003) for an in-depth discussion.
13. Hyper-corrected to 'à la bois'.
14. Pronounced /kamp/.
15. Initially they might, however, not always encode definiteness (see Granfeldt, 2003). Moreover, it should be added that, again contrary to the adult Swedes, these children, like monolingual children, pass through an extended early stage of determiner omission (Granfeldt, 2000b). If feature acquisition is incremental, as suggested by many scholars (e.g. Clahsen *et al.*, 1994; Say, 2001), it is plausible that activation of the gender feature interacts with the emergence of articles and, more generally, of determiners.
16. Interestingly, when overgeneralisations are reported in the literature on L1 acquisition (Chini, 1992 on Italian L1; Andersson, 1992), it seems as though a *particular gender* is overgeneralised, not individual articles as in L2. This supports the idea defended here that the children and the adults differ with respect to the initial stage of gender acquisition.

References

Andersen, R. (1984) What's gender good for anyway? In R. Andersen (ed.) *Second Languages: A Cross-linguistic Perspective* (pp. 77–99). Rowley, MA: Newbury House.

Andersson, A-B. (1992) Second language learners' acquisition of grammatical gender in Swedish. PhD thesis, University of Göteborg.

Bartning, I. (1997) L'apprenant dit avancé et son acquisition d'une langue étrangère. Tour d'horizon et esquisse d'une caractérisation de la variété avancée. *Acquisition et Interaction en Langue Etrangère* (AILE) 9, 9–50.

Bartning, I. (2000) Gender agreement in L2 French: Pre-advanced vs. advanced learners. *Studia Linguistica* 54 (2), 224–37.

Carroll, S. (1989) Second language acquisition and the computational paradigm. *Language Learning* 39 (3), 535–94.

Carroll, S. (1999) Input and SLA: Adults' sensitivity to different sorts of cues to French gender. *Language Learning* 49 (1), 37–92.

Chini, M. (1992) L'acquisizione del genere grammaticale in italiano L2: per un approccio comparativo. PhD thesis, University of Pavia.

Chini, M. (1995) Un aspect du syntagme nominal en italien L2: le genre. *Acquisition et Interaction en Langue Étrangère* (AILE) 5, 15–42.

Chomsky, N. (1995) *The Minimalist Program*. Cambridge, MA: MIT Press.

Chomsky, N. (1998) Minimalist inquiries: The framework. *MIT Occasional Papers in Linguistics* 15.

Clahsen, H., Eisenbeiß, S., and Vainikka, A. (1994) The seeds of structure: A syntactic analysis of the acquisition of case marking. In T. Hoekstra and B. Schwartz (eds) *Language Acquisition Studies in Generative Grammar* (pp. 85–119). Amsterdam: John Benjamins.

Clark, E. (1985) The acquisition of Romance with special reference to French. In D.

Slobin (ed.) *The Crosslinguistic Study of Language Acquisition.* Vol. 1. (pp. 687–782). Hillsdale: Erlbaum.

Corbett, G. (1991) *Gender.* Cambridge: Cambridge University Press.

Dewaele, J.-M. and Véronique, D. (2000) Relating gender errors to morphosyntax and lexicon in advanced French interlanguage. *Studia Linguistica* 54 (2), 212–24.

Dewaele, J.-M. and Véronique, D. (2001) Gender assignment and gender agreement in advanced French interlanguage: A cross-sectional study. *Bilingualism: Language and Cognition* 4 (3), 275–97.

Franceschina, F. (2001) Against an L2 morphological deficit as an explanation for the differences between native and non-native grammars. In S. Foster-Cohen and A. Nizegorodcew (eds) *EUROSLA Yearbook 1* (pp.143–158). Amsterdam / Philadelphia: John Benjamins.

Granfeldt, J. (2000a) The acquisition of the DP in bilingual and second language French. *Bilingualism: Language and Cognition* 3 (3), 263–80.

Granfeldt, J. (2000b) Le développement morphosyntaxique du syntagme nominal chez des enfants et des adultes. *PERLES 9.* MA thesis, University of Lund.

Granfeldt, J. (2003) L'acquisition des catégories fonctionnelles. Etude comparative du développement du DP français chez des enfants et des apprenants adultes. Etudes romanes de Lund, 67. Institut d'Etudes romanes de Lund, Université de Lund.

Granfeldt, J. and Schlyter, S. (submitted) Cliticisation in the acquisition of French as L1 and L2 Submitted for publication in Prévost, P. & Paradis, J. (eds) *Acquisition of French: Focus on Functional Categories.* Amsterdam: Benjamins.

Harley, B. (1979) French gender rules in the speech of English-dominant French-dominant and monolingual French-speaking children. *Working Papers in Bilingualism* 19, 129–56.

Hawkins, R. (1998) Explaining the difficulty of French gender attribution for speakers of English. Paper presented at EUROSLA 8, Paris, September.

Hawkins, R. (2001) *Second Language Syntax: A Generative Introduction.* Oxford: Blackwells

Hawkins, R. and Chan, C. (1997) The partial availability of Universal Grammar in second language acquisition: The 'failed functional features hypothesis'. *Second Language Research* 13 (1), 187–226.

Karmiloff-Smith, A. (1979) *A Functional Approach to Child Language: A Study of Determiners and Reference.* Cambridge: Cambridge University Press.

Lardière, D. (1998) Dissociating syntax from morphology in a divergent L2 end-state grammar. *Second Language Research* 14 (4), 359–75.

Lardière, D. (2000) Mapping features to forms in SLA. In J. Archibald (ed.) *Second Language Acquisition and Linguistic Theory* (pp. 102–29). Oxford: Blackwells.

Möhring, A. (2001) The acquisition of French by German pre-school children: An empirical investigation of gender assignment and gender agreement. In S. Foster-Cohen and A. Nizegorodcew (eds) *EUROSLA Yearbook 1* (pp. 171–94). Amsterdam / Philadelphia: John Benjamins.

Müller, N. (1990) Developing two gender assignment systems simultaneously . In J. Meisel (ed.) *Two First Languages. Early Grammatical Development in Bilingual Children* (pp. 193–234). Dordrecht: Foris.

Müller, N. (1994). Gender and number agreement within DP. In J. Meisel (ed.) *Bilingual First Language Acquisition: French and German Grammatical Development* (pp. 53–89). Amsterdam: John Benjamins.

Müller, N. (1995). L'acquisition du genre et du nombre chez des enfants bilingues (français-allemand). In S. Schlyter (ed.) *L'acquisition simultanée pré-scolaire.* Special issue of *Acquisition et Interaction en Langue Etrangère* (AILE) 6, 65–101.

Müller, N. (1999) Gender and number in acquisition. In B. Unterbeck and M. Rissanen (eds.) *Gender in Grammar and Cognition* (pp. 351–400). Berlin: Mouton de Gruyter.

Pienemann, M. (1998) *Language Processing and Second Language Development: Processability Theory.* Amsterdam: John Benjamins.

Prévost, P. and White, L. (2000) Missing inflection or impairment in second language acquisition? Evidence from tense and agreement. *Second Language Research* 16 (2), 103–33.

Radford, A. (2000) Children in search of perfection: Towards a minimalist model of acquisition. *Essex Reports in Linguistics,* 34. University of Essex.

Riegel, M., Pellat, J-C., and Rioul, R. (1997). *Grammaire Méthodique du Français.* Paris: Presses Universitaires de France.

Say, T. (2001) Feature acquisition in bilingual child language development. Unpublished ms.

Schlyter, S. (1993) The weaker language in bilingual Swedish-French children. In K. Hyltenstam and Å. Viberg (eds) *Progression and Regression in Language* (pp. 289–308). Cambridge: Cambridge University Press.

Schlyter, S. (1994) Early morphology in French as the weaker language in French-Swedish bilingual children. *Scandinavian Working Papers in Bilingualism* 9, 67–87.

Schlyter, S. (1997) Formes verbales et pronoms objets chez des apprenants adultes de français en milieu naturel. In C. Martinot (ed.) *Actes du Colloque International sur l'Acquisition de la Syntaxe en Langue Maternelle et en Langue Étrangère* (pp. 273–95). Paris: Annales littéraires de l'Université de Franche-Comté.

Schlyter, S. (2003) Development of verb morphology and finiteness in children and adults acquiring French. In C. Dimroth and M. Starren (eds) *Information Structure, Linguistic Structure, and the Dynamics of Learner Language* (pp. 15–44). Amsterdam: John Benjamins.

Schlyter, S. (this volume) Adverbes and Functional Categories in L1 and L2 French.

Sourdot, M. (1977) Identification et différenciation des unités: les modalités nominales. In F. François, D. François, E. Sabeau-Jouannet and M. Sourdot (eds) *La syntaxe de l'enfant avant 5 ans* (pp. 90–120). Paris: Librairie Larousse.

Surridge, M.E. (1993) Gender assignment in French: The hierarchy of rules and the chronology of acquisition. *International Review of Applied Linguistics* 31(2), 77–96.

Tucker, G.A. Lambert, W.E. and Rigault, A. (1977) *The French Speaker's Skill With Grammatical Gender: An Example of Rule-governed Behavior.* The Hague: Mouton.

Tsimpli, I-M. and Roussou, A. (1991) Parameter resetting in L2? *University College London Working Papers in Linguistics* 3, 149–69.

Appendix

Table 8.11 Types at different stages of development in Karl (N = 65)

Types at the 'default stage' (N = 14)	Types in development towards or at the end-stage (N = 31)	Types with only one type of marking (N = 20)
une champs (1) > le/une champ (3)	le/une pièce (1) > la pièce (5)	le aimant (1,3)
une nucléon (2) > le nucléon (3)	le porte (1) > une porte (2,3) > une/le porte (4,5) > (6x) la porte (5)	le bidon (1,5)
une chambre (1) > le chambre (4)	une source (1) > le source (3) > la source (5)	le fil (1,3)
une température (3) > le température(4)	le /une bateau (2) > le/un bateau (3)	une fois (2,3,5)le eau (1,3)
le surface (2,3) > le/une surface (4)	le machine (2,3) > la machine (3,5)	le froid (3,4)
le place (2,3) > une place (4)	une tempête (1) > le/une tempête (3) > (3x) la tempête	le gaz (1,3)le huit (2,3)
le château (1,3) > une château (3)	le mère (1) > la mère (3)	le île (1,2)
le/une chose (3) > une chose (4)	le côte (1,2) > la côte (3)	le jardin (2,3)
le/une église(2) > une église (3)	le/la cuisine (2) > la cuisine (3)	le loup (1,3)le mois (3,5)
le / une tension (2) > une tension (3)	le homme (2) > un/le/une homme (3) > le homme (4)	le moment (1,3,5)
le soir (1) > le/ une soir (3) > le soir (4)	une salle (2) > la salle (5)	le monde (2,3,4,5)
le gardien (3) > une gardien (4)?	une ville(3) > la ville (5)	le nom (1,2,5)
une canon (1) > une/la canon (2) > le/une canon (3)?	le mot (1) > le/un mot (3) > le mot (4,5)	une semaine (2,3)
le/une/la tente (3) > une tente (4)	le gens (1) > un gens (5)	le soleil (3,4)
	la femme (3) > la/une femme (5)un week-end (1) > le week-end (3)un/le bois (3) > le bois (5)	la Suède (1,5)
	la boîte (2) > une boîte (5)	le temps (1, 2, 3, 4, 5)
	la voix (2) > une voix (5)	le tissu (3,4)
	la voiture (2) > une voiture (3)	
	un truc (1,2) > le truc (3)le chaperon (1,3) / la chaperon (3)	
	le/une atome (2) > la atome (3)	
	le lit (1) > la lit (3)	
	une/le courant (1) > un/le/la courant (3) > la courante (3)?	
	le bobine (1) > le/une/la bobine (3)?	
	le carte (2) > le/la carte (3) > le carte (5)?	
	le/la grand-mère (1) > le/la grand-mère (3)?	
	la escalier (2) > la/le escalier (5)?	
	la maison (2) > un/une/la maison (3) > une maison (4) > la maison (5)?	
	le fuseau (1) > le/une fuseau (2) > une/le/la fuseau (3)	

Legend: Numbers in parenthesis = number of recording,? = uncertain classification

Chapter 9

From Speech Community Back to Classroom: What Variation Analysis Can Tell Us About the Role of Context in the Acquisition of French as a Foreign Language

VERA REGAN

Introduction

In second language research, what has been called 'context of acquisition' has been said to be one of the most important variables in learning another language. The notion of context of acquisition, although it is widely referred to in the literature of second language acquisition research and is seen to imply certain assumptions, is not always precisely defined and delineated as a term. Young (1999) cites Goodwin and Duranti (1992) as saying 'The notion of context (. . .) involves a fundamental juxtaposition of two entities: (1) a focal event, and (2) a field of action within which that event is embedded' (1999: 106). Young points out that (2) can vary according to the interest of the researcher. It can involve the 'setting of language use, participants' cultural background, first language, second-language proficiency, gender, social status' (1999: 106) and can be treated independently of language use. Ethnomethodologists, however, and conversational analysts view context as emerging and dynamic and believe it is through interaction that categories establish themselves. In the tradition of variation linguistics used in second language acquisition research, there has been a correlation of features of context (here independent variables) with variation in a linguistic form (the dependent variable). The study detailed in this chapter follows in this tradition and correlates variation in one variable with context, understood here as setting. It involves the traditional distinction between what is called the 'formal' context of acquisition (usually the classroom) and the 'naturalistic' context (usually the native speech community). It must be noted that the notion of community is increasingly seen as dynamic (Bayley & Schecter, 2003). These terms have been useful in making distinctions as to different conditions in which acquisition happens but they tend to be overly generalising and under-nuanced in relation to both the formal context (classrooms can be enormously variable in character) and the naturalistic setting (this can also mean very different experiences depending on the situation, for instance, how much contact does the learner actually have with native speakers?). An increasing number of learners of second languages throughout the world are spending time in the target-language community as well as in the classroom and it is increasingly important that we understand the nature of the various contexts in which acquisition takes place, as more and more resources are poured into '*stages*' for immersion students in native speech communities in Canada, or study abroad programmes for American students, or year abroad stays for British or Irish students,[1] or Erasmus/Socrates programmes for European students in general.

Study Abroad

Study abroad means, in general, the practice of student language learners spending a year in the target-language country. It has been seen as a 'special case of second language acquisition, one which offers a unique opportunity to observe the language learning process from a number of different perspectives' (Freed, 1995: 4). Recently, study-abroad research has thrown further light on the issue of context of acquisition. Freed (1995) says it has been assumed that the combination of immersion in the native speech community, integrated with formal classroom learning, creates the best environment for learning a second language: 'The strength of this assumption is so powerful that there has evolved a popular belief, one shared by students and teachers, parents and administrators, that students who go abroad are those who will ultimately become the most proficient in the use of their language of specialisation' (1995: 5). She laments the lack of empirical data that would permit us to examine the truth or otherwise of these popular beliefs. A related issue is the question of linguistic competences, and whether some types of linguistic competence are affected more than others by the stay in the speech community. Which linguistic competence is most affected by Study Abroad: grammatical competence, sociolinguistic competence, pragmatic competence, or pronunciation?

Since those remarks, we now do in fact have several studies of the linguistic behaviour of learners before and after the year abroad (Freed, 1995). What we do not have, however, are follow-up studies of these speakers: what happens when they return? This long-term evidence is undoubtedly necessary for a full understanding of how valid the popular faith in year-abroad experience actually is. If indeed there is evidence that living in the speech community is beneficial, is it also true that these benefits are lasting? This chapter charts the acquisition of a second language through three different phases, moving from one context to another and back again; in this case from the first phase where the learners learned mainly in a formal context, the classroom, then through the second phase where they spent a year in the native speech community, and finally the third phase where they return to the country of their first language, and to the language classroom once more. Freed indicates that '[p]ilot studies, as reported by Coleman and his colleagues (1994), provide, in addition to the usual support for linguistic progress during the year abroad, some new data which suggest that student growth in the target language slows down radically upon their return from a year abroad' (Freed, 1995: 10). Coleman (1996) suggests that 'language tuition following residence abroad might no longer raise proficiency'. A cross-sectional pilot study which he did of 136 students of Spanish across two post-residence years of study also failed to show any significant difference in proficiency. He suggests that it is possible that the C-Test used, does not measure the type of gains (i.e. the subskills) made by language students after residence abroad. Coleman (1996) notes that Raffaldini (1987) also found evidence of loss of proficiency upon return. He points out that 'further research is required, but it appears that return from residence abroad marks the high point of L2 proficiency, which can thereafter decay' (p. 191).

Other than Coleman's study, there is little evidence for the long-term effects of the year abroad and certainly no detailed, empirically verifiable research on linguistic effects. Even the largest studies (Brecht & Davidson, 1991; Brecht, Davidson & Ginsberg, 1990 and 1993) are all 'before and after' studies. Few, if any, so far, have information on long-term effects of the year-abroad experience. This chapter provides quantitative empirical evidence that can illuminate some of the issues surrounding long-term effects of the acquisition of one of the linguistic competences – sociolinguistic competence. It deals, in particular, with the acquisition of native patterns of variation by Irish L2 learners of French. The study described is part of a longer study of the acquisition of patterns of variation in French by Irish learners. Earlier phases in this study have been reported in Regan (1995, 1996, 1997, 1998) and Dewaele and Regan (2001, 2002).

Sociolinguistic Competence and the Acquisition of Native-Speaker Patterns of Variation in Second Language Acquisition

Variation is a natural, inherent feature of human language. Weinreich, Labov and Herzog (1968) refer to the concepts of 'inherent variability' and 'orderly heterogeneity'. Knowledge of a language necessarily involves knowledge of such variation. 'The fact that speakers have the ability to produce, perceive and understand the significance of linguistic variation is evidence that it is part of their linguistic competence' (Guy, to appear). To acquire native or near-native competence, the L2 learner must approximate the native pattern of variation. A fundamental assumption here is the view that 'a theory of language needs to explain variation as well as the invariant properties of language' (Guy, to appear). Variation analysis models language quantitatively. Second language learners, like native speakers, show patterns of 'orderly heterogeneity' in their speech (notwithstanding the fact that their speech is also highly variable). Like native speakers, they have, and are developing, tendencies – 'to what is preferred, disfavoured and more or less likely' (Guy, to appear). Research in SLA has generally focused on the acquisition of the invariant. Since Adamson and Regan (1991) there has been a distinct thread of research within sociolinguistic approaches to SLA which seeks to examine in a detailed way the acquisition of native patterns of variation by learners of a second language (see Rehner *et al.*, 2003 for a comprehensive overview).

In second language acquisition studies, therefore, we need to describe, at least, initially, the way in which the learner learns to produce the variable patterns which are part of native speech. The models and constructs that have been successful in sociolinguistics in relation to native speech have been shown to be appropriate for the analysis of L2 speech also. A probabilistic model can represent the choices speakers make in relation to particular variables, taking the context into account – both linguistic and extra-linguistic. The choice of a particular token may be affected by different features of its context. We therefore need a model that will deal with several simultaneous and sometimes conflicting contextual factors. A quantitative, probabilistic and multivariate model is ideally suited to representing speech which is at once highly variable and also systematic. The advantages of this approach in relation to SLA studies have been seen to be considerable (Bayley, 1996; Preston & Bayley, 1996; Preston, 1989; Young, 1991). This strand of research permits us to see how closely the L2 patterns of variation match the L1 pattern, the process whereby L2 patterns gradually approximate L1 patterns, and whether the constraints which cause the choice of one variant over another are the same for the L2 speaker as for the native. It permits us, in the case of a longitudinal study, to see whether these constraints change over time and we can chart the acquisition process. In the case of advanced learners, presumably, we would expect the patterns to be ever closer to native patterns (although there is much evidence that even advanced learners are rarely, if ever, completely native-like in their linguistic behaviour (Bartning, 1997; Freed, 1995 and others). In relation to the acquisition of sociolinguistic competence and especially of native variation patterns, advanced learners become close to, but are yet not quite, like natives (Bartning, 1997; Dewaele, 2002; Freed, 1995; Regan, 1995).

The study of the acquisition of variation by L2 learners has established itself as a distinct thread in second language acquisition research in the past ten years or so (Mougeon, Nadasdi & Rehner, 2002). Studies in this tradition were carried out in the 1990s: Adamson and Regan (1991) on the acquisition of patterns of in/ing usage in English by Asian learners; Bayley (1991) on the acquisition of past-tense marking by Chinese learners of English; Young (1991) on variation in plural marking by Chinese learners of English. Studies on the acquisition of variation by learners of French in particular began to proliferate in the mid-1990s: (Dewaele, 1992, 1999; Regan, 1995, 1996, 1997; Rehner & Mougeon, 1999; Sankoff *et al.*, 1997). There is a particularly strong line of research in this area in Canada in relation to immersion students of French L2 (Mougeon *et al.*, 2002; Mougeon & Rehner, 2001; Rehner, 2002). These studies specifically examined the acquisition of native patterns of variation. Whereas, previously, SLA research had generally focused on the learning of the invariant by learners, the aim of this particular thread of enquiry was to see how the learners acquired the aspects of the L2 which were variable for natives. These studies began to contribute to general knowledge of various issues in SLA; for example, Adamson and Regan (1991) showed that transfer from the L1 played a role in the acquisition of variation in the same way as it had for the invariant.

A Longitudinal Study of Advanced Learners and the Year Abroad

As we have seen, research on the year abroad has become both more abundant and more detailed in recent years. We now have a considerable body of literature in general, and in particular on the acquisition of French during the year abroad (see Coleman *et al.*, 1994; Freed, 1995; Towell *et al.*, 1996, etc.). Year-abroad studies have told us more about the role of differences in context of acquisition, the role of input and the debate about foreign vs. second language learners. In general, the studies show that a year abroad makes a considerable difference – although this varies depending on which aspect of acquisition we examine and on the proficiency level of the learner (Howard, 2001).

To date, most of the year-abroad studies are 'before and after'. They focus on the learners' performance before they go abroad and after they return. However, so far we have little information on what happens, for instance, when L2 learners return from the year abroad and find themselves once more in the classroom. This chapter reports specifically on a further stage in the process of language acquisition in year-abroad subjects.

This chapter is the final stage of a longitudinal study of sociolinguistic competence by advanced learners (Regan, 1995). It analyses the acquisition of native-speaker patterns of variation and especially of variables in contemporary spoken French which are sociolinguistically sensitive, and, in some cases, undergoing sound change in the language: for instance, the variable use of *nous* vs. *on* (see Coveney, 2000), the variable deletion of /1/ in clitic pronouns – and, in this instance, the variable deletion of the negative particle *ne*. The study was designed to highlight developmental stages in an acquisition process which included a stay in the native speech community by the speakers as well as learning in the traditional language classroom. The three stages of the study were charted by taped interviews with the speakers: the first set took place after their first year at university and before they spent a year in a French-speaking country; the second set of interviews were held after their return to Ireland and the third after a further year at university in Ireland.

Ne Deletion and the Second Language Learner

The deletion of *ne* was the variable chosen as a means of studying the acquisition of sociolinguistic norms in French as a second language. In spoken French, *ne* is deleted variably to a greater or lesser extent by all members of French-speaking communities throughout the world. *Ne* deletion appears to be a highly sensitive sociolinguistic variable and a powerful indicator of formality, issues of power and solidarity, style, register, and so on. It has a network of relationships with sociolinguistic factors such as age, sex and social class. It often co-occurs with other such sociolinguistically sensitive variables in French as the variable use of *tu* as opposed to *vous*, or *on* as opposed to *vous* and *nous*.

Subjects

The subjects of this study form a subset of five informants from a larger longitudinal study of the acquisition of sociolinguistic competence by seven Hiberno-English learners of French L2. These were advanced learners, university students who were studying French as one of two subjects for their BA degree. They had all studied French for five years at secondary school. Several had had short stays in France (two weeks to two months on average) but none had lived there for a long period. Most of them were studying a second European language and all had studied Irish from the age of four or five. They were all about the same age (from 19 to 21 years) and were mainly middle-class. They participated in a programme (Erasmus), funded by the European Union, which helped university students to spend an academic year in another European country. During the year abroad the students attended regular courses at the university and got credit for these. They generally lived in university residences. There was a system in place whereby the students were assigned a host French family who invited them on occasion to spend time in their home. This was taken up by the students with varying regularity. In general, the amount of contact with native speakers in interactive situations varied with the individual.[2] Only one of the speakers was male. This gender imbalance is an indication of the general proportion of males and females taking French as a subject, but obviously prevents any reliable conclusions being drawn regarding gender and second language learning. Another factor common to these speakers was that they had been selected as motivated students, on the basis of grades and evaluations, to take part in a year-abroad programme. Most of them reported an interest in working in and living in a French-speaking country eventually.

Two Previous Phases in the Study

Two earlier stages of this study have been reported (Regan, 1995, 1996, 1997). In relation to *ne* deletion, the study showed that the speakers deleted considerably more after their stay abroad. In other words, they were approximating roughly – though not exactly – the native-speaker norm. A multivariate analysis (VARBRUL) was used, and more specifically the Goldvarb 2.0 version for the Macintosh. This showed, amongst other things, the probability figures for *ne* deletion from Time 1 and Time 2. A separate factor group in the analysis contained two factors, Time 1 (before time abroad) and Time 2 (after time abroad), and the relative importance of each of these stages of development was estimated. A comparison was made which showed whether reweightings of these figures took place and which ones they were.

For the VARBRUL analysis, the factors believed to constrain the variation were specified. I hypothesised, following Ashby (1976, 1981) and Sankoff and Vincent (1977) in relation to native speech, and my own observations of the interlanguage of Irish speakers, that the following factors would affect *ne* deletion: Style, Lexicalisation, Following Phonological environment, Preceding Phonological Environment, Clause Type, Subject of Verb, Verb Tense, Presence of Object Clitic between *ne* and *pas*, Syntactic Structure of the Verb, Following Adverb. The factor groups were divided into constituent factors. Table 9.1 shows factor groups and factors in those groups with examples from the corpus gathered from the speakers.

Table 9.1 Factor groups and factors

Style		
	monitored	
	casual	
Following phonological segment		
	vowel	'je n'ai aucune idée (I have no idea)
	consonant	'elle ne travaille plus'(She doesn't work any more)
Preceding phonological segment		
	vowel	'je n'allais pas' (I didn't go)
	consonant	'elle ne va pas en France'(She doesn't go to France)
Syntactic structure of the verb		
	modal	'elle ne pouvait pas trouver'(She couldn't find)
	auxiliary	'j'ai entendu rien d'elle' (I haven't heard anything from her)
	copula	'c'est pas moi' (It's not me)
	main	'j'aimais pas' (I didn't like)
Time of interview		
	Time 1	prior to French visit
	Time 2	after return from France
Clause Type		
	main	'je dis rien contre elle' (I'm not saying anything against her)
	subordinate	'tout est bien s'il n'y a rien' (Everything is ok if there's no damage)
Subject		
	Pronoun	'je pourrais pas' (I wasn't able)
	full noun phrase	'les gens n'étaient pas contents' (People weren't happy about it)
Presence of object clitic		
	Absence	'je ne travaillais pas' (I wasn't working)
	Presence	'je ne l'aimais pas' (I didn't like him)
Lexicalisation		
	not a formula	'je ne voudrais pas sourire' (I didn't want to smile)
	lexicalised phrase	'il n'y a pas', 'je sais pas', 'il ne faut pas' (There isn't, I don't know, One must not)

Table 9.1 (*cont.*) Factor groups and factors

Individual		
1. Catherine (C)		
2. Donna (D)		
3. Joy (J)		
4. Judy (U)		
5. Miles (M)		
6. Nora (N)		
7. Sally (S)		

Data Elicitation

Three sociolinguistic interviews, of 45 minutes to an hour long for each speaker, were tape-recorded by myself. The speakers, students in the department where I taught, knew me to be a member of faculty, but were not students 0n courses I taught.[3] Prior to the study I was not acquainted with them, but, over the period of the study, a certain friendship was established. In their use of language, then, over this time, it is possible that the increased intimacy led to a slight decrease in formality.

The interviews were carried out with each speaker: one before they left for France, one after their return and the third a year later, after a further year in the classroom but without further contact with the native speech community. The interviews were transcribed orthographically using the methods developed by Blanche-Benveniste and Jeanjean (1978). Every token of negation was coded in a string which formed the input into the VARBRUL program. The production of *ne* in the data represents a choice for the speaker. A model for the choice which governs the outcome was postulated as a variable rule. The underlying form of the negation is *ne . . . pas*, which is variably changed to *0 . . . pas*.

To obtain the most parsimonious model of variation possible, each factor group in each data set was tested for significance. Individual factors within groups containing more than two factors were also tested for significance by comparing log likelihoods of runs with and without the factor. In a step-up, step-down analysis, the following factor groups were significant for the combined Time 1 and Time 2 data: Style, Lexicalisation, Individual speaker, Clause Type, Subject. A detailed account of the results can be found in Regan (1996). The general findings of the study were:

- The overall rate of *ne* deletion increases dramatically between Time 1 and Time 2.
- The rule strengthens for nearly all the factor groups from Time 1 to Time 2.
- The constraint ordering remains the same except for one factor group.
- The constraint ordering is generally the same as for native speakers and becomes even more similar to them for Time 2. It has become apparent from many variation studies of second language acquisition that in fact L2 learners 'observe, in general, the linguistic constraints on sociolinguistic variation found in L1 speech' (Rehner *et al.*, 2003: 134).

Given the dramatic increase in the rate of *ne* deletion after the stay in the native speech community, it seems clear that living abroad for an extended period does something to the learners' usage which classroom input does not. Also of interest is the fact that while the rate of deletion more than doubled, most of the linguistic factors that condition this deletion remained the same. Other studies, for instance, have found that the constraint ordering changed, for example from low-proficiency speakers to high-proficiency speakers (Young, 1991). It seems that, for these advanced learners of French, their structures in relation to negation remained basically the same, but their sociolinguistic knowledge increased significantly. This is consistent with Bartning's (1997) description of advanced learners in general. They have now almost acquired the vernacular grammar of the native speech community. They seem to understand the symbolic power of *ne* deletion for native speakers. In general, the VARBRUL analysis showed a close-up, detailed picture of the grammar of the learners.

Third Phase: A Year Later, Back in the Classroom

For the third and final phase of the study, a third set of sociolinguistic interviews was carried out, again by myself as researcher and in the same conditions as the first two. The interview topics were similar. They were, as in the previous two phases, the classic sociolinguistic interview designed and developed by Labov. The aim was to elicit spontaneous speech from the speakers by inviting them to discuss topics which tended to involve them emotionally. This time, however, the interviews contained more material about the current lives of the speakers. Nevertheless, the interviewees did talk frequently about their year in France. The procedure was the same as for the previous phases. The interviews were transcribed in full in orthography, again by myself, for consistency with the previous work.[4]

Each token of negation was coded using the same envelope of variation as for the previous stage. Finally, the coded strings were fed into the VARBRUL programme (GoldVarb 2.0).

The input that the students received during the third year back in the classroom was formal French in general, provided mainly through lectures and small-group seminars. The instructors were lecturers, and French 'assistants' who, though young people, would have used a relatively formal register in the classes they taught. The students did not maintain links with native speakers they met in France to any significant extent.[5]

Hypothesis

These learners of French L2 had spent a year in a native French-speaking environment. Their behaviour in relation to the native community dialect and in particular the native patterns of variation had altered considerably. On their return from France, they were now behaving almost like native speakers in relation to the one particular variable studied, the variable deletion of *ne*. As previously noted, several year-abroad studies have found similar improvements in proficiency in several areas of language competence. What has not been explored so far are the long-term benefits of such a stay in the community. Is attrition an issue in such a case? Do the students grow less native-like when back in their own country? Owing to the scarcity of research on this particular topic, there has been little theoretical material on the area on which to predicate hypotheses. Giles and Coupland (1991), when describing Speech Accommodation theory, would suggest, taking into account the importance of input, that once away from the native speech community and back in the classroom, the speakers would decolloquialise and behave less like native speakers in relation to *ne* deletion. This would mean that the rate of deletion would decrease. A second question was whether, for these advanced speakers, the constraint ordering remained the same (as it had in the previous two phases), given that for learners of different proficiency levels, the constraint ordering can change.

Results

Rates of *ne* deletion for the three years compared

The Varbrul probability figures for deletion rates for the three years compared were: Year 1: 0.36, Year 2: 0.59 and Year 3 was 0.54. So, where there was a dramatic increase in *ne* deletion after the year abroad (Phase 2), after a year back in the classroom and without further contact with the native speech community (Phase 3), the speakers seem to remain generally stable in their rate of deletion.

Table 9.2 The contribution of factor groups for *ne* deletion in Time 1, 2, 3 and native speakers

		Non–native Speakers			Natives*
		Time of Development			
		Time 1	Time 2	Time 3	
Factor group					
Style	monitored	0.35	0.44	0.44	0.47
	casual	0.63	0.57	0.65	0.52
Lexicalisation	non-formula	0.38	0.28	0.39	0.26
	formula	0.74	0.80	0.80	0.63
Subject	pronoun	0.53	0.55	0.54**	0.64
	full noun phrase	0.12	0.02	0.16	0.28
Following segment	vowel	0.51	0.32	ns*	na
	consonant	0.49	0.66	ns	na
Following segment	alveolar	0.76	0.45	ns	na
	non alveolar	0.41	0.52	ns	na
Object clitic	object clitic	0.37	0.21	ns	na
	no clitic	0.51	0.53	ns	na
Clause type	main clause	0.52	0.64	0.55**	0.70
	subordinate	0.36	0.32	0.23	0.40

*Native speaker figures derived from Ashby (1976). More recent studies of *ne* deletion by native speakers show a much higher rate of deletion. For instance, Armstrong (2002) finds in young people rates of 98.9% in informal style and 97.1% in formal style. These rates are similar to the very high deletion rates in Canadian French.
**these factor groups were almost but not quite significant at 0.05, but this is probably due to the smaller number of tokens available in phase three, as compared with phases one and two.

In addition, it appears that the constraint ordering remains the same for all three phases. So the grammar of these advanced speakers at the same level of proficiency remains stable in relation to negation throughout the three years of the study. Also, the rule for *ne* deletion in native speech, which had strengthened after the stay in France, appears not to weaken after the year at home, as was hypothesised, but to maintain itself as it was on return from the native speaker community.

The Year 3 data were analysed separately, and results were significant at 0.05. The significant factor groups were Style, Lexicalisation, and Individual. Clause Type was very close to significant. (These were also the factors that were found to be significant for native speakers.) The reason the factor group Clause Type was not significant was almost certainly that the speakers used very few subordinate clauses. This is not surprising, both because of their non-native status and possibly also because of the informal nature of the interview. Although advanced learners have been found to use more subordinate clauses than early learners (Towell, 1987), these advanced learners still used very few. The factor group Subject was again not significant, due to the small number of tokens of full NPs. Otherwise, the same factor groups were significant in Phase 3 as in Phases 1 and 2.

Discussion

Factors that were significant

Lexicalisation

Once again, as in Phase 1 and 2, and also for native speakers, lexicalisation has a strong constraining effect on *ne* deletion. Throughout the entire longitudinal study over three years, the results for lexicalised or formulaic phrases remain steadily similar. The pattern repeats itself. Lexicalised formulaic phrases strongly favour deletion. The rule, which had strengthened considerably after the stay in France (0.28 for not a formula, and 0.80 for formulaic phrases), remains substantially in place after a year in the classroom. (0.39 for non-formula phrases and 0.80 for formulae). The rule is the same one they have acquired in the speech community (for a fuller study of the role of formulaic phrases in advanced learners' speech, see Regan (1997), and for early classroom learners, see Myles *et al.* (1999)).

Style

According to whether monitored or casual style is used, the speakers delete very differently. When they are being casual, they delete considerably more than when they are being formal (unlike Dewaele's Dutch L1 learners in Dewaele & Regan (2002), who have not spent a year abroad and do not distinguish to any great extent between formal and informal registers in relation to *ne* deletion). Where the rule had strengthened considerably between Time 1 and Time 2, the figures for this factor group in Time 3 remain similar to those of the Time 2, except that the speakers delete even more now in casual style than in Phase 2. Deletion in casual style seems to be firmly fixed as a norm for the L2 speakers; now, like natives, they delete more in casual speech. They have not lost this pattern even after a year in the relatively formal context of the classroom.

Clause type

The effect of clause type is very strong throughout. Although this factor group turned out not to be significant (owing to insufficient numbers of tokens of subordinate clauses), it was in fact close to significance in the run for Phase 3. Once again, as for native speakers, main clauses caused significantly more deletion of *ne* than subordinate clauses. The rule strengthened slightly after the stay in France. In Phase 3, the constraint ordering remains the same.

Subject

Subject is a powerful effect for the non-native speakers and continues to be so in the third phase. The pattern remains similar throughout. It could be that the process of cliticisation in French where subject clitics of French are not noun phrases but constituents of the verb phrase and cause *ne* to be squeezed out from between clitic and verb has affected the non-natives. They have participated in this tendency to prosodic reduction from the beginning and know the general rule (this factor group was not significant for Phase 3 but this is certainly due to the fact of a small number of tokens of full noun phrases).

Individual

As in the previous phases, there is considerable variation between individuals in Phase 3. The figures vary from 0.85 for Judy to 0.14 for Donna. Comparing a subset of speakers from the previous study (Regan 1995), we find the following:

Table 9.3 Rates of deletion for individual speakers in Time 1, Time 2 and Time 3

	Time 1	*Time 2*	*Time 3*
Judy	0.79	0.93	0.85
Cathy	0.08	0.31	0.44
Sally	0.46	0.30	0.38
Donna	0.00*	0.22	0.14
Miles	0.15	0.39	0.56

[* in the first analysis, Donna did not delete at all, and so could not be included in the VARBRUL analysis. To run the programme it was necessary to collapse three speakers who deleted almost never.]

Of the five speakers, three increased from Time 1 to 2, and generally maintained their rates after their return to the classroom. Two, Miles and Cathy, increased their rates of deletion steadily during the three years, even after their return to Ireland. Of those who continued to increase, one reported from introspective accounts that they felt more confident once having the time to 'put into practice what they had learnt in France'. Interestingly, a similar effect was reported in a case study by Hashimoto (1993) of one student in the home environment which indicates that the student 'developed a sensitivity to the feature of variation in Japanese, but that it was not until her return to Australia that she began to incorporate variables of politeness into her speech' (1993: 14). Dewaele and Regan (2001) suggest that individual speakers have to take time to develop the courage to go against prescriptive norms of the classrooms and adopt what they have now learnt to be native-speaker norms. The only student who did not increase her rate of deletion after a stay in France reported that she had difficulty in making contact with natives. In addition, she was one of the highest deletors initially and had had short stays in France before the study began. In general, the least proficient speakers made the greatest gains in the acquisition of native patterns of deletion.

In relation to individual variation over the course of the whole study, between Time 1 and Time 2, there was less individual variation between speakers, and in Time 3 there was even slightly less.

Conclusion

This study set out to investigate the effect of context, specifically settings (classroom and speech community) on the acquisition of NS patterns of variation. My hypothesis was that the speakers, a year later and away from the native speech community would 'de-colloquialise'. The hypothesis was not supported. The VARBRUL figures for the whole group of speakers show that the rate of *ne* deletion was maintained a full year after the stay abroad. It appears that the speakers have acquired the native speech pattern of variation in relation to *ne* deletion after a year in France (though at slightly different rates). And further, a year later (Phase 3) they are still holding on firmly to this pattern. Essentially, despite a year away from the French-speaking community, and having input only from formal classroom French, they do not forget what they have learnt about native-speaker behaviour.

However, interestingly, in relation to individual speakers, two of the five speakers after a year at home in the classroom do not decrease but continue to increase in their rates of deletion. It is as if they have grasped that deletion is a good and a native-like thing to do, and despite 'formal' input in the classroom, which did not favour deletion, they continue to favour the deletion of *ne*. The pattern could also simply reflect normal development of the interlanguage. In relation to the role of instruction and its comparison to and/or interaction with naturalistic second language acquisition, Ellis (1994: 616) says 'there is support for the claim that formal instruction helps learners to develop greater L2 proficiency, particularly if it is linked with opportunities for natural exposure'. As far as the acquisition of sociolinguistic competence goes, Dewaele and Regan (2002), in relation to *ne* deletion, find that formal instruction for longer periods does not seem to advance the sociolinguistic competence of the learner. The present study suggests that time spent in the native speech community positively affects the development of sociolinguistic competence, and that further instruction in the classroom away from the community does not affect this.

The evidence from this study is encouraging in relation to time spent in the native speech community, at least in relation to one area of language acquisition. As regards the acquisition of native patterns of variation, it seems to have been worthwhile for the students to have invested time in living in the community and for language policy and language planners to be relatively encouraged by the outcome. In the light of accommodation theory, the results suggest that the learners do indeed accommodate to native speakers when they are in the native speech community, but that, equally, they do not lose these native-speaker patterns when they are in the formal classroom environment afterwards. Not only are the benefits immediately apparent on return but they seem to be retained.

Long-term effects of study abroad is a research area which has so far not attracted much attention in terms of either data or theory. This is despite the fact that it is quite common for many language learners to spend time in the native speech community and subsequently continue their language learning in a formal context. The present study is a start in the attempt to chart the process of acquisition of variation in both naturalistic and instructed contexts by following the progress of the same individuals over three years. It tells us more about the effect of two different contexts of acquisition, classroom and naturalistic, for Irish learners of French as a second language and their acquisition of sociolinguistic competence. It suggests that the process is a continuum through several different contexts rather than indicating any neat division of naturalistic as opposed to instructed learning. However, it is only by doing longitudinal studies and following the process over time that it is possible to get to a portrait of the learner over time in different learning contexts. The data from this study are small and would need further confirmation with larger studies. Nevertheless they provide material to form the basis for further studies and for theoretical discussion in the area.

Notes

1. Study abroad (SA) will be used as a general term to refer to the above-mentioned various types of experience of learning language in the native speech community.
2. Ethnographic survey provided general information on contact with native speakers.
3. Except for two, who, in the last year of the study, were part of an informal oral French class.
4. This analysis contained one speaker less, as it was not possible to locate this particular speaker for the final stage. The group of five speakers was thus compared to subsets of six or seven for the previous phases. The figures are therefore slightly different, but this did not, in fact, produce any significant changes to the overall figures patterns.
5. These were data obtained from ethnographic questionnaires.

References

Adamson, H.D. and Regan, V.M. (1991) The acquisition of community speech norms by Asian immigrants learning English as a second language. *Studies in Second Language Acquisition* 13, 1–22.

Armstrong, N. (2002) Variable deletion of French *ne*: A cross-stylistic perspective. *Language Sciences* 24 (2), 153–73.

Ashby, W. (1976) The loss of the negative morpheme *ne* in Parisian French. *Lingua* 39, 119–37.

Ashby, W. (1981) The loss of the negative particle in French. *Language* 57, 674–87.

Bartning, I. (1997) L'apprenant dit avancé et son acquisition d'une langue étrangère. Tour d'horizon et esquisse d'une caractérisation de la variété avancée. In I. Bartning (ed.) *Les apprenants avancés*. Special issue of *AILE (Acquisition et Interaction en Langue Etrangère)* 9, 9–50.

Bayley, R. (1991) Variation theory and second language learning: Linguistic and social constraints in interlanguage tense marking. PhD dissertation. Stanford University.

Bayley, R. (1996) Competing constraints on variation in the speech of adult Chinese learners of English. In R. Bayley and D. Preston (eds) *Second Language Acquisition and Linguistic Variation* (pp. 97–120). Philadelphia: Benjamins.

Bayley, C. and Schecter, S.R. (2003) (eds) *Language Socialisation in Bilingual and Multilingual Societies*. Clevedon: Multilingual Matters.

Blanche-Benveniste, C. and Jeanjean, C. (1978) *Le Français Parlé: Transcription et Edition* Didier Erudition.

Brecht, R.D. and Davidson, D. (1991) Language acquisition gains in study abroad: Program assessment and modification. Paper presented at the NFLC Conference on Language Testing, Washington D.C. March 1991.

Brecht, R., Davidson, D. and Ginsberg, R. (1990) The empirical study of proficiency gain in study abroad environments of American students of Russian. *American Contributions to the 7th International Congress of MAPRIAL* ed. by D. Davidson, 123–52. Washington, DC March 1991.

Brecht, R.D. Davidson, D. and Ginsberg, R. (1993) *Predictors of Foreign Language Gain During Study Abroad*. Washington DC: National Foreign Language Center.

Coleman, J.A. (1996) *Studying Languages: A Survey of British and European Students*.

The Proficiency, Background, Attitudes and Motivations of Students of Foreign Languages in the United Kingdom and Europe. London: CILT.

Coleman, J. Grotjahn, R. Klein-Braley, C. and Raatz, U. (1994) The European language proficiency survey: A comparative investigation of foreign language learners in schools and universities in several European countries. *Language Testing Update* 16, 49–55.

Coveney, S. (2000) Vestiges of *nous* and the 1st person plural verb in informal spoken French. *Language Sciences* 22, 447–481.

Dewaele, J.-M. (1992) L'omission du *ne* dans deux styles oraux d'interlangue française. *Interface. Journal of Applied Linguistics* 7, 3–17.

Dewaele, J.-M. (1999) Word order variation in interrogative structures of native and non-native French. *ITL Review of Applied Linguistics* 123–24, 161–80.

Dewaele, J.-M. (2002) Using sociostylistic variants in advanced French IL: The case of *nous/on*. In S. Foster-Cohen, T. Ruthenberg, M.L. Poschen (eds) *EUROSLA Yearbook 2* (pp. 205–26). Amsterdam/Philadelphia: John Benjamins.

Dewaele, J. M. and Regan, V. (2001) The use of colloquial words in advanced French interlanguage. In S. Foster-Cohen and A. Nizegorodcew (eds) *EUROSLA Yearbook 1* (pp. 51–68). Amsterdam: John Benjamins.

Dewaele, J. M. and Regan, V. (2002) Maîtriser la norme sociolinguistique en interlangue française: Le cas de l'omission variable de 'ne'. *Journal of French Language Studies* 12, 123–148.

Ellis, R. (1994) *The Study of Second Language Acquisition.* Oxford: Oxford University Press.

Freed, B. (ed.) (1995) *Second Language Acquisition in a Study Abroad Context.* Amsterdam/Philadelphia: John Benjamins.

Giles, H. and Coupland, N. (1991) *Language Contexts and Consequences.* Milton Keynes: Open University Press.

Goodwin, C. and Duranti, A. (1992) *Rethinking Context: Language As An Interactive Phenomenon.* Cambridge: Cambridge University Press.

Guy, G. (to appear) *Language Variation and Linguistic Theory: The Grammar of Language Use.*

Hashimoto, H. (1993) Language acquisition of an exchange student within the homestay environment. *Journal of Asian Pacific Communication* 4 (4), 209–24.

Howard, M. (2001) The effects of study abroad on the L2 learner's structural skills: Evidence from advanced learners of French. In S. Foster-Cohen and A. Nizegorodcew (eds) *EUROSLA Yearbook 1* (pp. 123–41). Amsterdam: John Benjamins.

Mougeon, R., Nadasdi, T. and Rehner, K. (2002) État de la recherche sur l'appropriation de la variation par les apprenants avancés du FL2 ou FLE. In J.-M. Dewaele and R. Mougeon (eds), *Appropriation de la variation en français langue étrangère.* Special issue of *AILE (Acquisition et Interaction en Langue Etrangère)* 17, 7–50.

Mougeon, R. and Rehner, K. (2001) Variation in the spoken French of Ontario French immersion students: The case of *juste* vs *seulement* vs *rien que*. *Modern Language Journal* 85, 398–414.

Myles, F., Mitchell, R. and Hooper, J. (1999) Interrogative chunks in French L2: A basis for creative construction? *Studies in Second Language Acquisition* 21 (1), 49–81.

Preston, D. (1989) *Variation and Second Language Acquisition.* Oxford: Blackwell.

Preston D. and Bayley, R. (1996) (eds) *Variation in Second Language Acquisition.* Amsterdam/Philadelphia: John Benjamins.

Raffaldini, T. (1987) Attrition of communicative ability among former year abroad students of French. PhD dissertation, Indiana University.

Regan, V. (1995) The acquisition of sociolinguistic native speech norms: Effects of a year abroad on L2 learners of French. In B. Freed (ed.) *Second Language Acquisition in a Study Abroad Context* (pp. 245–67). Amsterdam/Philadelphia: John Benjamins.

Regan, V. (1996) Variation in French Interlanguage. In R. Bayley and D. Preston (eds) *Variation in Second Language Acquisition* (pp. 177–201). Amsterdam/Philadelphia: John Benjamins.

Regan V. (1997) Les apprenants avancés, la lexicalisation et l'acquisition de la compétence sociolinguistique: une approche variationniste. In I. Bartning (ed.) *Les apprenants avancés.* Special issue of *AILE (Acquisition et Interaction en Langue Etrangère)* 9, 193–210.

Regan, V. (1998) Sociolinguistics and language learning in a study abroad context. *Frontiers: The Interdisciplinary Journal of Study Abroad* 4, 61–91

Rehner, K. (2002) The development of aspects of linguistic and discourse competence by advanced second language learners of French. Unpublished PhD thesis, OISE/University of Toronto.

Rehner, K. and Mougeon, R. (1999) Variation in the spoken French of immersion students: To *ne* or not to *ne*, that is the sociolinguistic question. *The Canadian Modern Language Review* 56 (1), 124–54.

Rehner, K. Mougeon, R. and Nadasdi, T. (2003) The learning of sociolinguistic variation by advanced FSL learners: The case of *nous* versus *on* in immersion French. *Studies in Second Language Acquisition* 25, 127–57.

Sankoff, G. and Vincent, D. (1977) The productive use of *ne* in spoken Montreal French. In G. Sankoff (ed.) *The Social Life of Language* (pp. 295–310). Philadelphia: University of Philadelphia Press.

Sankoff, G., Thibault, P., Nagy, N., Blondeau, H., Fonollosa, M.-O. and Gagnon, L. (1997) Variation in the use of discourse markers in a language contact situation. *Language Variation and Change,* 9, 191–217.

Towell, R., Hawkins, R. and Bazergui, N. (1996) The development of fluency in advanced learners of French. *Applied Linguistics* 17 (1), 84–119.

Weinreich, U., Labov, W. and Herzog, M. (1968) Empirical foundations for a theory of language change. In W.P. Lehmann and Y. Malkiel (eds) *Directions for Historical Linguistics* (pp. 95–189). Austin: University of Texas Press.

Young, R. (1991) *Variation in Interlanguage Morphology.* New York: Peter Lang.

Young, R. (1999) Sociolinguistic approaches to SLA. *Annual Review of Applied Linguistics* 19, 105–32.

Chapter 10

The Role of Psycholinguistic Factors in the Development of Fluency Amongst Advanced Learners of French

RICHARD TOWELL AND JEAN-MARC DEWAELE

Introduction

This chapter aims to increase our understanding of the potential role of various psycholinguistic factors in determining whether and how L2 learners are able to develop their ability to speak a foreign language fluently.

In the first section we will present the psycholinguistic production processes that are involved. From this starting point we will be able to isolate the main psycholinguistic factors that contribute to fluency.[1] This will enable us to formulate broad hypotheses about how fluency may develop in second language learners. In the second section we will present the results of a longitudinal study which bears on these issues.

Whilst it is clear that social and situational variables also make a significant contribution to fluency, the study on which we report in the second part of this chapter has limited these variables by adopting a longitudinal case-study methodology and we will therefore not discuss them here.

We begin by a description of the psycholinguistic processes that underlie language production.

A Model of Language Production

Levelt's (1989) model of speech production is widely accepted. It was designed as a representation of language production in a mature, monolingual native speaker, but de Bot (1992) has shown how it can be modified to deal with second language development.

It is represented by the following diagram.

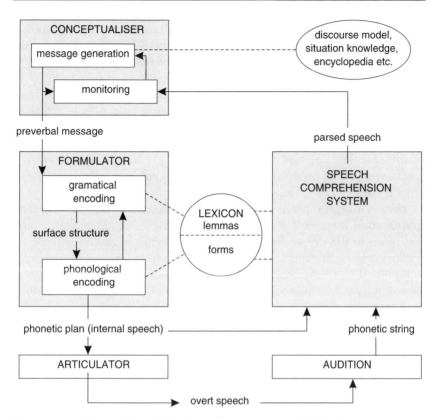

Diagram 10.1 Levelt's model of speech production (1989: 9)

The model distinguishes between two kinds of knowledge: declarative knowledge and procedural knowledge. These are represented in the diagram by round and square boxes respectively. Declarative knowledge is knowledge 'that' or knowledge 'about the world'. Procedural knowledge is knowledge 'how' or the knowledge that underlies skilled behaviour. Levelt argues that, for reasons to do with the nature of working memory (WM) and the speed with which speech is normally produced, fluent speech production requires procedural knowledge.

The three main elements on the production side, i.e. the conceptualiser, the formulator and the articulator, each contain procedural knowledge. Each functions by accessing different kinds of declarative knowledge.

In the conceptualiser the procedural knowledge takes the form of a production with the format of a condition / action pair: 'IF the intention is to commit oneself to the truth of √THEN assert √ Here √is some proposition the speaker wants to express as being the case and the indicated procedure is to build an assertion of that proposition' (Levelt, 1989: 10). In this way the speaker develops the propositional content of the message. This task is carried out by accessing declarative knowledge of the content to be expressed (encyclopedic knowledge), declarative knowledge of the situation (situational knowledge) and declarative knowledge of how discourse is organised (discourse knowledge). The output of the conceptualiser is expressed as a propositional pre-verbal message which acts as input to the formulator. De Bot and Schreuder (1993: 191) have shown how this mechanism can be modified to cope with bilingual speech production and strategy use.

The formulator must then give this propositional message an acceptable grammatical form in the language. It takes the semantic and pragmatic meanings in the pre-verbal message and searches in the lexicon for the means of expressing them. The lexicon contains form/meaning pairs called 'lemmas'. The formulator extracts the lemma which expresses a given meaning from the lexicon and builds utterances by combining the lemmas in a manner appropriate both to their syntactic requirements and to the meaning to be expressed (see Levelt, 1989: Ch. 5, 6, 7).

The grammatical encoding part of the formulator produces a set of surface syntactic forms and passes these to the phonological encoding part of the formulator. This then accesses the lower half of the lexical entry to obtain information about morpho-phonological form (see Levelt, 1989: Ch. 9).

The formulator delivers a phonetic plan to the articulator, which produces overt speech. The operations of the formulator are proceduralised in the production systems of mature monolingual native speakers.

This process is continuous: it permits no feedback between the pre-verbal message and the phonetic plan. This must be so because procedural knowledge has to run 'automatically' in order meet the speed requirements. The three processing components therefore operate autonomously in the speech production process. They work in parallel on different fragments of the message, which makes for a very efficient system (Levelt, 1989). The intermediate representations are stored in different facilities when they become available. Message, parsed, internal speech and pre-verbal messages are stored in the WM (see 1.3 below) which also monitors the speaker's own internal and overt speech (Levelt, 1989: 21). Bits of the surface structure are stored in the syntactic buffer and stretches of the articulatory plan are stored in the articulatory buffer for further execution as motor programs (Levelt, 1989: 28).

The Importance of Declarative and Procedural Memory for L2 Fluency

The declarative/procedural model may offer an optimal framework to account for differences in fluency in L1 and L2 production as it posits the existence of different brain memory systems as repositories of the mental grammar and the mental lexicon in L1 and L2.

According to this model, lexical memory depends upon declarative memory while aspects of grammar are subserved by procedural memory (Paradis, 1994, 1997; Ullman, 2001). Declarative memory, located in the temporal lobe structures (at the basis of the left hemisphere) including the hippocampus, has been implicated in the learning, representation, and use of knowledge about facts and events (Ullman, 2001). It is said to subserve 'an associative memory that underlies stored knowledge about words, including sounds, their meanings, and other memorized information' (Ullman, 2001: 106). All this information can be explicitly recollected.

Procedural memory is rooted in frontal basal ganglia structures. It has been implicated 'in the learning of new, and the control of long-established, motor and cognitive "skills" or "habits" (e.g. from simple motor acts to riding a bicycle to skilled game playing)' (Ullman, 2001: 106). It is also called 'implicit memory', because neither the learning nor the remembering of these procedures can be consciously recollected. The procedural memory 'subserves the non-conscious (implicit) learning and use of aspects of a symbol-manipulating grammar, across grammatical sub-domains, including syntax, non-lexical semantics, morphology and phonology. This system may be particularly important in the learning and computation of sequential and hierarchical structures (i.e. in grammatical structure building)' (Ullman, 2001: 106).

Support for the declarative/procedural model also comes from the investigations in the development of automaticity in second language word recognition by Segalowitz and Segalowitz (1993) and Segalowitz *et al.*, (1998). It is important to note that these authors claim to have demonstrated that underlying cognitive processing mechanisms are restructured in the direction of increased automaticity with extended learning experience and not simply speeded up, thus implying the cognitive recoding of knowledge and not just faster retrieval or activation.

One of the important areas of debate in L2 acquisition is to do with whether the declarative and procedural knowledge systems operate in the same way in the L1 and in the L2. Whereas lexis is universally believed to be declarative knowledge in L1 and L2, some would argue that there may be two ways of learning grammar. L1 learners almost certainly learn grammar implicitly by integrating their linguistic knowledge with parsing mechanisms, but L2 learners may learn varying amounts of their L2 grammar explicitly or declaratively by consciously automatising their explicit knowledge e.g. from classroom instruction.

The Importance of Long-term and Short-term Memory and Working Memory in L2 Fluency

All input and output in language comprehension and production must transit through memory systems. Any constraints imposed by memory systems therefore have the potential to greatly influence the processes involved. The relationship between memory and language has been shown to have a central role to play.

Speaking involves a constant use of both long-term memory (LTM) and short-term memory (STM) (Caspari & Parkinson, 2000; Fabbro, 1999, 2002; Levelt, 1989). Fluent speech production requires: (1) the presence and quick accessibility of the required information in LTM; (2) efficient preparation of new messages (which need to be coherent and relevant in the interaction); (3) a correct allocation of resources between both operations; and (4) enough capacity in the STM (and WM) in order for it to act as a repository.

Recent non-invasive neuroimaging techniques have revealed that several brain structures are involved in memory-processing (Perani, 1999). Dewaele (2002) argued that if individual differences in L2 production are linked to differences in the architecture and the functioning of STM and LTM, one needs to consider complex neuroanatomical and neurochemical evidence: STM, WM and LTM seem to be situated in various brain areas and regulated by various neurotransmitter systems (Izquierdo et al., 1998). The dorsolateral pre-frontal cortex plays a key role in WM as it maintains information and is involved in the preparation of actions (Lieberman, 2000), while the basal ganglia play a central role in procedural memory formation (Saint-Cyr & Taylor, 1992).

The question of whether WM can be pinpointed in a particular part of the brain is still being hotly debated (Kosslyn & Koenig, 1992; Miyake & Shah, 1999; Lieberman & Rosenthal, 2001).

Models of STM and WM

The most widely used model of WM is that developed by Baddeley (1986), Gathercole and Baddeley (1993) and Baddeley and Logie (1999). WM is defined as a specialised cognitive system that is involved in 'temporary processing and storage of information' (Gathercole & Baddeley, 1993: 2). It contains three components: a central executive that processes information and supervises temporary memory systems including a phonologically based store (the phonological loop) and a visuospatial store (the visual sketchpad) (Baddeley & Logie, 1999: 28). The phonological loop itself consists of two separate subsystems or processes. These are a storage component – the phonological store that can hold information for about two seconds – and an articulatory subvocal rehearsal process. Information in the phonological store suffers from being forgotten over time, but this can be countered by active subvocal rehearsal which refreshes items within the store (Jarrold *et al.*, 2000).

Fluent verbal comprehension and production in the L1 (and by extension the L2) has been clearly linked to capacity in STM. Just & Carpenter (1992) showed that individual differences in WM capacity for language, related to the amount of activation, can account for qualitative and quantitative differences in several aspects of language comprehension. A larger WM capacity permits interaction between syntactic and pragmatic information and allows individuals to maintain multiple interpretations in cases of syntactic ambiguity. Emerson *et al.*'s (1999) study on individual differences in integrating and coordinating multiple sources of information (visuospatial and verbal) also lends support to the idea that a central construct such as the central executive with a limited capacity could create 'a possible bottleneck in which the visuospatial and verbal sources of information may compete for common resources involved in conversion when an overlap occurred' (Emerson *et al.*, 1999: 1301).

Rosen and Engle (1997) found that only high-memory-span participants could perform complex verbal tasks in their L1 fluently while monitoring their output. The low-memory-span participants on the other hand committed more errors because of a supposed lack of controlled attention. Cowan *et al.* (1998) conclude that rehearsal efficiency and STM retrieval efficiency determine an individual's memory span. This generally confirms an earlier study by Roodenrys *et al.* (1994), who found that accessibility and articulation rates of words retrieved from STM were determined by their frequency (high-frequency words being articulated faster) and by the age at which the speaker had acquired the word (words acquired later in life being articulated more slowly).

Individual differences have therefore been shown to be linked to the speed with which an individual can rehearse and output items: 'on the one hand, the faster one rehearses, the more items one can refresh in the phonological store. In addition, the more rapidly one can output the to-be-remembered item in a verbal serial recall task, the less decay will degrade items that have yet to be verbally recalled' (Jarrold *et al.*, 2000: 234).

Differences in STM, more specifically in digit span, have been found to vary across languages. Chincotta and Underwood (1997) found that Chinese speakers obtained a larger digit span than did speakers of English, Finnish, Greek, Spanish, and Swedish, who did not differ among themselves. However, under articulatory suppression, these differences were eliminated and suppressed – digit span was equivalent across the languages. The authors attribute these cross-linguistic differences in digit span to variation in the articulatory duration of digit names and the rate of subvocal rehearsal between languages. Chincotta and Underwood (1998) moderated the view that the variation in bilingual short-term memory capacity is determined by differential rates of subvocal rehearsal between languages after observing equivalent memory span between the languages of Finnish-Swedish bilinguals despite a shorter articulation time in Finnish than Swedish. The authors conclude that there is also an influential contribution from factors related to language fluency and the strength of lexicosemantic representations.

Cheung *et al.* (2000) analysed cross-language variation in WM processing among Chinese-English bilinguals and concluded that both articulatory and non-articulatory processes contribute to the cross-language variation. They attribute the language effect to a difference in consonant-vowel structures of the items from the two languages. Their conclusion is that the phonological loop model is applicable to cross-language WM processing.

STM in L1 and L2 processing and learning

Most research in L1 as well as L2 deals with the relationship of the phonological loop to learning rather than to processing (Baddeley *et al.*, 1998; Papagno & Vallar, 1995). More capacity in the STM seems to be the key to better language learning. Ellis and Sinclair (1996) argue that WM is heavily involved in foreign-language acquisition because (1) language learning demands the learning of sequences, (2) WM allows short-term maintenance of sequence information, and (3) short-term rehearsal of sequences promotes LTM.

There seems to be no reason to believe that there are fundamental differences in the architecture of the STM in L1 and L2 processing: 'the phonological basis of STM could be established on the same grounds in L2 processing as in L1 processing' (Cook, 1997: 284). Indeed, an adult L2 user does not have to recreate the system from scratch in STM. However, L2 users do seem to have a STM deficit compared to L1 users, and this deficit is more pronounced in beginners than in advanced learners (Brown & Hulme, 1992; Cook, 1977). Research into cross-linguistic STM spans showed that participants can hold fewer L2 items than L1 in the STM (Cook, 1997). Chincotta and Underwood (1996) found that digit span is linked to levels of familiarity and practice in particular language among bilinguals. Constant bilinguals (for whom the mother tongue was also the language of schooling) obtained faster reading rates and larger digit spans in their dominant language than compound bilinguals. This was confirmed in research by Thorn and Gathercole (1999) who found that STM performance in English and French mirrored bilingual childrens' familiarity with these languages.

Paradis (1997) argues that a shortage of STM capacity in the L2 user hampers not only production but also reception of long or complex utterances. L2 speech production needs more WM, with attention directed at virtually every stage of processing (Cook, 1997; Temple, 1997; Temple, 2000). Temple suggests that in L2 production WM 'is being used to store and coordinate fragments processed by the formulator, before the next stage of processing' (Temple, 1997: 87). As the WM capacity is strictly limited (Gathercole & Baddeley, 1993), parallel processing breaks down and is replaced by serial processing with word-by-word or phrasal type of production (Temple, 1997, 2000).

Fortkamp (1999) examined whether WM capacity correlates with fluent L2 speech production. This notion is based on Daneman (1991), who found that WM capacity can explain individual variations in verbal fluency in the first language. Adapting Daneman's methodology, Fortkamp developed a set of seven experiments with 16 advanced speakers of English as a foreign language. WM was assessed by means of the Speaking Span Test and the Reading Span Test in both Portuguese and English. L2 fluency was assessed by means of the Speech Generation Task, the Oral Reading Task, and the Oral Slip Task. WM capacity, as measured by the Speaking Span Test in English, correlated significantly only with the Speech Generation Task, which was aimed at assessing fluency at the discourse level. WM capacity, as measured by the Reading Span Test, in both Portuguese and English, correlated significantly only with the reading-related task, the Oral Reading Task, aimed at assessing fluency at the articulatory level.

The results support a task-specific view of WM capacity, which posits that this capacity is functional, varying according to the individual's efficiency in the processes specific to the cognitive task with which it is being correlated.

Some L2 verbal processing tasks may suffer more when speakers run out of STM resources. Dewaele and Furnham (2000) argue that speakers can prioritise particular sub-tasks by allocating extra resources drawn from elsewhere. It also possible however that a speaker has relatively little conscious choice for certain tasks. Caplan and Waters (1999) for example found evidence that syntactic processing happens outside the dorsolateral prefrontal cortex where the WM is situated and that it escapes conscious attention.

In addition to limitations in STM capacity, the question arises as to whether any other factors might exacerbate the problems in the STM. Just and Carpenter (1992) point to inefficient processing as a possible cause for an STM deficit, delays mean degradation of the data supplied between the components, thus, 'a slow or errorful component robs other processes not only of good data but also of resources' (Just & Carpenter 1992: 145). Hirst and Kalmar (1987) argue that insufficient segregation of information generated by the components causes cross-talk that hampers the parallel processing. One could argue that, in L2 processing, some lemmas, when activated, may appear to lack morphological or syntactic information, forcing the speaker to improvise in order to find an acceptable alternative (Dewaele, 2001). This delay would mean that the storage time of other items in the phonological loop would be exceeded, interrupting production and forcing the speaker to reconceptualise the pre-verbal message. It is difficult, however, to pinpoint the cause of the STM deficit in L2 processing with certainty.

Segalowitz (1997) points out that L2 speakers are required to demonstrate not only fluency but also flexibility of processing: 'the ability to shift attention from one stimulus dimension to another, as the occasion requires, so as to remain sensitive to the pragmatic, social, semantic, syntactic, and phonological cues one is receiving and sending' (Segalowitz, 1997: 103). The need for flexibility is especially marked in situations where the speaker is already struggling to maintain fluency. This flexibility could include the ability to suppress irrelevant information and the control of relative activation levels of two or more languages (Michael, 1999). An overstretched STM might therefore lead to a breakdown in both fluency and flexibility.

The evidence cited above therefore suggests that individuals may have physiological differences in STM or WM capacity and that these differences have been shown to contribute to differences in performance. This has been seen to take various forms including: (1) a reduced STM capacity for storing an amount of data in the L2; (2) an inability to deal with more complex forms; (3) an inability to process data in parallel but instead a reliance on serial processing; (4) a variable ability to perform tasks depending on the demands they make on WM; (5) a lack of fluency and / or flexibility in situations where irrelevant information is present.

How Learners Deploy their Psycholinguistic Abilities in the Development of L2 Fluency

Bearing in mind the factors mentioned in Section 1, there are three main ways in which the growth of fluency has been envisaged. For ease of reference we will call these the automatisation of knowledge model, the processing model and the implicit vs. explicit learning model.

Position One: The automatisation of knowledge

This view assumes that the two kinds of knowledge present in the Levelt model become more accessible as a result of frequency of use. Fluency is seen as the result of the automatisation of knowledge. Learners would be seen to build up more and more knowledge of the grammar and the lexicon and to make that knowledge available more and more quickly as a result of practice. Both declarative and procedural knowledge develop in this way: there is general agreement that knowledge is in some way strengthened as a result of use. Views differ, however, as to how this process is carried out. Anderson (1983, 1993), for example, claims that the same knowledge may be held in both procedural and declarative form. He argues that declarative knowledge can become proceduralised to a point where it becomes autonomous. On the way it is restructured in 'productions'. Segalowitz *et al.* (1998) claim that increased automatisation does not just lead to the speeding up of recognised processes but can also lead to restructuring of knowledge. Others would claim that only certain kinds of skill-based knowledge can become automatic and would see the process mainly as one of speeding-up.

In terms of our study here, if this view is correct we would expect there to be continuous development in the L2 for each individual in both knowledge and fluency over time. The critical variable for fluency would be the extent of the linguistic knowledge and/or the extent to which that knowledge had been automatised. More knowledge and more automatisation would lead to swifter passage through WM. Both would depend on exposure. There would be no barrier to prevent development and there would be no reason to expect much variation between mature speakers of the L1.

Position Two: The processing model

Under the second view, the relationship between knowledge and processing is reversed. This view is associated with the work of Pienemann (1998). He claims that the development of the knowledge of language depends on the ability to process the L2. He attaches particular importance to the creation of linguistic relationships across phrase boundaries and argues that learners cannot develop knowledge of such relations unless they have already attained a certain level of processing capability. The reason why individuals may not have that ability may be physiological, such as a less well-developed WM (see above). As we have seen in Section 1, there is good evidence to show that differences in WM can affect language learning.

With regard to our study here, if this view is correct this physiological difference would become the critical variable. It would be critical because it would determine the amount and kind of knowledge that can be built up. In this case we would expect learners to vary individually and in a parallel way in the L1 and the L2. Their linguistic knowledge would develop once they have attained a certain level of processing ability.

Position Three: The implicit versus explicit learning model

Paradis (2000) insists on the fact that implicit competence is qualitatively very different from explicit knowledge: 'explicit knowledge is conscious awareness of some data (utterances) and/or of their explicit analyses (structure). Implicit competence, on the other hand, is a set of computational procedures (of which the speaker is unaware) that generates sentences' (Paradis, 2000). A crucial point is that 'metalinguistic knowledge does not evolve or change into implicit linguistic competence . . . We have (. . .) two different sources of knowledge (. . .) one that remains explicit, the other that independently develops in the form of implicit competence' (Paradis, 2000).

This distinction can be applied to L1 learning and L2 learning. Thus, it can be argued, as indicated above, that the learning of L2 grammar is qualitatively different from the learning of L1 grammar. Linguistic forms 'whose grammatical computation depends upon procedural memory in L1 are posited to be largely dependent upon declarative / lexical memory in L2' (Ullman, 2001: 105). These linguistic forms may be stored in declarative memory and/or constructed through the use of explicit rules. This would imply that L2 relies to a much greater extent on declarative memory.

Evidence for a declarative/procedural distinction for learning of L2s as against L1s has been provided by Perani *et al.* (1996). The researchers used PET scans (Positron Emission Tomography) to measure activation levels in the left hemispheric areas of the brain of Italian L1 – English L2 bilinguals during listening tasks and found that stories in Italian engaged the temporal lobes and temporoparietal cortex more extensively than L2 English. In a further study, Perani *et al.* (1998) discovered that patterns of cortical activity in highly proficient bilinguals listening to stories in their L1 and L2 were comparable, whereas very different patterns emerged in low-proficiency subjects.

This also has implications for the role of the memory systems. If L2 users rely more on declarative knowledge, then this undoubtedly increases the load on the STM. This could account for the larger variation in fluency of even relatively advanced L2 users compared to that of native speakers and learners at intermediate level (Largeau, 2000). Indeed, as Paradis (2000) points out, 'speeded-up control over explicit rules is not the same as automatic use of implicit competence' (2000: 8).

It is therefore argued that because the computation of linguistic forms relies more on declarative/lexical memory in the L2, fluency in the L2 will be lower: a heavier use of declarative/lexical memory implies a higher cost in cognitive resources.

As regards our study here, this view would lead us to expect all subjects to perform at a lower level in the L2 than in the L1. In the L1, learners have acquired the grammatical knowledge and proceduralised it in one natural implicit process. In the L2, learners may have acquired the grammatical knowledge by a different, explicit route and automatised it by general cognitive learning mechanisms. This view therefore implies that there is a differently balanced combination of declarative and procedural knowledge. The critical variable here would be the amount of linguistic knowledge learnt through the implicit as opposed to the explicit route.

Research Questions

This understanding of the psycholinguistic factors that contribute to fluency gives rise to four specific research questions to be examined in the context of our longitudinal study.

The first two questions establish the baseline information:

(1)   Does knowledge of the L2 (as determined by grammatical judgement scores) remain constant between Time 1 and Time 2, the period during which the learners were exposed more intensively to the L2? Are there individual or group differences?

(2)   Does fluency in the L2 as determined by performance on defined tasks remain constant between Time 1 and Time 2 as defined above? Are there individual or group differences?

The third question investigates whether any learners who gain higher accuracy scores earlier on are thereby enabled to gain greater fluency, thus establishing a link between the amount of knowledge and the growth of fluency. We therefore ask:

(3)   If it can be shown that some learners have greater knowledge of the L2 at Time 1, can it also be shown that this greater knowledge correlates with greater fluency at Time 1 and Time 2?

Under the hypothesis that there may be a physiological basis for differences in fluency we would expect those differences to be visible in the L1 performance. The fourth question therefore deals with whether L1 and L2 performance levels correlate. If individuals have similar degrees of fluency in both languages, there may well be a physiological explanation.

(4)   Are knowledge and fluency in the L2 linked to fluency in the L1?

Method

The investigation from which this information is drawn was a four-year longitudinal study into the acquisition of linguistic knowledge and linguistic processing. It set out to follow a group of 12 students over a four-year period and to test at different times their linguistic knowledge and their fluency. Data were collected that related to different aspects of learners' capacities both in knowledge and fluency, as described below.

Subjects

In the group there were four males and eight females, all studying French at the University of Salford, Great Britain. The subjects were selected on the basis of a degree of homogeneity in their scores in pre-university examinations and in a cloze test carried out for selection purposes. They were all aged between 18 and 19 at the beginning of the study. They had all followed the British secondary-school curriculum over the previous seven years.

Data collection

The data reported in this article were obtained from the subjects at three different points during their period of study. These students all spent six months in a French-speaking country. It was assumed that this would be the time of greatest exposure to the language. The first test (Time 1) in each data set took place before the subjects went abroad: this may have been in the first or the second year of their course depending on the activity involved. The second test (Time 2) took place at the end of or after the period of residence abroad, normally towards the end of their third year. Performing relevant tasks in English took place right at the end of their course, towards the end of their fourth year.

Knowledge based task: Grammaticality judgement tests

Subjects were asked to complete grammaticality judgement tests at regular intervals during their course. The tests focused on the use of clitic pronouns, the use of negation and the use of adverbs. Each test consisted of randomised sentences and the subjects were asked to indicate their acceptance or otherwise of the sentences on a five-point scale. The product of the test is an individual score for knowledge of these specific aspects of the language at different times. It is assumed that the knowledge revealed by these tests represents the learners' linguistic competence at that time. This leaves open the question as to the degree of automatisation of that knowledge.

Fluency based tasks

It has been shown above that there are three variables which are constantly implicated in fluency: the amount of knowledge, the degree to which knowledge has been proceduralised, and the extent to which L2 knowledge is automatised explicitly learnt knowledge as opposed to implicit knowledge. It is not possible to devise credible authentic tests that test only one of the variables, but the three fluency tasks described below call on each aspect to a greater or lesser degree allowing us to gain some insight into the relative contribution of each.

Global fluency: Speaking rate

Subjects were shown a short cartoon film which relates a short story. It was used in this investigation to elicit continuous free production from the subjects. The subjects watched the cartoon film and then recounted the story in their own time and in their own words. The data were then transcribed in detail and temporal variable counts carried out. The Speaking Rate (SR) is calculated by dividing the total number of syllables produced in a given speech sample by the amount of total time (including pause time), expressed in seconds, required to produce the speech sample. The resulting figure is normally then multiplied by 60 to give a figure expressed as syllables per minute.

This task is not intended to put pressure on any particular aspect of fluency. It measures the speed at which the speakers undertake the complete process described by Levelt from conceptualisation to articulation.

Different scores between L1 and L2 on this activity were thought to reflect differential storage of knowledge on the implicit/explicit lines and different scores between Time 1 and Time 2 to reflect increases in the amount and/or degree of proceduralisation of knowledge stored.

Fluency in the context of working memory: Shadowing

Subjects were required to listen to a tape recording of a text and to repeat what was being said. The recording was continuous: therefore the subject had to repeat what he or she had just heard at the same time as listening to the next part of the text. The simultaneous tasks of listening and speaking can be expected to overload the WM. The level of overload can be measured by the extent to which the learner manages to carry out the task successfully. The quantitative product is expressed as a percentage of the text which has been successfully reproduced by the subject. The text of the language produced on each occasion is measured against the target forms. The percentage scores were thought to give an indication of the extent to which the speaker could cope with the two tasks in their WM and therefore to be a measure of WM.

If WM has a key role in on-line processing and is variable by individual, we would expect variation in performance on this task. If this is a physiological trait, i.e. a non-modifiable characteristic, we would expect learners with low WM capacity to score lower in both L1 and in L2 at Time 1 and Time 2.

If WM is a critical variable for learning as well as on-line processing, we might well expect that any learner who had low ability in the L1 on this task might display low proficiency in the L2.

Fluency in the context of automatised knowledge: mini-story recall

Subjects were required to repeat a mini-story. This consists of four sentences which together provide an account of some kind of event. An investigator reads the mini-story to the subject, who is then asked to reproduce as much of it as he or she can immediately after hearing it.

The mini-stories are deliberately too long to be held in WM. The subject has to decode the meaning and then recode it using linguistic knowledge which they possess in their own linguistic storage systems. This task places the emphasis on the retrieval process which is taken to be essential for fluency. The quantitative product consists of percentage scores indicating the amount of exact repetition of the forms offered.

The intention is to reveal the degree of automatisation of knowledge. If it is correct to assume that L1 knowledge is more 'implicit' than L2 knowledge, then the L1 performance will be higher. We would also expect that between Time 1 and Time 2 the necessary L2 language will have become more automatised and that this would give rise to increased scores.

Analysis/Results

Linguistic knowledge at Time 1 and Time 2

We look first at the group average results of the three grammaticality judgement tests (dealing with negation, clitic pronouns and the placement of adverbs) at Time 1 and Time 2.

It can be seen that the group as a whole significantly improved its scores on each of the tests. The group average scores on all three grammatical judgement tests increased significantly: negation ($t = -4.0$, $p < 0.002$), adverb ($t = -3.2$, $p < 0.008$), and object clitic ($t = -2.8$, $p < 0.018$).

However, there were important differences between the individual subjects' performance at Time 1 on these tests, despite the similarities in

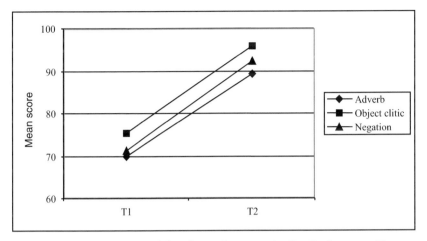

Figure 10.1 Mean scores of the three Grammaticality Judgement Tests at Time 1 and Time 2

their scores in examinations and on the cloze tests used to select the population for this study.

This would suggest that, although the group can be regarded globally as being within a defined range of overall language proficiency, some subjects had not at Time 1 acquired knowledge of some fairly basic French syntax. Three groups were therefore distinguished: five participants were labelled 'High' (scores > 80%); four participants were labelled 'Medium' (scores between 60% and 80%); and three participants were labelled 'Low' (scores < 60%).

A one-way ANOVA with proficiency level as fixed effect and average score at Time 1 as dependent variable confirms that the differences between the three groups are highly significant (df = 2, 9, F = 229.6, $p <$ 0.0001): Mean High = 91.8% SD = 5.6; Mean Medium = 71%, SD = 3.9; Mean Low = 40.7%, SD = 3.2. A Fisher's PLSD post-hoc analysis confirms that the differences are highly significant between the three groups ($p <$ 0.0001).

Given the small sample size and the danger of the data not being normally distributed, we repeated the analysis with non-parametric statistics (the Kruskal-Wallis ANOVA by ranks). This confirmed that the difference between the three proficiency groups is highly significant (2, N = 12; H = 9.7; $p <$ 0.008). When the averaged results for the three tests at Time 1 were compared with the averaged results at Time 2, it was clear that the three groups had not evolved over time in the same way.

The High group, having attained a very high score at Time 1 has only

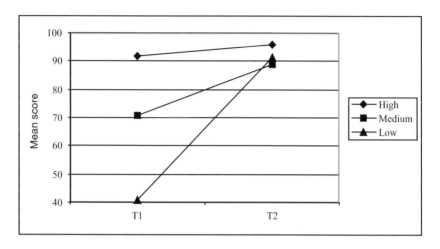

Figure 10.2 Mean scores for high, medium and low groups

slightly improved its score. The Medium group has improved considerably and the Low group has more than doubled its average.

In the context of our specific questions above, however, what is particularly interesting is that at Time 2 the differences between the groups had all but disappeared and the Low group had overtaken the Medium group.

A one-way ANOVA with proficiency level at Time 1 as fixed effect and average score at Time 2 as dependent variable shows that the differences between the three groups are still significant ($df = 2, 9$; F = 5.5 $p < 0.027$) but that the Low group has overtaken the Medium group. However, a post-hoc analysis (Fisher's PLSD) shows that the difference between the High and the Medium group is the only one to be highly significant ($p < 0.001$). The difference between the Low group and the High group is only marginally significant ($p < 0.083$).

A Kruskal–Wallis ANOVA by ranks suggests that the difference between the three proficiency groups is in fact only marginally significant at Time 2 (2, N = 12; H = 5.4; $p < 0.068$). A Spearman Rank correlation between average grammatical judgement scores at Time 1 and Time 2 is positive but only marginally significant: (R = 0.52; $p < 0.08$) confirming that the rank order of the participants for this variable has shifted between Time 1 and Time 2.

Fluency at Time 1 and Time 2 and comparison with L1 performance

Our second question addresses the development of fluency. A paired-samples *t*-test was used to determine whether the values of the fluency variables had increased significantly on each of the fluency based tasks between Time 1 and Time 2. The six-month stay in a French-speaking environment can be seen to have had a significant impact for each of the groups as well as for the group as a whole.

Speaking rate

There was a significant increase for Speaking Rate for the whole group ($df = 11$, $t = 3.6$, $p < 0.004$). However, the mean Speaking Rate at Time 2 is still significantly lower than L1 values, (Mean = 186.6, SD = 29, $t = 4.8$, $p < 0.0005$). None of the groups attains the same Speaking Rate as they have in the L1, although all increase their scores and the low group increases the most. Figure 10.3 shows how each group evolved.

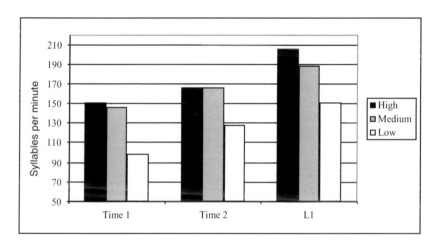

Figure 10.3 Mean Speaking Rate at Time 1 and Time 2 in French, and in the L1 for the High, Medium and Low proficiency groups

This graph shows that the High and the Medium proficiency groups virtually came together at Time 2 having been marginally separated at Time 1, but that the Low group, although it increased the score more than the two others, continued to score at a significantly lower absolute level. A post-hoc (Fisher's PLSD) reveals that the Speaking Rate of the Low group is significantly lower than that of the High group at Time 1 ($p < 0.050$) and this is still (marginally) the case at Time 2 ($p < 0.076$). This is also reflected in a low Speaking Rate in the L1. The difference between the Low and Medium groups is marginally significant at Time 1 ($p < 0.080$) and remains so at Time T2 ($p < 0.087$). The Medium group is seen to have a lower L1 Speaking Rate than the High group.

Shadowing

Similar significant increases were noted for Shadowing ($t = 4.5$, $p <$ 0.001). Here also the values at Time 2 are significantly lower than the corresponding L1 values (Shadowing L1: Mean = 95, SD = 4.9, $t = 7.3$, $p < 0.0001$). The very large standard deviation for the low group at Time 1 is linked to the fact that some participants could hardly shadow at all at Time 1. The increased mean at Time 2 is the result of a very great increase on the part of one or two individuals, hence a narrower dispersion of means within that group. Figure 10.4 shows the evolution of each group. Shadowing ability in the L1 remains considerably above Shadowing ability in the L2 for all groups, although this is the area where all groups show the steepest rise in scores between Time 1 and Time 2. An important feature of this graph is the high score in the L1 by the Low group.

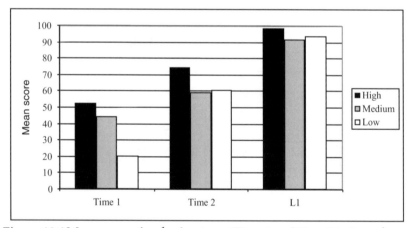

Figure 10.4 Mean scores for shadowing at Time 1 and Time 2 in French, and in the L1 for the High, Medium and Low proficiency groups

The graph shows that the values for Shadowing of the Low group are significantly lower (Fisher's PLSD) than those of the High group at Time 1 ($p < 0.019$) but no longer so at Time 2. The differences between the Low and Medium groups is marginally significant at Time 1 ($p < 0.075$) but no longer so at Time 2. It can be seen that by Time 2 the Low group catches up with the Medium group through a very sharp increase in scores but does not quite catch up with the High Group.

Recall

The overall pattern is repeated for Recall ($t = 2.4$, $p < 0.037$). Recall ability for the overall group also increased significantly between Time 1 and Time

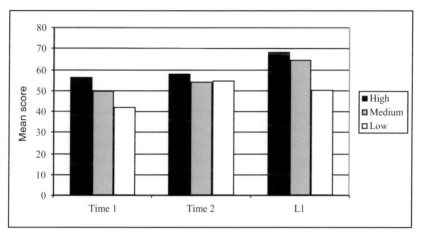

Figure **10.5** Mean scores for Recall at Time 1 and Time 2 in French, and in the L1 for the High, Medium and Low proficiency groups

2 but nonetheless lagged behind the Recall ability in the L1 (L1 Mean = 62.7, SD = 10, t = 2.7, p < 0.021). It can be seen from the graph, however, that the differences between Time 1 and Time 2 and the differences between L2 and L1 performance are not so great as in the other two fluency tests. An interesting and possibly significant feature is the fact that the Low group has actually performed worse on the L1 Recall task than it did on L2 at Time 2.

The values for Recall of the Low group are significantly lower (Fisher's PLSD) than those of the High group at Time 1 (p < 0.031) but no longer so at Time 2. There are no significant differences between the other groups, although the High group still maintains an absolute score advantage.

Summary commentary on the fluency measures

There are four specific observations that can be drawn from the evidence presented in the three graphs above and which will guide our interpretation of this evidence in Section 7 below.

(1)   All three groups score higher on all three tasks in the L1 (with the exception of the Low group on Recall – see 3 below) than in the L2 at Time 2. This would suggest that, whatever knowledge and skills underlie L2 fluency, they are different from those underlying L1 fluency.

(2)   The groups were established on the basis of proficiency scores at Time 1 and **not** on initial fluency scores. Yet each of the three groups thus identified has been shown to develop fluency in a parallel way albeit

at different levels of performance. Fluency is thus seen to develop in parallel with knowledge at a differentiated level for each of the proficiency groups. This would suggest that increased knowledge is playing a 'background' role in fluency development as each group increases its knowledge from its differentiated starting point.

(3)   The Low group consistently scores significantly lower than the High group on all L2 fluency measures at both times. However, by Time 2 the proficiency difference has evaporated. This would suggest that there must be a different, perhaps physiological, basis for the continuing difference in fluency. This claim is reinforced by the evidence of relatively low performance on L1 Speaking Rate and very much lower L1 Recall by the Low group: the L1 score for Recall by the Low group is lower than the group's score in the L2 at Time 2.

(4)   Although, as just noted, the Low group scores significantly lower on L1 Speaking Rate and L1 Recall, this is not true of the L1 Shadowing score. If we are correct in assuming that Shadowing requires a certain amount of WM, this evidence would contradict any attempt to attribute the Low group's low scores to a WM deficit.

Before attempting to integrate these observations into an overall interpretation of the evidence, we need to respond to our third question: If it can be shown that some learners have greater knowledge of the L2 at Time 1, can it also be shown that this greater knowledge correlates with greater fluency at Time 1 and Time 2?

One-way ANOVAs with Proficiency level (determined by the grammaticality judgement tests at Time 1) as single categorical independent variable and Speaking Rates, Shadowing and Recall in the L2 as single dependent variables, revealed non-significant or only marginal differences at Time 1 and Time 2. This suggests that the link between grammatical intuitions in the L2 and fluency in the L2 is at best weak. The Kruskal–Wallis ANOVA by ranks reveals a very similar picture. This in itself weakens the view that fluency is a simple product of increases in automatised knowledge. The fact that, as we have seen above, at Time 2 the groups cannot really be distinguished in terms of knowledge and yet there remain significant differences in fluency also suggests that the main reason for persistent differences in fluency lie elsewhere.

We will therefore move on to our fourth question: Are knowledge and fluency in the L2 linked to fluency in the L1?

A one-way ANOVA with proficiency in the L2 at T1 as fixed effect, and Speaking Rates, Shadowing and Recall in the L1 as dependent variables yields results that are similar to the ones obtained for L2.

The L1 results are visually displayed in Figures 10.3, 10.4, and 10.5.

Table 10.1 One-way ANOVAs with Proficiency level as single independent variable and Speaking Rates, Shadowing and Recall in the L2 as single dependent variables

Speaking rates	F	p
T2	2.4	0.14
T1	2.8	0.11
Shadowing		
T2	1.4	0.28
T1	4.1	0.053
Recall		
T2	0.75	0.58
T1	3.3	0.084

Table 10.2 One-way ANOVA with proficiency in the L2 at T1 as fixed effect and fluency variables in the L1 as single dependent variables

	F	p
Speaking rates	6.8	0.015
Shadowing	2.5	0.13
Recall	6.4	0.018

Analyses confirm that the high proficiency group had higher Speaking Rates in the L1 and had better Recall compared to the Medium and Low groups. The Kruskal–Wallis ANOVA by ranks generally confirms the previous results: they are marginally significant for Speaking rates ($H = 5.3$; $p < 0.07$) and Recall ($H = 5.7$; $p < 0.06$) but not significant for Shadowing ($H = 2.7$; $p < 0.26$). The values for Speaking rate in the L1 of the Low group are significantly lower (Fisher's PLSD) than those of the High group ($p < 0.005$) and at T2 ($p < 0.016$) and those of the Medium group ($p < 0.039$). Marginally significant differences also appear for Shadowing between the High and Medium group ($p < 0.054$) and significant differences emerged for Recall between High and Low groups ($p < 0.007$) and Low and Medium groups ($p < 0.025$).

In order to judge the relationship between fluency in the L1 and fluency in the L2, the Spearman rank correlations were calculated between L1 values and L2 Time 1 and Time 2 values (Table 10.3). They are highly significant for Speaking Rate, and marginal to non-significant for Shadowing and Recall.

Table 10.3 Spearman Rank correlations between L1 fluency values and L2 T1 and T2 fluency values

Variable	Speaking Rates L2 T2	Speaking Rates L2 T1
Speaking Rates L1	$r = 0.73$	$r = 0.81$
	$p < 0.007$	$p < 0.002$
Shadowing L1	Shadowing L2 T2	Shadowing L2 T1
	$r = 0.51$	$r = -0.42$
	$p < 0.084$	$p < 0.17$
Recall L1	Recall L2 T2	Recall L2 T1
	$r = 0.36$	$r = 0.55$
	$p < 0.24$	$p < 0.063$

Table 10.4 One-way ANCOVA with proficiency in the L2 at T1 as fixed effect, fluency variables in the L2 at T1 and T2 as single dependent variables, and fluency variables in the L1 as covariants

Speaking rates	F	p
T2	0.41	0.67
T1	0.29	0.75
Shadowing		
T2	0.41	0.67
T1	3.35	0.087
Recall		
T2	1.2	0.34
T1	0.52	0.61

In order to focus on the effect of L2 proficiency only (and filter out L1 effects), we repeated the analyses in an ANCOVA design (cf. Hulstijn & Bossers, 1992), with L1 fluency values as covariants and L2 fluency values as single dependent variables (see Table 10.4).

The effect of L2 knowledge (as tapped by these grammaticality judgement tests) on L2 fluency variables weakens considerably once the effect of fluency in the L1 is cancelled out. Only in Shadowing at Time 1 is there a marginal significant effect. This suggests that the amount of grammatical knowledge in the L2 is at best indirectly linked to fluency. Fluency in the L2 reflects fluency in the L1, most directly in Speaking Rate.

Discussion

The presentation of the results in the previous sections has answered our four specific questions to a large extent. We now need to interpret those answers first in the context of the three 'positions' and then in relation to the existing literature.

We begin with a brief summary of the results in response to our research questions. The subjects in this investigation have been shown to increase their knowledge and their fluency between Time 1 and Time 2. In almost all cases the performance in the L2 at Time 2 was lower than the performance in the L1. At Time 1 we found significant differences based on grammaticality judgement tests as measures of linguistic knowledge or proficiency between three groups. These groups were shown to develop in parallel both their knowledge and fluency. Those who had greater knowledge at Time 1 performed with greater fluency at Time 1, but this was not the case at Time 2. Although the knowledge differences ceased to exist, the fluency differences persisted. We also noted several supplementary differences in performance between the groups: in the L1 the Low group performed at a lower level than the other groups on both Speaking Rate and Recall but not on Shadowing. On Recall, the Low group performed less well in the L1 than in the L2 at Time 2.

In a search for further explanations, we first looked for correlations between grammatical knowledge and levels of fluency. We were not able to find such correlations. We then compared the fluency performance in the L1 and the L2 in more detail. It was shown that the performance in the L2 and the performance in the L1 are linked in the case of Speaking Rate but not in the case of Shadowing and Recall.

What can this tell us in relation to our three positions? To recap, position one suggests that increased fluency is a product of increased knowledge both in the sense that that more knowledge will lead to more fluency and that more automatised knowledge will lead to more fluency. This position is supported by the parallel growth of the knowledge and fluency of each of the groups but undermined by the lack of correlation between linguistic knowledge and fluency especially at Time 2. We have to recognise, of course, that these tests only measure syntactic knowledge. A more comprehensive notion of linguistic knowledge or proficiency would have improved the comparison, especially one which encompassed lexical proficiency.

Position two suggested that knowledge might not grow until and unless learners had acquired certain levels of processing ability. This position is supported by the evidence to a large extent. The groups defined in terms of proficiency were shown to have corresponding levels of fluency. At Time 1 the most proficient group was the most fluent and the least proficient the least fluent. This relation, however, disappears over time. This does not, however, undermine position two: this would assume that, once a certain processing threshold was attained, knowledge would grow rapidly. The performance of the Low group rather supports that interpretation.

The question arises, however, as to why greater knowledge does not lead to a uniform level of greater fluency, as might be expected if there were no other barriers to overall L2 fluency. An explanation may be provided by position three. Greater knowledge as tested by grammaticality judgement tests may not be not the same as greater implicit knowledge or even greater automatised or proceduralised knowledge. The evidence that the groups (with one exception on one task) are not able to attain the same levels of fluency in the L2 as they have in the L1 suggests that L2 knowledge may not be not the same as L1 knowledge. Whilst this evidence cannot unambiguously show that the L2 knowledge held by these learners has more declarative knowledge which has been automatised than is the case for their L1 knowledge, it certainly supports such an interpretation. If L2 automatised declarative knowledge requires more WM space than L1 knowledge, this would explain why, for example, the Low group can score so high on L1 Shadowing but not attain anywhere near the same level in the L2. The L1 score rules out a physiological explanation in terms of a WM deficit. But if we then acknowledge that none of these learners has a deficit in the WM, we have to explain why they still cannot process the L2 in the same way. One good explanation would be that the knowledge is automatised declarative knowledge in areas where in the L1 it is implicit procedural knowledge.

However, whilst we have an almost universal set of lower performances in the L2 compared with the L1, which may be explained by the explicit/ implicit knowledge distinction, we have also observed differences between the groups which have persisted over time and carried over into the L1, except as noted above in the area of Shadowing. These individual differences are sufficiently consistent and persistent to suggest that they are physiological. But they are seemingly not to do with WM, our initially favoured explanation on the basis of previous literature. The finding that individual differences in L2 can be accounted for by individual differences in the L1 is not new. Hulstijn and Bossers (1992) analysed the performance of 65 Dutch learners of English in reading aloud tasks in the L1 and L2. Covariance analyses revealed that most of the differences in L2 performance due to grade and academic levels disappeared when performance in L1 was accounted for. The authors therefore concluded that non-L2-specific factors contributed significantly to L2 reading performance.

Speaking Rate measures the ability to conceptualise, formulate and articulate messages, i.e. the full process as described by Levelt. Shadowing measures the ability to reproduce specific linguistic forms whilst the WM is occupied by other knowledge. It does not assume that the speaker has to call on his or her existing knowledge, rather that s/he re-cycles the linguistic forms. Recall measures the ability to bring back into WM knowledge which is stored. The factor that differentiates Recall from Shadowing and Speaking Rate is therefore the reliance on stored knowledge.

One possible interpretation of this part of the evidence is that the less able L2 learners have difficulty in storing knowledge. The problem is not so much that the less able learners can't learn forms but that they have difficulty in storing language forms and procedures. A salient and unexpected fact is that the Low group performed less well on Recall in the L1 than they did in the L2 at Time 2. This would suggest that any storage difficulty that these subjects may have could also apply in their L1. It may be that these learners have difficulty in creating, storing and recalling language productions whether implicit or explicit in any language.

Finally, we will seek briefly to integrate the findings of this experiment with some of the experiments cited in Section 1. Despite what has just been said, it is likely that how WM actually works and how it may fail to function as well in the L2 as in the L1 remain key issues. There are many views as to why this may be the case, and some of these have produced evidence similar to this study. There are similarities with some of the evidence presented in Roodenrys *et al.* (1994) as they suggest that performance may be influenced by the age at which the speaker acquired knowledge. All these learners have learned their L2 after the age of seven. Rosen and Engle (1997) point to high-memory-span participants as those who can complete tasks whilst monitoring. This is similar to our observation that only the High group was able to perform Shadowing well at Time 1. Fortkamp (1999) noted that WM capacity correlated significantly only with a Speech Generation task which was aimed at assessing fluency at the discourse level. It was noticeable amongst our learners that Speaking Rate varied considerably among individuals and that performance varied by task. We have not introduced the issue of errorful performance into this discussion but it is certainly possible that learners have had to improvise on occasions and that this has caused them to lose information stored in WM and thus to have to begin processing again, as suggested in Dewaele (2001).

We would hope that the evidence presented here can contribute to further investigations into how L2 learners develop their fluency. Obviously, the results presented in this study are based on very small numbers indeed and the extent to which the results would generalise cannot be known without larger-scale studies. These indicative data and the methodology employed may help, however, to formulate better hypotheses and better research questions in the future in our collective attempt to understand the forces that govern second language development and second language fluency in particular.

Acknowledgements

We would like to thank Alex Housen, Scott Jarvis, Peter Skehan and Liz Temple for their feedback on earlier versions of this chapter. Thanks also to Kees de Bot and Willem Levelt for their clarifications on the speech-production model.

Note

1. In this chapter we have chosen to deal with those aspects of fluency which are related to the speed of language production (cf. Schmidt, 1992; Towell *et al.*, 1996). We are aware of the multiple interpretations of this concept (cf. Chambers, 1997; Wood, 2001).

References

Anderson, J.R. (1983) *The Architecture of Cognition.* Cambridge, MA: Cambridge University Press.

Anderson, J.R. (1993) *Rules of the Mind.* New Jersey: Lawrence Erlbaum.

Baddeley, A. (1986) *Working Memory.* Oxford: Clarendon.

Baddeley, A. and Logie R. H. (1999) Working memory. The multiple-component model. In A. Miyake and P. Shah (eds) *Models of Working Memory. Mechanisms of Active Maintenance and Executive Control* (pp. 28–61). Cambridge, MA: Cambridge University Press.

Baddeley, A., Gathercole, S. and Papagno, C. (1998) The phonological loop as a language learning device. *Psychological Review* 105, 158–73.

Brown, G. and Hulme, C. (1992) Cognitive psychology and second language processing: The role of short-term memory. In R. Harris (ed.) *Cognitive Processing in Bilinguals* (pp. 105–21). Amsterdam: Elsevier.

Caplan, D. and Waters, G.S. (1999) Verbal working memory and sentence comprehension. *Behavioral and Brain Sciences* 22 (1), 77–94.

Caspari, I. and Parkinson, S.R. (2000) Effects of memory impairment on discourse. *Journal of Neurolinguistics* 13, 15–36.

Chambers, F. (1997) What do we mean by fluency? *System* 25, 535–44.

Cheung, H., Kemper, S. and Leung, E. (2000) A phonological account for the cross-language variation in working memory processing. *Psychological Record* 50, 373–86.

Chincotta, D. and Underwood, G. (1996) Mother tongue, language of schooling and bilingual digit span. *British Journal of Psychology* 87, 193–208.

Chincotta, D. and Underwood, G. (1997) Digit span and articulatory suppression: A cross-linguistic comparison. *European Journal of Cognitive Psychology* 9, 89–96.

Chincotta, D. and Underwood, G. (1998) Non temporal determinants of bilingual memory capacity: The role of long-term representations and fluency. *Bilingualism: Language and Cognition* 1, 117–30.

Cook, V. (1977) Cognitive processes in second language learning. *International Review of Applied Linguistics* 15, 73–90.

Cook, V. (1997) The consequences of bilingualism for cognitive processing. In A.M.B. de Groot and J.F. Kroll (eds) *Tutorials in Bilingualism. Psycholinguistic Perspectives* (pp. 279–300). New Jersey: Lawrence Erlbaum.

Cowan, N., Wood, N., Wood, P., Keller, T., Nugent, L. and Keller, C. (1998) Two separate verbal processing rates contributing to short-term memory span. *Journal of Experimental Psychology: General* 127 (2), 141–60.

Daneman, M. (1991) Working memory as a predictor of verbal fluency. *Journal of Psycholinguistic Research* 20 (6), 445–464.

De Bot, K. (1992) A bilingual production model: Levelt's 'Speaking' model adapted. *Applied Linguistics* 13: 1, 1–24.

De Bot, K. and Schreuder, R. (1993) Word production in the bilingual lexicon. In R. Schreuder and B. Weltens (eds) *The Bilingual Lexicon* (pp. 191–214). Amsterdam: Benjamins.

Dewaele, J.-M. (2001) Activation or inhibition? The interaction of L1, L2 and L3 on the language mode continuum. In U. Jessner, B. Hufeisen and J. Cenoz (eds) *Cross-linguistic Influence in Third Language Acquisition: Psycholinguistic Perspectives* (pp. 69–89). Clevedon: Multilingual Matters.

Dewaele, J.-M. (2002) Individual differences in L2 fluency: The effect of neurobiological correlates. In V. Cook (ed.) *Portraits of the L2 User* (pp. 221–49). Clevedon: Multilingual Matters.

Dewaele, J.-M. and Furnham, A. (2000) Personality and speech production: a pilot study of second language learners. *Personality and Individual Differences* 28, 355–65.

Ellis, N.C. and Sinclair, S.G. (1996) Working memory in the acquisition of vocabulary and syntax: Putting language in good order. *Quarterly Journal of Experimental Psychology, Section A: Human Experimental Psychology* 49a (1), 234–250.

Emerson, M.J., Miyake, A. and Rettinger, D.A. (1999) Individual differences in integrating and coordinating multiple sources of information. *Journal of Experimental Psychology: Learning, Memory, and Cognition* 25 (5), 1300–321.

Fabbro, F. (1999) *The Neurolinguistics of Bilingualism. An Introduction.* Hove: Psychology Press – Francis and Taylor Group.

Fabbro, F. (2002) The neurolinguistics of L2 users. In V. Cook (ed.) *Portraits of the L2 User* (pp. 199–218). Clevedon: Multilingual Matters.

Fortkamp, M.B.M. (1999) Working memory capacity and aspects of L2 speech production. *Communication and Cognition* 32 (3–4), 259–295.

Gathercole, S. and Baddeley, A. (1993) *Working Memory and Language.* Hove: Lawrence Erlbaum.

Hirst, W. and Kalmar, D. (1987) Characterizing attentional resources. *Journal of Experimental Psychology: General* 116, 68–81.

Hulstijn, J. and Bossers, B. (1992) Individual differences in L2 proficiency as a function of L1 proficiency. *European Journal of Cognitive Psychology* 4 (4), 341–53.

Izquierdo, I., Izquierdo, L.A., Barros, D.M., Mello e Souza, T., de Souza, M.M., Quevedo, J., Rodrigues, C., Kauer-Sant'Anna, M., Madruga, M. and Medina, J.H. (1998) Differential involvement of cortical receptor mechanisms in working, short-term and long-term memory. *Behavioural Pharmacology* 9 (5–6), 421–27.

Jarrold, C.; Baddeley, A.D. and Hewes, A.K. (2000) Verbal short-term memory deficits in Down Syndrome: A consequence of problems in rehearsal? *Journal of Child Psychology and Psychiatry and Allied Disciplines* 41 (2), 223–44.

Just, M. and Carpenter, P. (1992) A capacity theory of comprehension: Individual differences in working memory. *Psychological Review* 99 (1), 122–49.

Kosslyn, S. M. and Koenig, O. (1992) *Wet Mind: The New Cognitive Neuroscience*. New York: Free Press.

Largeau, C. (2000) Apprendre et utiliser une règle en langue étrangère: la procéduralisation. Paper presented at the Instructed Second Language Colloquium, Free University of Brussels, August 2000.

Levelt, W. J. M. (1989) *Speaking. From Intention to Articulation*. Cambridge, MA – London: ACL-MIT Press.

Lieberman, M.D. (2000) Introversion and working memory: Central executive differences. *Personality and Individual Differences* 28, 479–86.

Lieberman, M.D. and Rosenthal, R. (2001) Why introverts can't always tell who likes them: Social multi-tasking and non-verbal decoding. *Journal of Personality and Social Psychology* 80, 294–310.

Michael, E. (1999) The consequences of individual differences in cognitive abilities for bilingual language processing. Unpublished PhD, The Pennsylvania State University.

Miyake, A. and Shah, P. (1999) Towards unified theories of working memory. Emerging general consensus, unresolved issues, and future research. In A. Miyake and P. Shah (eds) *Models of Working Memory. Mechanisms of Active Maintenance and Executive Control* (pp 442–79). Cambridge: Cambridge University Press.

Papagno, C. and Vallar, G. (1995) Verbal short-term memory and vocabulary learning in polyglots. *Quarterly Journal of Experimental Psychology* 48A, 98–10.

Paradis, M. (1994) Neurolinguistic aspects of implicit and explicit memory: Implications for bilingualism and SLA. In N. Ellis (ed.) *Implicit and Explicit Learning of Languages* (pp. 393–419). London, San Diego: Academic Press.

Paradis, M. (1997) The cognitive neuropsychology of bilingualism. In A. M. B. de Groot and J. F. Kroll (eds.) *Tutorials in Bilingualism. Psycholinguistic Perspectives* (pp. 331–354). New Jersey: Lawrence Erlbaum.

Paradis, M. (2000) Awareness of observable input and output – not of linguistic competence. Paper presented at Odense University, Denmark, April 2000.

Perani, D. (1999) The functional basis of memory: PET mapping of the memory systems in humans. In L.-G. Nilsson and H.J. Markovitsch (eds) *Cognitive Neuroscience of Memory* (pp. 55–78). Seattle: Hogrefe and Huber Publishers.

Perani, D., Dehaene, S., Grassi, F., Cohen, L., Cappa, S.F. and Dupoux, E. (1996) Brain processing of native and foreign languages. *Neuroreport* 7, 2439–444.

Perani, D., Paulesu, E., Galles, N. S., Dupoux, E., Dehaene, S., Bettinardi, V., Cappa, S. F., Fazio, F. and Mehler, J. (1998) The bilingual brain: Proficiency and age of acquisition of the second language. *Brain* 121, 1841–852.

Pienemann, M. (1998) *Language Processing and Second Language Development: Processability Theory*. Amsterdam–Philadelphia: Benjamins.

Roodenrys, S., Hulme, C., Alban, J. and Ellis, A. (1994) Effects of word frequency and age of acquisition on short-term memory span. *Memory and Cognition* 22 (6), 695–701.

Rosen, V.M. and Engle, R.W. (1997) The role of working memory capacity in retrieval. *Journal of Experimental Psychology: General* 126 (3), 211–27.

Saint-Cyr, J.A. and Taylor, A.E. (1992) The mobilization of procedural learning: The 'key signature' of the basal ganglia. In L. R. Squire and N. Butters (eds)

Neuropsychology of Memory (2nd edn) (pp. 188–202). New York: The Guilford Press.

Schmidt, R. (1992) Psychological mechanisms underlying second language fluency. *Studies in Second Language Acquisition* 14 (3), 357–85.

Segalowitz, N.S. (1997) Individual differences in second language acquisition. In A.M.B. de Groot and J.F. Kroll (eds) *Tutorials in Bilingualism. Psycholinguistic Perspectives* (pp. 85–112). New Jersey: Lawrence Erlbaum.

Segalowitz, N.S. and Segalowitz, S.J. (1993) Skilled performance, practice, and the differentiation of speed-up from automatization effects: Evidence from second language word recognition. *Applied Psycholinguistics* 14, 369–85.

Segalowitz, N.S., Segalowitz, S.J. and Wood, A.G. (1998) Assessing the development of automaticity in second language word recognition. *Applied Psycholinguistics* 19 (1), 53–67.

Temple, L. (1997) Memory and processing modes in language learner speech production. *Communication and Cognition* 30, 75–90.

Temple, L. (2000) Second language learner speech production. *Studia Linguistica* 54 (2), 288–97.

Thorn, A.S.C. and Gathercole, S.E. (1999) Language-specific knowledge and short-term memory in bilingual and non-bilingual children. *Quarterly Journal of Experimental Psychology: Human Experimental Psychology* 52a (2), 303–24.

Towell, R., Hawkins, R. and Bazergui, N. (1996) The development of fluency in advanced learners of French. *Applied Linguistics* 17 (1), 84–119.

Ullman, M.T. (2001) The neural basis of lexicon and grammar in first and second language: the declarative/procedural model. *Bilingualism: Language and Cognition* 4 (1), 105–22.

Wood, D. (2001) In search of fluency: What is it and how can we teach it? *Canadian Modern Language Review / Revue canadienne des langues vivantes* 57 (4), 573–89.

Index

Subjects

Authors